The greening of golf

Manchester University Press

Globalizing Sport Studies

Series editor: **John Horne, Professor of Sport and Sociology, University of Central Lancashire, UK**

Public interest in sport studies continues to grow throughout the world. This series brings together the latest work in the field and acts as a global knowledge hub for interdisciplinary work in sport studies. While promoting work across disciplines, the series focuses on social scientific and cultural studies of sport. It brings together the most innovative scholarly empirical and theoretical work, from within the UK and internationally.

Books previously published in this series by Bloomsbury:

Global Media Sport: Flows, Forms and Futures
David Rowe

Japanese Women and Sport: Beyond Baseball and Sumo
Robin Kietlinski

Sport for Development and Peace: A Critical Sociology
Simon Darnell

Globalizing Cricket: Englishness, Empire and Identity
Dominic Malcolm

Global Boxing
Kath Woodward

Sport and Social Movements: From the Local to the Global
Jean Harvey, John Horne, Parissa Safai, Simon Darnell and Sebastien Courchesne-O'Neill

The greening of golf

Sport, globalization and the environment

Brad Millington and Brian Wilson

Manchester University Press

Copyright © 2016 Brad Millington and Brian Wilson

The right of Brad Millington and Brian Wilson to be identified as the authors of this work has been asserted by them in accordance with the Copyright, Designs and Patents Act 1988.

Published by Manchester University Press
Altrincham Street, Manchester M1 7JA
www.manchesteruniversitypress.co.uk

British Library Cataloguing-in-Publication Data
A catalogue record for this book is available from the British Library

An electronic version of this book is also available under a Creative Commons (CC BY-NC) licence.

ISBN 978 1 7849 9327 6 hardback
ISBN 978 1 5261 0703 9 open access
ISBN 978 1 5261 4366 2 paperback

First published by Manchester University Press in hardback 2016
This edition first published 2019

The publisher has no responsibility for the persistence or accuracy of URLs for any external or third-party internet websites referred to in this book, and does not guarantee that any content on such websites is, or will remain, accurate or appropriate.

Typeset by Out of House Publishing

Contents

Series editor's preface	vii
Acknowledgements	ix
List of abbreviations	xi
Preface	xiii

Part I: Introduction and tools for seeing golf sociologically 1

1 Introduction: approaching golf and environmental issues 3
2 Light green to dark green: how to make sense of responses to environmental problems 27

Part II: Background and history 49

3 Waging a war on pests: golf comes to America 51
4 Golf in consumer culture and the making of Augusta National syndrome 71

Part III: The light-greening of golf 89

5 The turn to responsible golf and the roots of golf's light-green movement 91
6 Environmentalism incorporated: professionalization and post-politics in the time of responsible golf 109
7 Light-green regulation? Environmental managerialism and golf's conspicuous exemption 131

Part IV: The dark-greening of golf 151

8 Anti-golfers across the world unite! Global and local forms of resistance to golf course development 153
9 Organic golf 'on the fringe': the potential and challenges of a chemical-free golf alternative 177

Part V: Conclusion **197**

10 Reflections, recommendations, and minor utopian visions
    for a game we love   199

References   217
Index   237

Series editor's preface

There is now a considerable amount of expertise nationally and internationally in the social scientific and cultural analysis of sport in relation to the economy and society more generally. Contemporary research topics, such as sport and social justice, science and technology and sport, global social movements and sport, sports mega-events, sports participation and engagement and the role of sport in social development, suggest that sport and social relations need to be understood in non-Western developing economies, as well as European, North American and other advanced capitalist societies. The current high global visibility of sport makes this an excellent time to launch a major new book series that takes sport seriously, and makes this research accessible to a wide readership.

The series **Globalizing Sport Studies** is thus in line with a massive growth of academic expertise, research output and public interest in sport worldwide. At the same time, it seeks to use the latest developments in technology and the economics of publishing to reflect the most innovative research into sport in society currently under way in the world. The series is multidisciplinary, although primarily based on the social sciences and cultural studies approaches to sport.

The broad aims of the series are to: *act* as a knowledge hub for social scientific and cultural studies research in sport, including, but not exclusively, anthropological, economic, geographic, historical, political science and sociological studies; *contribute* to the expanding field of research on sport in society in the United Kingdom and internationally by focusing on sport at regional, national and international levels; *create* a series for both senior and more junior researchers that will become synonymous with cutting edge research, scholarly opportunities and academic development; *promote* innovative discipline-based, multi-, inter- and trans-disciplinary theoretical and methodological approaches to researching sport in society; *provide* an English language outlet for high quality non-English writing on sport in society; *publish* broad overviews, original empirical research studies and classic studies from non-English sources; and thus attempt to *realize* the potential for *globalizing* sport studies through open content licensing with 'Creative Commons'.

With *The greening of golf* Brad Millington and Brian Wilson offer a pioneering work in critical studies of golf. Golf is a sport that is broadly popular as an adult participation sport and as a professional spectator sport. It is of truly global reach – and it is precisely the clash of its profitable economics and its punishing environmental costs that make it so important. This is in fact the central question of the book: can golf ever become both economically viable and environmentally benign? Does economic health collide inevitably with environmental and human health? Is 'corporate environmentalism' (a claim made, of course, in a great many settings beyond golf) an oxymoron?

The authors explore key issues pertaining to golf and the environment, outline relevant debates within the field of environmental sociology and make clear links to wider research on sport, globalization and social movements. The book assesses golf's turn to reflexive environmental stewardship as well as golf-related protest movements since the 1980s, focusing on both global and local forms of protest activity. Millington and Wilson conclude with a set of recommendations intended to inspire critical thinking about how to promote healthier and more ethical relationships between the golf industry and its numerous stakeholders.

The book offers a wealth of case studies and contextualization in a modern history of golf. In it the authors explore the current global reach of the sport and provide an array of interviews to support their claims and analysis. They offer a persuasive theorization of the politics of the environmental economics of the sport, drawing from the interrelated fields of sociology, critical ecology, organizational studies and social movement studies. Overall their argument is coherent, provocative, and has significance for much broader issues of sport and environmental politics.

John Horne,
Preston and Edinburgh, 2015

Acknowledgements

We first acknowledge the support offered through a Social Sciences and Humanities Research Council of Canada Standard Research Grant (funding reference number 410-2008-2749). We cannot overstate the importance of this sort of financial assistance for endeavours such as this one that are time-intensive and aim ultimately for positive social and environmental outcomes.

We would also like to express our immense gratitude to everyone who generously agreed to share their experiences and perspectives on golf and environmental issues with us over the course of our research. Although we have offered our own 'take' on these issues in the book, through our work we developed a great deal of respect for the many individuals working in, around, and against the golf industry with particular goals in mind. We hope that our document does justice to the issues that these individuals are concerned with, even if our final arguments and conclusions are not necessarily agreeable to everyone.

We are also grateful for the research assistance we received from Kaitlin Gray, Shawna Lawson, and Liv Yoon – for their hard and thoughtful work on so many of the tasks that are needed for the production of a document like this. Kaitlin, Shawna, and Liv were all students at The University of British Columbia at the time of their involvement with the project.

Of course, we cannot forget to thank our fantastic editor John Horne for the support he provided from the book proposal stage through to its completion. We are also greatly appreciative of John's outstanding leadership in general in the excellent Globalizing Sport Studies book series. Gratitude is owed here to those at Manchester University Press who agreed to publish this manuscript and offered help in a range of ways throughout the publishing process. Thanks are also owed to those who offered encouraging and insightful reviews of the book proposal and the final draft of the manuscript. We similarly appreciate the excellent copy-editing work of Chris Steel.

Finally, we both acknowledge that none of what we produced here would have been possible without the support of a range people in our lives. Brian would like to thank Desiree for her consistent and remarkable love, support, and encouragement (and tolerance during the writing process!) – and Bailey for the daily heart-warming reminders to keep it playful and real. He'd also like to express gratitude to his Mom and Dad, who fostered his interest and ongoing appreciation of golf – an appreciation that is at the core of Brian's pursuit of 'better' (i.e. more socially and environmentally friendly) golf. Brad would like to thank Katie for her unwavering love and support and her inspirational strength and work ethic, and Theo for giving new insight into life. Huge thanks are owed as well to Brad's Mom and Dad for that first set of irons (never quite used correctly) and for being a constant source of comfort and guidance. Thanks too to Rob, Scott, Suneeta, and Brad's friends for being supportive without fail and for entertaining matters both trivial and important over the years.

List of abbreviations

BMP	Best Management Practices
CBS	Columbia Broadcasting System
CGSA	Canadian Golf Superintendents Association
CPI	Chemical Processing Industry
CPO	Compulsory Purchase Order
CTRF	Canadian Turfgrass Research Foundation
EIFG	Environmental Institute for Golf
EM	Ecological Modernization
EPA	Environmental Protection Agency
FIFRA	Federal Insecticide, Fungicide, and Rodenticide Act
GAGM	Global Anti-Golf Movement
GCM	Golf Course Management
GCSAA	Golf Course Superintendents Association of America
GEO	Golf Environment Organization
GNAGA	Global Network for Anti-Golf Course Action
IOC	International Olympic Committee
IPM	Integrated Pest Management
IPMAP	IPM Accreditation Program
LEACHM	Leaching Estimation and Chemistry Model
MIT	Massachusetts Institute of Technology
NAGA	National Allied Golf Association
NBC	National Broadcasting Company
NGF	National Golf Foundation
NGO	Non-Governmental Organizations
NHL	Non-Hodgkin Lymphoma
PAAR	Pro-Alter-Anti-Response
PCPA	Pest Control Products Act
PESP	Pesticide Environmental Stewardship Program
PGA	Professional Golfers' Association
PMRA	Pest Management Regulatory Agency
PR	Public Relations
Q&A	Question and Answer

SME	Sport Management Environmentalist
SNWA	Southern Nevada Water Authority
SSHRC	Social Sciences and Humanities Research Council of Canada
SSSI	Site of Special Scientific Interest
TUT	Tripping up Trump
UNEP	United Nations Environmental Programme
UNESCO	United Nations Educational, Scientific and Cultural Organization
USGA	United States Golf Association
WCED	World Commission on Environment and Development

Preface

We golf

Brian grew up a few blocks from a nine-hole golf course in a small city in Ontario, Canada – and spent many an afternoon, evening, and sometimes night (i.e. junior hours) playing rounds, chipping, and putting on greens long-abandoned by those who had completed their rounds. Brian vaguely remembers friends who joked that you should "not lick your golf balls" because they would be coated with the chemicals that were sprayed on the course.

Brad played golf in the Ontario suburbs as much as possible too. Golf was and remains a social activity as much as a sporting endeavour – a reason to spend time with family and friends. The site of lush greens and fairways was a sign that winter had thawed.

We both grew up enamoured with the pristine courses we saw on television. Brian's parents took him to see the Canadian Open golf tournament at Glen Abbey Golf Club in Oakville, Ontario in the early 1980s, where he saw Jack Nicklaus, Greg Norman and others manoeuvre a golf course that Brian remembers as a utopian landscape – with fairways that looked like putting greens, and putting greens that looked like billiard tables. Brad's memories of golf are tied as much to watching tournaments such as the Masters on TV as they are to experiences actually playing the game.

Golf is a game we both grew up with, and one we genuinely enjoy and appreciate. We have golfed together many times. We tell you this at the outset because this book, and the research and arguments that are featured within it, unsettled how we see the game of golf. Specifically, this work raised serious questions for us about golf's evolving relationship with the environment, and how various stakeholders in golf have responded to pressing environmental concerns. By raising these questions in the pages that follow, we might be seen by some as social scientists (i.e. critics) who don't like and don't 'know' golf. This couldn't be further from the truth. However, as social scientists who are ultimately interested in and concerned with the *factors that influence those who make decisions that have important consequences for public health and the health of the world's natural environments* we feel obligated to tell the story that emerged from our research into golf's environmental history – and its environmental present.

The good, the bad – and the ambiguous and complex

As you will see, this book includes many storylines, some optimistic and hopeful, and others more pessimistic and cynical. On the more positive side, we discuss how an industry – the golf industry – that at one time vehemently denied its potentially negative impacts on the environment, has come to proclaim leadership on environmental issues (see Chapters 5, 6, and 7). This leadership stems in large part from the ability of key decision makers to assess the latest research related to turfgrass management and to deploy a range of technologies en route to delivering a sustainable golf course environment. This is a 'success story' akin to that outlined by Andrew Hoffman (2001) in his book *From Heresy to Dogma: An Institutional History of Corporate Environmentalism*. Hoffman described the success of the chemical and oil industries in moving from a state of denial on their negative environmental impacts (in the early 1960s) to a moment (i.e. the current moment) when foregrounding pro-environment initiatives has become the status quo. What Hoffman is really telling is an evidence-based story about industrial and organizational behavioural change. This story is nicely summarized in Hoffman's use of the phrase "from heresy to dogma" in the book's title to refer to the industry's early view that acknowledging environment-related problems was *heretical*, and to the current situation whereby pro-environment agendas and programs are 'par for the course' (i.e. are *dogma*). We argue here in *The greening of golf* that Hoffman's observations on the oil and chemical industries align well with our findings pertaining to the evolution of golf industry responses to similar issues.

The view that industry has made great progress on environmental issues is certainly something to be optimistic about. However, in this book we also contend that there are important reasons to be concerned about some of the claims made by industry about their leadership on environmental issues. We investigate how and why industry members and profit-seeking stakeholders in other industries (such the chemical industry, which produces pesticides for on-course use) are in a position to influence and sometimes make important decisions that have implications for environmental and public health. Our answers to these questions are not always the answers we would hope for. We note that the pursuit of economic prosperity sometimes seems to outweigh health-related concerns, and that astute strategies are commonly used to generate consent for decisions that are meant to simultaneously satisfy economic and environmental mandates. We ultimately suggest that some well-publicized claims about the 'best' options for dealing with (golf-related) environmental problems are deeply unsatisfactory.

It is here that we are especially attentive to ways that sociological research and theory can help us make sense of how and why people might make decisions that are sometimes against their own best interests – or that at least defy a precautionary approach to public health – and how the policies and belief systems that guide the activities of some governments and industries might facilitate such decision-making. In Chapter 2 we discuss these theories in detail; in later chapters we put these theories to work in making sense of our empirical findings on golf-related practices. Theory in this way is a 'lens' for seeing the world around us.

Thus, in this book we document both optimistic and pessimistic views on golf's environmental record. But even in our critical moments we find reasons to be hopeful. We found hope, for example, in the emergence of 'organic golf' courses that are offering and promoting a chemical-free golf experience, as we describe in Chapter 9. We also appreciated the efforts of various social movement groups to challenge the status quo around golf-related developments, and to question commonly accepted and often problematic claims by golf industry advocates. Last, but certainly not least, we also came across many superintendents who maintained courses with attention to the most strategic and environmentally friendly ways of using chemicals and water – following guidelines approved by an 'Integrated Pest Management' (IPM) board that is mandated to promote responsible turfgrass maintenance. While we outline our concerns about this 'responsible' approach to golf course maintenance in Chapters 5 to 7, our critiques are of the systems and structures that require chemical inputs in the first place, and of the reasons why golf and chemical industry members would have such influence on public and environmental health-related issues. In many respects, these concerns have little to do with the often-inspiring individuals we met who were doing their best within circumstances that were not of their own choosing.

Globalization, golf, and the environment

It is with this last point in mind – the idea that there are broader forces at play facilitating potentially environmentally compromising behaviours – that we came to some of the key topics underlying the Globalizing Sports Studies series of which our book is a part. Specifically, we began to think more deeply about how globally relevant developments associated with mass media and tourism were at the core of the issue we were studying. We are referring here especially to what has come to be known as 'Augusta National syndrome', a term that refers to the desire for uniformly pristine golf courses reminiscent of Augusta National Golf Club where the Masters major golf tournament is held. As we discuss in Chapter 4, one of the many problems with this 'syndrome' is that pristine, Augusta-like conditions are quite difficult to attain without significant chemical and water inputs.

Our main point here is that the explanations for the emergence and ongoing relevance of Augusta National syndrome can be traced to ongoing processes associated with globalization. For example, widespread exposure to Augusta National's 'ideal' aesthetic first occurred thanks to a major globalizing medium: television. Augusta National syndrome also resonates in many parts of the world, what with the desire to create uniform, predictable, and ultimately marketable (golf) tourism experiences. Furthermore, golf's global growth across the twentieth century, and particularly in the post-war years, reflects the neoliberal idea that little should stand in the way of cross-border development. Neoliberalism is also relevant to the idea that consumer-golfers should ultimately be the ones who decide whether a golf course is environmentally friendly enough to play – consumers, that is, and not governments armed with regulatory authority. Links between the policies and ideologies of neoliberalism are directly related to globalization, since deregulation, unmitigated economic growth, and the opening of borders for cross-border trade and private industry manoeuvring are fundamental neoliberal tenets.

It is not a stretch to see how such developments are relevant to the theoretical work of one of the major globalization theorists of recent years, Arjun Appadurai. Appadurai (1996) developed an influential model for understanding globalization as the transnational 'flows' of various globalizing 'forces', including the flow of people, ideas, finances, media, and technologies. Appadurai used the term 'scapes' to describe the various global flows mentioned above – e.g. ethnoscapes (movement of people); financescapes (movement of money); technoscapes (movement of technology), mediascapes (how media of all kinds are implicated in globalization); and ideoscapes (movement of ideas, perspectives, and political ideologies like neoliberalism). One might consider here how golf-related practices move about the globe, and why we need rich and comprehensive analyses of how these practices have environmental implications in various local contexts. Indeed, using Appadurai's model as a guide, we can draw connections between golf and global environmental issues and topics, including: golf tourism (i.e. 'ethnoscapes' and 'financescapes'); ideologies pertaining to golf-related environmental regulation and to technology-focused approaches to dealing with environmental problems ('ideoscapes' and 'technoscapes'); the representation of 'pristine' golf courses on television ('mediascapes'); internet enabled anti-golf activism ('mediascapes'); and ways that neoliberal ideologies and forms of governance are pertinent across and within contexts ('ideoscapes').

In the conclusion to this book, we make a case for thinking about how studying golf in particular 'local contexts' (e.g. like the golf industry in Canada, or as an event at the 2016 Rio Olympics) can inform analyses of global issues and enhance our understanding of how global forces and trends play out and are interpreted across various settings. We also stress the importance of seeing the natural environment as something that 'flows' – both materially and discursively – within and around the social world itself, and of adopting a form of analysis that privileges not just human interests, but those of other species and the planet as well. The final part of our concluding chapter is based on a set of recommendations that we hope will help inspire a radical rethinking of golf's relationship with these sorts of global and local environmental concerns in mind. Our ultimate goal here is to provoke a global Contextual Golf Movement – a movement that is reminiscent of the transformational global movements described in Harvey et al.'s recent book *Sport and Social Movements: From the Local to the Global*. We use the term 'contextual golf' to mean situations and environments where *really* green golf is truly viable. We suggest that golf courses should only exist in particular situations and environments where *really* healthy relationships between golf and the humans, flora, and fauna that have a stake in golf course development and maintenance practices exist and can be fostered. This means being open to the existence and value of golf, but also to its many problems.

We golf. We are fans of the game. And yet researching and writing this book opened our eyes to golf's lingering environmental problems – and to potential pathways forward. We hope with all modesty that this book can help make golf better – *really* green – and that readers will have a similar experience to our own.

PART I

Introduction and tools for seeing golf sociologically

1
Introduction: approaching golf and environmental issues

In a 1964 edition of *The Golf Course Reporter*, a premiere journal for course superintendents in North America, journal editor Gene C. Nutter wrote a scathing review of Rachel Carson's 1962 book *Silent Spring*. Carson, whose now-renowned book included criticisms of chemical companies for their environment-damaging behaviours, was admonished by Nutter for loading her arguments with emotional rather than scientific pleas, and for using "isolated examples" of pesticide-induced harms. Nutter went so far as to suggest that "the threat of increased governmental controls [e.g. on chemicals] is a threat to greater freedom of action in our country and to the necessary use of essential agricultural tools" (Nutter, 1964: 50). For Nutter, this "threat to greater freedom of action" was also a threat to the freedom of golf industry members – members who, to a great extent, saw pesticides (i.e. chemicals) as necessary tools for superintendents committed to keeping golf courses playable and pristine.

Almost 40 years later, in 2001, another article appeared in this same journal – by this point renamed *Golf Course Management* – that had a very different take on golf-related environmental issues and Rachel Carson's book. The article, written as part of the celebration of the seventy-fifth anniversary of the Golf Course Superintendents Association of America (GCSAA), included the following excerpt:

> For generations, greenskeepers went about their jobs more or less without regulation and a kind of environmental innocence, or ignorance, if you will. But that all began to change in 1962 when Rachel Carson's book, 'Silent Spring,' hit the shelves. The ground-breaking work, a treatise on the dangers of pesticide use, caused much of society to take notice. (Ostmeyer, 2001: 41)

What happened?

What happened in and around the golf industry between the early 1960s and early 2000s that led to this change in tone and content? What role do the pesticides that Nutter so vehemently defended continue to play in golf course maintenance – and what did the change from 'ignorant' to (presumably) 'responsible' practices on the part of golf course superintendents look like? What did we know – and what do we now know – about the impacts of pesticides used on golf courses on humans, animals, and the natural environment? How are golf-related pesticides currently regulated, who enforces these regulations, and what ethical stance underpins these regulations (i.e. is a 'precautionary' approach driving regulation, or a 'cost-benefit' one)? How is the problem of excessive water usage, another major environmental concern associated with golf course maintenance, dealt with and viewed by industry, governments, and others? Why is it so important to have pristine conditions on golf courses? How have governments, activists, and various golf industry members responded to golf-related environmental concerns over time? How viable is 'organic golf' (i.e. chemical-free golf) as an alternative to synthetic chemical-dependent golf course management?

These are the sorts of questions we explore in this book. In pursuing answers, we trace the evolution of the golf industry's response to environmental concerns and describe how the practices of golf superintendents have changed over time. We also outline how changes in the golf industry have been justified. This means examining the maturing public relations strategies of golf industry members and highlighting how industry representatives have come to market themselves as leading figures in what we term the 'responsible golf' movement.

More than a study of golf-related institutional change, though, we also examine how it is that the golf industry has been so effective in some contexts in minimizing government regulation. We discuss, among other developments, the major and highly publicized legislation that was introduced by the provincial government in Ontario, Canada in 2008 – legislation that essentially banned pesticide use for cosmetic reasons across the province, *except when used on golf courses*. As we will note, Ontario is not alone in offering this exemption to golf. In this regard, we pursue questions on power relations and government policy, asking why it is that golf would receive 'special status' in recent legislation and what problems lie in forms of governance that give such latitude to industry.

Why single out golf?

Golf is a major global industry. Though estimates vary, it is generally assumed that more than 60 million people play golf worldwide, and that there are more than 32,000 courses across the globe in 140 countries (IBISWorld, 2008; Rees,

2008; Wheeler and Nauright, 2006). This includes courses in 'emerging market' regions of Africa and in countries such as Kazakhstan, Nicaragua, Myanmar, and Afghanistan. Golf's professional tournaments have been major spectator events for some time now, and the sport has also been extremely successful in attracting recreational golfers from a range of demographics (although it is still a sport that is most accessible to the wealthy). While in recent years wider economic problems have impacted the sport's rate of growth, especially in North America (e.g. see Hutheesing, 2013; Lansner, 2013), the overall impact and presence of the industry remains immense.

Along with this success has come criticism. Concerns about golf's potential impacts on the environment have come from many directions, as we explore in later chapters. Some argue that the chemicals used on golf courses have negative effects on wildlife and humans (although it is difficult to measure the precise risks), while others note the potentially negative implications of course construction for natural habitats, and the problem of excessive water usage in course irrigation (Kross *et al.*, 1996; Kunimatsu *et al.*, 1999; Mallin and Wheeler, 2000; Wheeler and Nauright, 2006; Winter *et al.*, 2002). The golf industry has, over time, responded to these and other concerns in various ways. Most recently, as we shall see, a primary response tactic has been to stress the industry's capacity for recognizing and dealing with environmental problems from within. Golf industry representatives are now self-professed environmental leaders.

There are, however, reasons to be sceptical about the golf industry's proclaimed leadership on environmental issues – and, indeed, about corporate environmentalism in general. In broad terms, research conducted outside the golf industry on pro-environment measures adopted by major corporations has shown: (a) that these measures are in many cases attempts to prevent the government from implementing guidelines that might be more stringent (i.e. more environmentally responsible and economically inhibiting) than the 'voluntary' guidelines created and implemented by industry (Gibbons, 1999); (b) that industry, almost without exception, adopts a 'sustainability' approach to their environmental work – a not-uncontroversial approach that sees environmental progress and economic growth as compatible (Wilson and Millington, 2015); (c) that some industries overstate the extent to which they are, in fact, implementing pro-environment practices (i.e. they are greenwashing); and (d) that decisions to change environment-related practices within industries tend to be driven by a 'cost-benefit' analysis – where the economic costs of 'going green' are weighed against the legal and public relations costs of eschewing a corporate environmentalist agenda. This cost-benefit logic sits uncomfortably alongside the 'precautionary' approach to environment-related risks that is most often preferred by public health officials.

All of these concerns are pertinent to the case of the golf industry. Put simply, there are many unanswered questions about why and when environmentally questionable strategies for maintaining and constructing golf courses are considered necessary, who says they are necessary, who benefits from this form of risk taking, and who might be negatively affected. This book was written to address these questions and others; to address what we see as a gap in our understanding of the politics of the 'greening of golf'.

What we did: background and research

The following chapters are based on information we collected as part of our ongoing research on corporate environmentalism and the golf industry. Our study included interviews with various stakeholders in the golf industry with a vested interest in environmental issues – in particular, representatives of influential health and environmental organizations and golf course superintendents from courses that have earned environmental certification from Audubon International, an independent organization. We also visited one of the very few 'organic' golf courses in North America (located in British Columbia, Canada) and the lone organic course in England, conducting in-depth interviews in both cases with course owners and superintendents. Also included herein is an analysis of published interviews with the head superintendent of the highly publicized Vineyard Golf Club in Edgartown, Massachusetts. This is an organic course too, one that US President Barack Obama has been known to play.

Our study also took us north of Aberdeen in the UK, where we met with members of the 'Tripping up Trump' resistance group, including its founder. This activist group protested the development of a golf course in Menie Estates because of both its environmental impacts and its effects on homeowners in the areas targeted for development. It was a high-profile case – unsurprisingly so, given celebrity businessman Donald Trump's leadership in the course's planning and development. Our research here included interviews with 'Tripping up Trump' group members as well as a 'tour' of the disputed areas around the course.

Beyond interviews and site visits, a main source of information for our study came from an in-depth analysis of trade publications produced for golf industry representatives in Canada and the United States. We drew especially from the publications *GreenMaster* (Canada) and *Golf Course Management* (USA), both directed towards golf superintendents, and from the United States Golf Association's (USGA's) *Green Section* family of publications, aimed towards a broader industry audience.[1] We found the information in these publications particularly informative in that they were written in large part "by golf industry members for golf industry members". As such, these publications were in some respects more revealing than any of our interviews, as they detailed behind the scenes information about industry motivations and practices. We focus to a great extent on information from these publications from the 1960s to the present, recognizing that it was in the early 1960s when the environmental movement truly began. We do, however, also look back to industry trade documents from the early 1900s to help understand the full trajectory of golf's environmental evolution. The publication *The Golf Course* – one laden with directives on how golf could modernize in the early twentieth century – is especially valuable in this regard. Finally, information from trade publications was supplemented by searches for newspaper coverage of golf-related environmental issues in the *New York Times* and major Canadian newspapers from 1962 to the present, and by a broader examination of key articles from other news media outlets around the world. Chapter 7 also contains analysis of government policies relevant to golf and the environment – in particular, the Cosmetic Pesticide Ban Act, recently instituted in the Canadian province of Ontario.

Although the interviews conducted for the study were mostly with stakeholders in the Canadian golf industry, overall the broader topics dealt with herein are international in their scope. The anti-golf and organic movements discussed in Chapters 8 and 9, respectively, are global movements. At the same time, strategies adopted by the golf industry for dealing with environment-related concerns are shared by industry members in various parts of the world. Questions about how and whether to regulate environment-related activities on golf courses are also being dealt with in many countries (though the case study featured in this book focuses on the Canadian context). Indeed, commentators around the world remain concerned about the problems and tensions that emerge when governments are mandated to both regulate the environmental impacts of industrial practices and, at the same time, promote economic growth without fail. All told, golf is now a global sport, and the environment a global issue. Any analysis of the two is bound to be wide reaching in its focus.

What is known about the health and environmental implications of golf?

While this book is mainly about how golf industry members, governments, and activists have responded to golf-related environmental issues, we acknowledge that our central arguments are based on the assumption that golf-related activities – namely the construction and maintenance of golf courses – pose potential threats to the health of humans and non-humans alike. We spend some time here, at the outset, establishing what is known and not known about these impacts. This discussion of existing research on the science of golf-related environmental impacts segues into our explanation of why it is that a sociological analysis of golf-related environmental issues is sorely needed.

We begin this overview by suggesting that, in some respects, our assumptions about golf's potential and real impacts on the environment and public health are uncontroversial and straightforward. That is to say, in recent years members of the golf industry have readily admitted that some golf course development and maintenance practices have been and can be damaging if not carried out responsibly. This is the reason that industry members have, since the 1980s especially, actively positioned themselves as leaders when it comes to dealing with golf-related environmental issues. It is also well known that some chemicals that were previously used on golf courses (e.g. DDT) came to be seen as 'too risky' for use when considering the health of non-humans and/or humans, and have therefore been outlawed (see Chapter 5).

In this way, it is widely acknowledged that golf-related activities are *potentially* damaging to the environment. Differing views still exist, however, when it comes to questions about what has been 'proven', and what remains in doubt, in regards to the risks associated with chemicals still used on golf courses today. Related questions about whether and when golf courses might be environmentally friendly spaces (e.g. as wilderness and conservation areas), and when they might be viewed as the opposite (e.g. as disrupters/destroyers of ecosystems) are also relevant here, and are discussed below.

Chemicals, golf, and health

By the United States Environmental Protection Agency (EPA)'s definition, a pesticide is a substance or mixture of substances designed to prevent, destroy, repel, or mitigate pests (EPA, 2014a). Insecticides, herbicides, and fungicides are the most well-known pesticide variants. Historically, the synthetic production of these chemicals has proven highly effective, but also deeply controversial.

In terms of risks associated with chemical usage, a number of studies have been designed and carried out to examine the potential impacts of the pesticides, herbicides, and fungicides used on golf courses on human and non-human health. Few of these studies, however, focus directly on how exposure to these chemicals may be impacting golf course superintendents (and other on-course workers) or regular golfers who may have more intense and longer-term exposure to the chemicals used specifically on courses. A study by Kross *et al.* (1996) is noteworthy in this sense because it specifically examined the consequences of chemical usage for those who work on courses. The study – that was supported by the GCSAA – compared mortality rates for 686 golf course superintendents to rates for the general population. The researchers were especially interested in the reasons for and levels of mortality for the Caucasian male superintendent group they studied, compared to the general Caucasian male population in the United States. Kross *et al.* ultimately found that death rates attributable to non-Hodgkin lymphoma and to cancers associated with the brain, large intestine, and prostate were higher than would be expected for golf course superintendents when compared to those with similar characteristics who were *not* superintendents. Reflecting on how their results compare with other, similar studies, the researchers noted that similar patterns of "elevated NHL [non-Hodgkin lymphoma], brain, and prostate cancer mortality along with excess deaths from diseases of the nervous system has been noted among other occupational cohorts exposed to pesticides" as well (Kross *et al.*, 1996: 501). That is to say, other groups that had long-term and fairly intense exposure to the chemicals identified in Kross *et al.*'s study are, according to the research reviewed by these authors, more likely to have higher rates of the cancers identified above.

Other research, while not specifically focused on the effects of exposures to chemicals on golf courses themselves, still offers pertinent health-related information about exposure to chemicals sometimes used on golf courses. Knopper and Lean's (2004) review of existing research on the topic – entitled 'Carcinogenic and genotoxic potential of turf pesticides commonly used on golf courses' – is especially helpful in this context because the authors not only highlight concerns about chemical exposure, but also point out the limitations of existing studies on the topic. For example, they describe how difficult it is to determine a clear and causal relationship between pesticide exposure and health problems such as cancer because "even the most unbiased and stringent studies cannot account for all variables" (Knopper and Lean, 2004: 276). They note also that cohort studies – i.e. studies where groups exposed to particular pesticides are compared to cohorts not exposed in the same way – are commonly criticized for underestimating pesticide-related cancers because there is not a long enough follow-up with these groups. This is a problem because the effects of such exposures may take several years to show up, so it is assumed that some cases where cancer(s) did eventually appear would be missed in these studies. Conversely, case control studies – i.e. studies where the exposure histories of people with particular cancers are compared with histories of those who have not developed cancer – are at times thought to overstate exposure effects: "individuals may want to lay blame on a specific cause for their condition (e.g. pesticide exposure), and as such tend to overreport their exposures compared to controls" (Knopper and Lean, 2004: 276).

Even while acknowledging these limitations, Knopper and Lean saw enough evidence to strongly assert the need for future research on the topic, and to stress their bona fide concerns about the effects of exposure to golf-related chemicals. As they state:

> There appears to be convincing in vitro and in vivo laboratory and epidemiological evidence to support the claim that under certain circumstances, iprodione, chlorothalonil, PMA, and 2,4-D [chemicals commonly used on golf courses at the time this research was conducted] have been associated with cancer in humans and animals. Carcinogenicity from these pesticides seems to be related to genotoxic and epigenetic effects. As is pointed out by some opponents of pesticide bylaws, although some studies may find associations between cancer and exposure to pesticides, these associations are usually very weak ... [Still], weak associations are very much different than no association at all, and studies presenting these results should not simply be disregarded or misinterpreted as meaning that exposure to the compound in question is not related to any health concern ... Weak associations should be used to highlight concern over the effects of exposure to the chemical or chemicals under study and lay the foundation for future work. (Knopper and Lean, 2004: 276–277)

Let us repeat a key statement from the above passage – "*weak associations are very much different than no association at all, and studies presenting these results should not simply be disregarded or misinterpreted as meaning that exposure to the compound in question is not related to any health concern*" (p. 276). We emphasize this point because it speaks to Knopper and Lean's views on how to interpret the results of studies that are conducted on something as difficult to discern as the effects of chemical exposure on human and animal health. In essence, their argument – that it is irresponsible and unwise to dismiss studies because they do not offer conclusive evidence – is the same argument that underscores the position taken by those who advocate for a precautionary approach to policy making around potentially risky chemical usage.

It is also worth noting here that Knopper and Lean are certainly not the only researchers coming to these sorts of conclusions. For example, Alavanja and Bonner, authors of a 2012 review of research on occupational pesticide exposures and cancer risk, summarized their findings by saying that "chemicals in every major functional class of pesticides including insecticides, herbicide, fungicides, and fumigants have been observed to have significant associations with an array of cancer sites" (Alavanja and Bonner, 2012: 238). While Alavanja and Bonner also responsibly note that alongside the chemicals associated with cancer are many chemicals that did not show associations, they still go on to assert that, in light of existing research, "it is reasonable and timely for the scientific community to provide a multidisciplinary expert review and evaluation of these pesticides and their potential to produce cancer in occupational settings" (p. 238). In this way, and like Knopper and Lean, Alavanja and Bonner assert that something potentially serious is going on with chemical usage, and more attention should be paid to this issue.

Public health groups, influenced by this research, have made efforts to summarize these claims and concerns in ways that will be useful for the public and policymakers. The Canadian Cancer Society, for example, outlined their position as follows:

> Research to date does not show a definite link between pesticides and human cancer, but it does suggest an increasingly likely connection with cancers such as non-Hodgkin lymphoma (especially among farmers), multiple myeloma, and prostate, kidney and lung cancers. Studies on pesticides and childhood cancer show a possible connection with leukemia, brain tumours and non-Hodgkin lymphoma. (Canadian Cancer Society, n.d.)

Responding to these claims, some governments have implemented legislation that outlaws the use of chemicals for cosmetic purposes. For example, the provincial government of Ontario, Canada did just this in 2008 when they introduced the aforementioned Cosmetic Pesticides Ban Act. However, and as we discuss in Chapter 7 of this book, the golf industry was exempted from this legislation in Ontario, and has recently received similar treatment in other provinces as well.

While the golf industry has received such exemptions in a context where industry members are also claiming to be responsible users of pesticides, recent research in the United States has led to questions about chemical safety as well. We are referring here to a 2011 study by Arcury-Quandt *et al.* that focused on golf course superintendents and grounds maintenance workers who were required to handle chemicals as part of their duties. The researchers paid particular attention to the knowledge that these individuals had about safe chemical usage. They were also interested in whether these golf course workers were, in fact, following safety guidelines pertaining to chemical applications on courses. The safety guidelines Arcury-Quandt *et al.* were especially concerned with, known as 'Right-To-Know', requires course superintendents to offer appropriate education on chemical use for on-course workers, and to be sure that workers understand and comply with existing best practice guidelines. Arcury-Quandt *et al.* (2011) were straightforward in their assessment of findings from interviews with a sample of ten golf course superintendents in five states, and with sixteen Latino grounds maintenance workers in four states:

> Few superintendents were in compliance with Right-to-Know regulations or did pesticide safety training with all of their workers. Few workers had any pesticide safety knowledge. Most safety training on golf courses was rudimentary and focused on machine safety, and was usually conducted in the off-season or on rainy days, not before workers were assigned tasks. (Arcury-Quandt, 2011: 474)

This appraisal by Arcury-Quandt *et al.* is important on two levels. First, it calls into question claims of expertise and accountability by at least some members of the golf industry. That is to say, while this relatively small study in the United States should not be taken to mean that the sort of negligence Arcury-Quandt *et al.* identified is necessarily widespread, it does raise the familiar concern that what industries say they do in the name of environmental and public health may not always align with what is happening in practice. As will become evident throughout this book, we think that there are excellent reasons to interrogate the claims made by some golf industry members about the effectiveness of current attempts to respond to golf-related environmental problems. Second, the focus on the occupational health of immigrant workers in Arcury-Quandt *et al.*'s study is significant for our purposes because it directly links golf-related environmental issues with the matter of social inequality. We reflect on this in greater detail later, but suffice it to say here that this study suggests that the risks associated with chemical use are not always evenly distributed. The fact that the groups in Arcury-Quandt's study are immigrant Latino workers is relevant in the sense that it speaks to broader concerns about the social and cultural problems commonly experienced by some (especially less wealthy) newcomers to the USA

Golf's water usage and its implications

Pesticide usage stands out as perhaps the predominant issue when it comes to golf's relationship with the game's wider surroundings. This is reflected in our own analysis herein. Pesticides are, by the above definition, designed to 'destroy'; the potential risks that follow from this 'destructive' imperative have commanded the attention of governments, industry, and the public alike. Indeed, pesticides were a key focus in the industry trade publications we assessed in our research. It is also noteworthy that our study unfolded at the same time that landmark pesticide legislation was developed and instituted in Ontario, Canada; something we discuss further in the pages that follow.

To be clear, though, this focus on pesticides in *The greening of golf* should not be taken to mean that we ignored other environmental issues in our research – golf's consumption of water among them. Indeed, the issue of water use is unavoidable when examining golf's environmental impacts. In the most obvious and straightforward sense, golf courses around the world use massive amounts of water, a point that varies in relevance and urgency depending on the context in question. For example, water demands can fluctuate greatly depending on the location of the course, with a golf course in Nevada, USA (for instance) likely demanding much more water than a course in the USA's rainier north-west region or on the west coast of Canada (GCSAA, 2009). The onset of drought conditions is also a contextual factor that can shed light on golf's water demands. Ongoing problems with water scarcity in California – and related questions about the implications of this shortage for golf courses and the ethical responsibilities of courses in this region – is but one high-profile and recent example of this (Bliss, 2015). Important too in this regard is the source from which irrigation water is derived, recognizing here that some courses effectively use recycled water (generally deemed a sound environmental practice) while others still draw from municipal drinking water sources, among others (e.g. see GCSAA, 2009).

Even with the qualifier that water usage is highly contextualized, when it comes to water consumption the numbers are still staggering. According to an oft-quoted statistic from the Washington, DC-based environmental research organization, World Watch Institute, the amount of water used per day to irrigate the world's golf courses is 2.5 billion gallons – the same amount of water that is needed to support 4.7 billion people at the United Nations' daily minimum (WorldWatch, 2004). The Golf Environment Organization (GEO) adds that golf's water consumption is doubling every twenty years. For GEO, golf's 'water footprint' is significant; it includes, among other things, golf's irrigation needs, the use of potable water in places like clubhouses, and the production of fertilizer, pesticides, and turf (Golf Environment Organisation, n.d.c). Historically, golf's demand on water resources has been a source of consternation in parts of the global South in particular. Indeed, when it comes to golf tourism in many parts of the world, water is *the* main issue. The United Nations Educational, Scientific and Cultural Organization (UNESCO) addressed this point in a newsletter on water and tourism:

> An increasing number of low-income countries have actively promoted a large increase in tourism activities to foster their economic development. While there are clear economic benefits, there is also a downside. Problems of excessive water consumption in tourist complexes in water-scarce areas, especially where golf courses are involved, an increase in marine pollution in coastal areas from inadequate wastewater treatment and loss of crucial marine biodiversity, including coral reef destruction, have all occurred. (UNESCO, 2006)

We focus on these sorts of global concerns especially in Chapter 8's discussion of the Global Anti-Golf Movement and protests that directly address the impacts of golf-related tourism around the world.

Of course, it is not only activists and organizations such as UNESCO that have recognized the significance of golf's heavy consumption of water. A key theme of this book is the golf industry's insistence that golf's environmental impacts are 'under control', thanks to the industry's proactive efforts at achieving environmental sustainability. As we shall illustrate in upcoming chapters, the turn to 'responsible golf' from roughly the 1980s onwards involved careful consideration of how water might be conserved and/or used more efficiently on golf courses. Two excerpts from a 2009 article from the magazine *Golf Digest* entitled 'Drying out: America's courses are curbing their addiction to water' show this 'water awareness' at work:

> The director of golf course maintenance at Spanish Trail is John Pollok, who came to Las Vegas in 2008 from a golf course in Los Angeles. In L.A., Pollok's annual water bill was $250,000; at Spanish Trail, it's six times as high ... Pollok's crew constantly monitors soil moisture and can adjust irrigation levels, sprinkler head by sprinkler head, to make sure they're never putting out more than just enough. Irrigation costs have made Spanish Trail an enthusiastic participant in

the SNWA's [Southern Nevada Water Authority] Water Smart Landscape programme, which, among other things, pays cash rebates to water customers who convert turfed areas into 'xeriscapes'. (The word comes from the Greek xeros, meaning 'dry'.) In 2007, the club renovated one of its three nines under the programme and, in the process, removed 38 acres of turf, mostly from the periphery of the course. (Owen, 2009)

Angel Park Golf Club, a 45-hole public facility about five miles north of Spanish Trail, has removed 76 acres of grass, replaced much of the turf on its driving range with pinkish, pea-size gravel, turned off a fountain and eliminated three lakes. (Water features, because of evaporation, can require more irrigation than fairways do.) An important element of southern Nevada's water conservation efforts has been the conversion of golf course irrigation systems to recycled wastewater. For a decade, Angel Park irrigated with potable water, which the city pumped from Lake Mead, 30 miles to the southeast and 1,500 feet lower in elevation. During an especially dry year, in the mid-1990s, the club used 650 million gallons. Not long afterward, the Las Vegas Valley Water District (one of the seven municipal agencies that make up the SNWA) built a wastewater recycling plant a short distance from the course, and the club connected to the new main and built a reservoir. (Owen, 2009)

Practices of this kind have not gone unannounced, with the golf industry over time devising formal campaigns to stress that golf courses are indeed responsible when it comes to water use.

Even so, and without dismissing measures such as the making of 'xeriscapes', we emphasize throughout this book that it is imperative to think critically about industry claims of environmental leadership if 'greener' responses to golf-related environmental problems are to be developed and supported. This means, say, considering the potential for more efficient uses of water alongside golf's still significant overall water demands – a relevant point in light of the fact that the golf industry has, and continues to, push for its own overall expansion (potentially offsetting efficiencies in a 'big picture' sense). Consider also that the amount of land deemed irrigable on individual golf courses can change with time. On this last point, for example, a 2009 report from the GCSAA's Environmental Institute for Golf noted that between 2001 and 2005 approximately 31,877 acres (net) of irrigated turfgrass were added to the country's existing golf facilities, with superintendents citing the demand among consumers to change non-irrigated rough into irrigated rough as a reason (GCSAA, 2009: 15).

All told, water remains a pressing issue for golf – one that has been dealt with in ways that are reminiscent of industry responses to pesticide-related concerns. We shall return to the 'water question' and to issues such as the tension between economic growth and environmental sustainability in later chapters of this book.

Golf and environmental health

Finally, beyond pesticides and water, the body of research on golf's environmental impacts also includes studies focused on the well-being of non-humans and broader ecosystems. For example, and returning to research on pesticides especially, Post *et al.* (2010) state that "pesticides can adversely affect wildlife by exerting sublethal effects, by killing them outright, and indirectly by damaging their habitat or food supply" (Post *et al.*, 2010: 116). Following research from Ewald *et al.* (1998), Post *et al.* point to the ways that the use of insecticides and herbicides "contribute to eliminating insect populations that are essential for the growth of newly hatched birds" – while noting that of the twenty-nine pesticides most commonly used on golf courses, four of these are known to be highly toxic to birds.[2] Post *et al.* (2010) also describe how the pesticide-containing water that runs off of pesticide-treated turf into streams can have negative impacts on fish and other aquatic organisms (see Nimmo and McEwen, 1994). They note, for example, that sixteen out of the twenty-nine pesticides most commonly used on golf courses are classified as 'highly' or 'very highly toxic' (see Nimmo and McEwen, 1994). Benbook (2008), reflecting on his examination of how the science of chemical use on golf courses has influenced environmental regulation in the United States, suggests that "in the real world of pesticide regulation, birds, fish and bees are expendable" (Benbrook, 2008: 13, quoted in Post *et al.*, 2010: 117). Course construction too has the capacity to impact on natural habitats. In Chapter 4 we will investigate a case where a beaver dam was 'blown to bits' to make way for a new golf course landscape.

All told, in offering this synopsis of a vast body of literature pertaining to golf-related environmental impacts, we recognize that there are always gaps and controversies. Most of all, it is difficult to 'prove' the extent of chemical-related impacts and problems generally and/or to isolate the impacts of chemical use on golf courses specifically. This is especially the case with the study of an open system like a golf course, where the health of golfers, golf course workers, and other inhabitants of courses are always going to be influenced by a variety of factors.

Acknowledging these limitations, though, we still return to Knopper and Lean's (2004) especially rigorous and balanced assessment of existing research on golf course chemicals and the reasons they offer for remaining extremely wary of chemical effects. What Knopper and Lean raised for us were some fairly straightforward social and political questions, including: Even if existing studies are inconclusive, why would we take any changes with the health of humans and non-humans by using non-essential chemicals on golf courses? Who benefits and who does not from the status quo in the golf industry, and especially in the continued use of chemicals for golf course maintenance? In the next section, we suggest that social scientists have much to offer when it comes to addressing these bigger questions about why we would take on environmental risks to support a sport and leisure activity from which only some people benefit – an activity, moreover, that could be played and enjoyed without chemicals!

The need for a sociological perspective on sport and the environment

This book is an attempt to address these sorts of questions as part of our broader goal of better understanding how the golf industry has responded to environmental concerns over time. In carrying out this analysis, we look to fields that have developed tools for examining questions of social change, power relations, and inequality. Specifically, we draw herein from the interrelated fields of sociology, critical ecology, organizational studies, and social movement studies.

The sociology and critical ecology literature is useful in the first instance in situating golf-related environmental practices in their wider contexts, and especially in aiding understandings of the relationship between environmental and economic activity. In one sense, the work of commentators such as David Harvey (2005) is helpful because it outlines and appraises the broad shift towards neoliberal governance in recent years – a shift that, generally speaking, has privileged the deregulation of industry activity and market-driven solutions to social and environmental problems. Insight of this kind overlaps with the work of critical ecologists such as Schnaiberg and Gould (2000), who use the metaphor of the 'treadmill of production' to help them explain the process and consequences of privileging economic concerns over environmental ones. As we shall see in Chapter 7, John Hannigan (2006) makes a similar case through the concept of 'environmental managerialism'. This concept bespeaks the way in which governments are often 'dually mandated', on the one hand charged with environmental protection and on the other with stimulating economic growth. The key point is that the latter mandate, especially in neoliberal times, has a tendency to override the former. The sociology and critical ecology literature is also helpful in assessing industry efforts at impression management in a post-war context marked by growing concerns over environmental sustainability. The assumption here is that public relations campaigns are socially constructed and ideological to the extent that they tend to reinforce a set of power relations through the promotion of key messages – messages that might, for example, promote an industry-friendly version of sustainability as the common sense approach to dealing with environmental problems (Hannigan, 2006).

These conceptualizations of power relations and the socio-political context for corporate decision-making will be adopted alongside a framework that offers a nuanced explanation for institutional change, known loosely as 'institutional theory' (Hoffman, 2001; Zucker, 1988). Drawing especially on the work of Andrew Hoffman and his 2001 book *From Heresy to Dogma: An Institutional History of Corporate Environmentalism*, this framework offers a foundation from which to map various influences on any organization or industry, and to aid attempts to find the various reasons that decisions are made (or not made) to change environment-related practices. In the case of golf, these influences have come from various directions: from chemical and equipment industries, suppliers of golf's 'tools' for course development and management; from governments concerned with environmental issues and seeking ways of fairly regulating golf industry practices; from environmental non-governmental organizations (NGOs) who are themselves naturally concerned with the environment, though are perhaps less likely to see environmental problems through the prism of economic growth; from concerned citizens mounting activist campaigns in the face of golf's post-war expansion; from journalists covering golf, whether in a positive or negative light; and, of course, from golfers themselves who wield power in the perception that they demand 'ideal' playing conditions, as we shall see. Chapters 5, 6, and 7 especially draw on this organizational studies literature.

Finally, our book also draws from social movement studies, especially when we reach Chapter 8 and attempt to understand the emergence of golf-related protests. Most influential in this regard is a foundational article by sociologists of sport Jean Harvey, John Horne, and Parissa Safai (2009), published in the *Sociology of Sport Journal* and focused on the characteristics of various sport-related global social movement organizations (see Harvey *et al.*, 2013). The authors categorize each movement along a spectrum, with neoliberal globalization at one end, alter-globalization movements in the middle, and anti-globalization movements at the far end. Our own typology of responses to golf-related environmental issues is similarly inclined. At one end, we outline what we term 'pro-golf' responses: 'pro' in that they are 'for' golf, but also 'pro' in that they are 'Promethean', meaning based on the idea that humankind has an inherent right to manipulate the earth. This is a business-friendly response and, as we shall see, one that grew increasingly unpalatable in the post-war years. We also map out two different types of 'alter-golf' responses herein. The first of these is reformist (i.e. less radical) in nature. From roughly the 1980s onwards, the golf industry recognized that denial of golf's potential environmental impacts was itself unsustainable, and thus actively took steps towards altering course development and maintenance practices as a way of positioning the industry as environmentally responsible. Moving further across our spectrum, Chapter 9 examines organic golf, an alter-golf response in that golf itself is still valued, yet a more transformist approach in that golf's connection to the chemical industry is (for the most part) severed – recognizing that chemical industries may still supply 'organic' ingredients to courses that choose to use them. Finally, we also map out 'anti-golf' responses akin to the anti-globalization movements described by Harvey and his colleagues. All told, and with a nod to golf's scoring system, our own typology is named the PAAR (pro-alter-anti-response) continuum: **p**ro-golf, **a**lter-golf, and **a**nti-golf **r**esponses.

The rise of 'critical golf studies'

Although we aim to make a novel contribution to thinking about golf-related environmental issues using the tools outlined above, we respectfully acknowledge that our research builds on a small but emerging body of sociology-influenced studies that focus on golf and its various sociological dimensions. A special 2010 issue of the *Journal of Sport and Social Issues* was especially significant in this regard. Contributors to this compendium highlighted the pressing need for sociologists to take golf seriously, given its economic, social, and environmental repercussions. They specifically focused on exclusionary practices around golf (Vamplew, 2010; see also Crosset, 1995; McGinnis *et al.*, 2005; Nylund, 2003), on how identities are performed on golf courses (Perkins, 2010), on the symbolic meaning of golf in the world of business (Ceron-Anaya, 2010), and, most pertinently for our purposes, on golf and the environment (Briassoulis, 2010; Neo, 2010). In doing so, these authors contributed to 'critical golf studies' – a name coined by the special issue editors (Perkins, Mincyte, and Cole, 2010).

Indeed, in their introduction to the special issue, Perkins *et al.* (2010) express their surprise at the lack of sociological research on golf. They also offer a compelling synopsis of why golf deserves attention from researchers:

> [T]he characteristics of golf make it a fascinating sport for investigation: its stereotypically conservative image; its sometimes explicit and other times more insidious sexist, racist, and ablist norms; its strongly class-associated practices; and its links to global business interests. The diversity of kinds of golf that are

played and the tensions between regulation and a strongly individual ethos also suggest a rich field for research. Golf's institutional contexts are intriguingly diverse: American Country clubs, municipal public courses, golf resorts, and golfing communities. Its richly variable geographies embody productive tensions with the uniformly regulated global practice. The wider social reception of the game verges from media triumphalism and lionizing, with golf stars now firmly entrenched in celebrity culture, as evidenced by the demonizing and moral panic occasioned in the fall from grace of Tiger Woods. Moreover, golf's wider social reception entails contentious issues related to development, environmentalism, water, land-use, displacement, and labor. As the most land-hungry sport, golf development poses not only questions about justice, access, and environmental preservation but also the issues of responsibility for long-term transformations in ecological systems and landscaping politics. (Perkins *et al.*, 2010: 268)

To the extent that this special issue of the *Journal of Sport and Social Issues* addresses golf's intersections with the environment and the environmental movement, it furthers some key earlier works focused on this same topic. In a prescient *Sociology of Sport Journal* article published in 1990, Stoddart pointed to the environmental compromises that underlie attempts to attract tourists to pristine (i.e. chemically maintained) courses. "The central problem, of course," writes Stoddart, "is that golf is resource hungry in demanding large spaces and substantial water supplies" (Stoddart, 1990: 380). His arguments anticipate more recent work by Wheeler and Nauright (2006) that is likewise focused on golf's environmental implications. Having outlined golf's rather stark environmental demands, Wheeler and Nauright (2006) also describe the emergence of protest movements expressing consternation over prevailing golf industry practices – a theme we address later on as well. Furthermore, they discuss what has come to be known as 'Augusta National syndrome', the 'affliction' whereby golfers expect perfectly green playing conditions without fail, having been exposed to media representations of these same conditions on TV. Golf's relationship to media and, more broadly, consumer culture is indeed crucial in affecting the shaping and treatment of the sport's 'modern' landscapes.

Even with these initial critical studies of golf in tow, it is fair to say that golf is still understudied from a sociological perspective. We say this while recognizing that golf's environmental implications have received some attention from journalists writing in both mainstream publications and golf-focused outlets. Still, this remains an issue in need of detailed exploration. By our reading, the lack of scholarly attention given to golf is only somewhat surprising. It is perhaps curious that sociologists of sport have not paid more attention to golf, yet it is well known that sport's relationships with 'serious' social (and environmental) issues have not received the consideration they merit in general. The common explanation for this is that serious societal problems sometimes 'fly under the radar' when they are sport-related because of sport's inherent associations with play, leisure, and other 'non-serious' pursuits. Sport is for entertainment, in other words, and not a subject for critical scrutiny. As social scientists ourselves, our goal here is to begin to address this shortcoming in the following chapters as it pertains to golf and the environment. Golf is for entertainment for sure, but it is meaningful in other important ways as well.

This book

Our synopsis herein unfolds across five connected parts. The current chapter and the next comprise the first section of the book, entitled 'Part I: Introduction and tools for seeing golf sociologically'. The current chapter, as you have seen, sketches out key issues pertaining to golf and the environment, establishes the central questions we pursue in the book, and introduces the structure and logic of our analysis. The next chapter (Chapter 2), entitled 'Light green to dark green: how to make sense of responses to environmental problems', outlines key debates within the field of environmental sociology. The main debate we focus on involves the view, on one side, that environmental problems can be solved through business-friendly innovations and the development of new technologies, and the view, on the other side, that corporate-driven solutions are rarely stringent enough to foment substantial (and necessary) environmental changes. In this context, we also explain the theoretical concepts mobilized on each side of this debate. The former, corporatist side tends to be underpinned by the theory known as 'ecological modernization' (EM) – a theory that positions technological ingenuity as a viable avenue towards 'cleaner' forms of industrialization. This is countered by the aforementioned treadmill of production concept whereby the 'need' for ongoing consumption and global expansion (e.g. of golf-related tourism) is problematized for putting constant and perhaps unsustainable stresses on the natural environment. In Chapter 2, we also map out our PAAR continuum in greater detail, explaining more thoroughly its links to the work of Harvey *et al.* (2009) on globalization and social movements.

The next section of the book – 'Part II: Background and history' – contains Chapters 3 and 4. Chapter 3, entitled 'Waging a war on pests: golf comes to America', outlines changes in golf course maintenance that emerged as golf moved across the Atlantic from the UK in the late 1900s. We specifically describe how the increasing use of chemicals on golf courses and the adoption of highly invasive and at times destructive practices for altering golf course landscapes aligned well with the modernizing practices under way beyond the golf industry itself at this point in time. Golf's 'move' to America inspired discussion among key industry representatives on how to develop 'modern', predictable playing terrain, as opposed to the 'primitive' conditions of old. In the post-war years, this modernist sentiment reached its apotheosis in the use of the highly potent synthetic chemical DDT in the quest to eradicate unwanted 'pests'.

Chapter 3 fits with Chapter 4, the latter entitled 'Golf in consumer culture: the making of "Augusta National syndrome"'. Chapter 4 describes how media depictions of ideal golf playing conditions effectively provided further rationale in the post-war years for the deployment of highly impactful course management tactics. This is where we build from Wheeler and Nauright (2006) in outlining the arrival of Augusta National syndrome, named after the Augusta National golf course in Augusta, Georgia, home of the annual Masters men's golf tournament. With the televising of golf, Augusta's seemingly unblemished course aesthetic was widely disseminated. The outcome – or at least the perceived outcome – was the expectation among golfers that Augusta's lush fairways and greens could be easily achieved elsewhere. In this chapter we also highlight the economic growth imperative that has long sat at the golf industry's core. Together, Chapters 3 and 4 outline an initial 'pro-golf' response to environmental concerns, marked in large part by denial that golf must become more environmentally responsible.

The next section of the book – 'Part III: The light-greening of golf' – includes an overview of responses to environmental problems from members of the golf industry and governments both. In Chapter 5, 'The turn to responsible golf and the roots of golf's light-green movement', we take initial steps in documenting the golf industry's move towards a 'responsible' and leading position on environmental issues – in other words, towards adopting a reformist alter-golf approach. We are concerned in this chapter mainly with best practices, and even more specifically with the adoption of technology-aided protocols for turfgrass management such as integrated pest management, or IPM. As the 1980s grew near, IPM was adopted from the wider agricultural sector as a formal system for reducing (albeit voluntarily) the application of synthetic chemicals in the treatment of 'pests'. At the same time, organizations such as the GCSAA were fortifying their scientific research agenda, in part by strengthening their relationship with chemical companies who acted as funding donors. The golf industry, then, while long interested in modernization, was effectively adopting an *ecological modernist* position as the twentieth century neared its end.

Chapter 6 further advances this narrative of enhanced environmental responsibility. Entitled 'Environmentalism incorporated: professionalization and post-politics in the time of responsible golf', Chapter 6 turns to the issue of professionalization, looking specifically at the development of formal educational and impression management campaigns around golf. The former were aimed at training golf industry representatives in environmental best practices, including those discussed in Chapter 5; the latter went towards managing impressions among key audiences, meaning the public and government officials in particular. The point here is not that the golf industry had never before been concerned with training its labour force or with how golf was perceived externally. Rather, the point is that professionalization grew ever more important as the post-war period unfolded, what with the environmental movement and its problematizing of practices (e.g. pesticide spraying) gathering steam.

As its name suggests, Chapter 7, 'Light-green regulation? Environmental managerialism and golf's conspicuous exemption', looks at governments' responses to concerns about golf's environmental impacts. If the golf industry has indeed sought to manage impressions of their environmental record in the post-war years, the question becomes, how have those with regulatory authority responded to this? It is here where we focus especially on recent legislation in Ontario, Canada that exempted the golf industry from an otherwise stringent law on pesticide use for cosmetic reasons. In Chapter 7, though, we also look beyond Ontario to understand the nature of environmental regulation at present in more general terms. As noted, Chapters 5, 6, and 7 make up the third part of this book, and fit together under the heading of 'light-green' approaches to environmental sustainability. We spend time at the end of each of these chapters thinking critically about how the golf industry moved, beginning roughly in the 1980s, towards reflexive environmental stewardship, though it is at the end of Chapter 7 that these critical perspectives come together. Most of all, we suggest that golf's self-proclaimed leadership on environmental matters has been met by a desire among governments to find industry-friendly mechanisms for environmental regulation – one fits 'hand in glove' with the other. This has fomented what has been termed a 'post-political' situation whereby alternative, perhaps 'radical', ways of addressing environmental problems fall by the wayside in favour of light-green environmental strategies.

And yet Chapters 8 and 9 suggest that alternative perspectives still exist, even if they are not always valued. These chapters make up 'Part IV: The dark-greening of golf', which deals with responses to golf-related environmental issues that reflect a 'darker-green', or ecocentric, environmental approach. In Chapter 8, entitled 'Anti-golfers across the world unite! Global and local forms of resistance to golf course development', we discuss golf-related protest movements, focusing on both global and local forms of protest activity. Much of our attention here is given to the Global Anti-Golf Movement, which emerged in the 1990s from the collaborative work of prominent environmental groups in East Asia. In the view of the Global Anti-Golf Movement, golf tourism (especially in developing countries) displaces indigenous peoples from their land, unduly impacts on local resources, disperses toxins (e.g. through chemical spraying), and, in the end, funnels profits towards transnational companies and away from local communities. And while golf course developers, designers, and managers increasingly make claims regarding their 'friendlier' environmental practices, the Global Anti-Golf Movement sees many light-greening practices as mere 'greenwashing': "nothing more than a hollow attempt to make golf courses appear less toxic than they are."[3] When it comes to local protests, our attention turns mainly to original research we conducted on a resistance campaign in Menie, Scotland against a golf course proposed (and eventually built) by a group led by US businessman, and now presidential candidate, Donald Trump. This Scottish case is compelling for a number of reasons; what it tells us in large part is that protesters can (and do) take up their own range of tactics to present a persuasive case about golf's sometimes-negative social and environmental impacts.

Following this, in Chapter 9, entitled 'Organic golf "on the fringe": the potential and challenges of a chemical-free golf alternative', we focus on organic, or chemical-free, golf as another alter-golf response to golf-related environmental issues. It is here where we discuss our site visits to organic courses in Canada and the UK, and describe a more transformative approach to changing golf than that led by the mainstream golf industry to date. In Chapter 9 we also note how some organic golf proponents are interested not only in changing established golf industry practices, but in inspiring golfers themselves to judge the quality of golf courses differently. This might involve, for example, recognizing that pristine courses may not be 'healthy' courses and environments. We suggest that this sort of cultural shift is crucial if an organic, alter-golf movement is to take hold. Far from celebrating organic golf *tout court*, however, we close this chapter by acknowledging that organic golf is not immune to criticism (e.g. over the exclusivity of golf based on its high cost to consumers) and is not free of environmental concerns of its own. We suggest instead that organic golf is a tentative move in the right direction for the golf industry, one that should not languish 'on the fringe' of golf as it has to a great extent so far.

Finally, 'Part V: Conclusion', gives our final thoughts on golf and the environment. This part of the book includes Chapter 10, 'Reflections, recommendations and minor utopian visions for a game we love'. In this final chapter we offer an overview of the main findings that emerged in our research and that we present over the course of this book. We also present a set of recommendations that are intended to inspire critical thinking on how to promote healthier and more ethical relationships between the golf industry and its numerous stakeholders, paying particular attention, of course, to golf's many environmental issues. We conclude the chapter and book by acknowledging the many relevant topics and issues we were unable or chose not to pursue and, in turn, by offering suggestions for future research on golf, the environment, and globalization. The 'greening of golf' is an ongoing matter, just as the *study* of golf and the environment should be ongoing too.

Notes

1 The trade publications studied here have in some cases undergone name changes over time. For example, *Golf Course Management*, the flagship publication of the Golf Course Superintendents Association of America (GCSAA), has been known in the past as *The National Greenkeeper*, *The Greenkeeper Bulletin*, *The Golf Course Reporter*, and *The Golf Superintendent*. The GCSAA itself has previously been known as the National Association of Greenkeepers of America, the Greenkeeping Superintendents Association, and the National Greenkeeping Superintendents Association (NGSA). The USGA's key publication is the *Green Section Record*. But the USGA has also published materials under other names, including the *Bulletin of the Green Section of the US Golf Association*, *Turf Culture*, and *Timely Turf Topics* (see Turfgrass Information File, n.d.b). For simplicity, we generally use the latest names for these trade publications and associations in the main text of this manuscript.
2 These are the insecticides chlorpyrifos, imidacloprid and trichlorfon (termed 'very highly toxic') and the herbicide 2,4-D (termed 'highly toxic').
3 For information about GAGM and an outline of its manifesto, see http://www.antigolf.org/english.html.

2

Light green to dark green: how to make sense of responses to environmental problems

When we began to explore how particular groups responded to golf-related environmental problems, we encountered a range of viewpoints, actions, and suggestions for change. We came across those who think that golf courses should be abolished outright, those who think that golf courses should not be built close to where they live, and those who see the need for radical transformation in how golf courses are maintained (see Chapters 8 and 9). We also came across those who see golf as *potentially* beneficial. For example, we met members of a local activist group fighting to save a golf course built on a former landfill site – a meeting that led us to find literature supporting the idea that, under particular circumstances, golf can provide green space for flora and fauna to thrive, and may even help environmental recovery on particular sites (see Colding *et al.*, 2009; Ede, 1990; Misgav *et al.*, 2001; Price *et al.*, 2013). Furthermore, we encountered views from golf industry representatives stressing how course development and maintenance techniques are guided by the latest science and best practices. Thus, while practices such as chemical spraying might seem risky at first glance, according to many industry members golf is, in fact, 'in good hands' when it comes to its environmental implications.

However, it was when we began to consider *why* particular groups responded to golf-related environmental problems the way they did, and especially why some approaches have become dominant and others marginal, that we began to notice some especially interesting, and at times troubling, themes and tensions. These themes and tensions pertained especially to questions about how chemicals should be used on golf courses, or if they even should be used at all. Related to this, we encountered different views on the level of risk to which humans and non-humans should reasonably be exposed for the sake of a leisure activity – albeit a sometimes lucrative activity for some industry stakeholders. We also saw that different groups had varying levels of 'faith' in the latest studies on the health and environmental impacts of chemicals, and also quite distinct interpretations of existing research on this topic. These same groups also differed when it came to their faith in the ability of humans to find innovative solutions to longstanding environmental issues.

For sociologists who study the assumptions that underlie particular responses to environmental problems, it is not difficult to see how these different perspectives are associated with common, and in many ways competing, stances on how environmental problems should be dealt with in general. On the one side, we have those aligned with what is commonly termed a 'sustainability' approach to dealing with environmental problems – an approach that is based on principles associated with a theory known to sociologists as 'ecological modernization'. Of course, sustainability has become a buzzword for businesses, governments, and even many environmentalists in recent years. As we will show, it is often interpreted in a business-friendly or 'light-green' way (Lenskyj, 1998). On the other side are perspectives that more closely align with a 'dark-green' approach to dealing with environmental issues. Those working from this more ecocentric perspective typically point to flaws in the logic underlying business-friendly solutions to environmental problems, emphasizing how the incentive system driving business-friendly environmentalism can be exploited by those motivated, above all, by economic goals. Those adopting a dark-green position are also more likely to recognize the various inequalities relevant to environmental issues (Maguire *et al.*, 2002). These include both intergenerational inequalities, whereby future generations are impacted by the environmentally damaging activities of the present day, and inter-species inequalities, which pertain to the impacts of human behaviour on 'voiceless' non-humans such as flora and fauna. Ultimately, supporters of a dark-green position argue that these inequalities need be taken seriously by those who make decisions that impact on the environment. They also suggest that the health of the environment – that is, the Earth and its ecosystems – should account for more than 'one third' of the triple bottom that is allotted by advocates of a sustainability approach (alongside social and economic concerns).

Put another way, the assumptions underlying light and dark-green responses to environmental problems in general tell us a great deal about the assumptions underlying responses to golf-related environmental problems in particular. To help us explain the principles guiding these different responses, in this chapter we explore the details and taken-for-granted aspects of different stances on environmental issues. We also discuss how, once it is recognized by all that environmental concerns indeed merit our attention, we might explain why particular perspectives on and responses to these concerns are dominant and taken for granted, and others are marginalized. We expound in this chapter on the

PAAR spectrum we developed through our research. This is a heuristic tool we use to map different ways of dealing with golf-related environmental issues, ranging from **p**ro-golf to **a**lter-golf to **a**nti-golf **r**esponses.

This chapter is the lynchpin of the book in the sense that understanding different approaches to environmental decision-making and the assumptions that underpin these approaches is crucial if we are to offer a perceptive and rigorous assessment of how the golf industry has responded to environmental concerns over time. That is to say, when the assumptions underlying different approaches to environmentalism are highlighted and appreciated, then particular environmental practices begin to 'make sense'. From here, we are then better positioned to consider who benefits and who (or what) might be adversely affected when certain environmental pathways are chosen – and to begin to think about recommendations for promoting forms of environmentalism that do not undermine social and environmental goals in the name of economic progress. We ultimately provide such recommendations in the book's final chapter.

'Light-green' environmentalism: an ecological modernist narrative

We begin this chapter in earnest, then, with a review of ecological modernization (EM) and its links to the notion of sustainability. As a theory guiding environmental decision-making, EM stems in large part from German, Dutch, and British writing on the evolution of industrialization and its environmental impacts. At its core, EM theory rests on the simple premise that economic growth and environmental degradation can effectively be 'decoupled': the former need not necessarily engender the latter. The EM narrative is therefore distinguishable from the narratives offered by proponents of theories such as 'limits to growth' and the 'treadmill of production' (both described below) who assert that economic productivity in the post-Second World War years set the stage for ecological collapse. Indeed, it was the perceived failure of this critical (i.e. Marxist-informed) theorizing in the 1970s that, to a great extent, spurred the arrival of EM as a viable theoretical construct.

As EM advocate Arthur Mol described in his 2003 book *Globalization and Environmental Reform: The Ecological Modernization of the Global Economy*, the institutional changes stemming from the transformative sensibilities of limits to growth proponents in the 1970s and 1980s were 'meagre', thus paving the way for an era of more pragmatic thinking and more conciliatory efforts at resolving environmental problems. In fact, one of the most attractive aspects of EM is the apparent optimism that underlies its message of progress: that a consumer society can be a sustainable society. This feature of EM made it preferable to the 'bad news' stories offered by those who see many of EM's premises to be illusory, and who advocate for broad-based economic and lifestyle changes that are not easily digestible for businesses and many consumers. Gould, Pellow, and Schnaiberg (2004) – proponents of some of the more critical perspectives outlined below – readily admit that their narrative on environmental degradation and consumption is especially depressing reading for those wishing to believe that environmental sustainability is achievable.

While criticisms of EM abound, we do not want to underestimate what this theory has to offer, nor dismiss the compelling arguments that EM advocates continue to make. Perhaps the most intriguing assumption contained in EM theorizing is that human ingenuity in the name of environmental sustainability can light a pathway out of the 'darkness' of environmental degradation. To be precise, in the EM imagination it is technological innovation that has traditionally stood as the 'silver bullet' for resolving environmental problems (Davidson, 2012). This was especially true in early writing on EM – particularly the work of Huber (1982, 1985) – that envisioned a technology-aided switch from 'dirtier' forms of industrialization to 'clean', super-industrial methods of production. Innovation is, in this sense, a propulsive force. Moreover it fits together with a deregulatory sensibility. Indeed, for those championing 'weak' or techno-corporatist versions of EM, government intervention is seen as a last resort, to be taken when voluntary and market-based mechanisms fail (Davidson, 2012: 37; also see Christoff, 1996; Hajer, 1995). This deregulatory sensibility is also a hallmark of neoliberalism – with neoliberalism referring here to a form of governance and an ideology that is based on the idea that market mechanisms can best lead to the resolution of economic, social, and environmental problems (Harvey, 2005). The idea, in other words, is that consumers who value pro-environment work will support businesses that are leading the development and implementation of 'green' products and services. This, in turn, will inspire further innovation among businesses, who will continue to serve the needs of the environment as a logical result of their economic self-interest (Wilson, 2012a, 2012b). 'Weak' EM also sits alongside stronger versions of this theory. The latter impress the need for government intervention in cases where industries are unreceptive to adopting cleaner technologies or where more socially just environmental outcomes might be achieved (see Christoff, 1996; Davidson, 2012). In both cases, though, the market stands as a driver of positive environmental outcomes, given its place as a site par excellence for innovation.

Although the term ecological modernization has not (yet) achieved mainstream cachet, as noted earlier, EM is closely affiliated with the widely recognized concept of sustainable development and its more politically palatable variant, sustainability (politically palatable in that its drops the reference to development, and thus more easily avoids the critique that economic motives are in fact driving environmental decision-making). The origins of sustainable development lie with the 1987 World Commission on Environment and Development (WCED) (also known as the Brundtland Commission) where the term was defined as follows: "meeting the needs of the present without compromising the ability of future generations to meet their own needs" (WCED, 1987: 8; also see Chernushenko *et al.*, 2001). Said another way, through the prism of sustainable development, economic, social, and environmental concerns – the 'triple bottom line' – are inseparable, and as such must be dealt with in an integrated manner. In the late 1980s and early 1990s, this was an appealing logic to governments and businesses alike in the face of more radical formulations urging the curtailment of economic expansion. 'Third sector' organizations, and especially more mainstream environmental NGOs, have largely embraced sustainable development as well – a point we explore in later chapters. By the mid-1990s, sustainability discourses had achieved mainstream integration to the point that Campbell (1996) was moved to proclaim that, in the 'battle' of public ideas, sustainability had won: "the task of the coming years is simply to work out the details, and to narrow the gap between theory and practice" (Campbell, 1996: 312, cited in Krueger and Gibbs, 2007: 1).

Of course, sustainable development, as a theoretical concept, is linked with a range of practices when it comes to its 'real' applications. It is possible, therefore, to emphasize the latter half of the concept's definition: "meeting the needs of the present *without compromising the ability of future generations to meet their own needs*". This could serve as a rationale for limiting industrial expansion in the name of protecting future generations against, for example, dangerous levels of atmospheric carbon dioxide. In other words, it could justify a 'limits to growth' approach, and *demodernization*. One might also interrogate how 'needs' is interpreted in this definition. Are golf courses, and particularly conspicuously 'green' ones, a need of present generations? The key point for the time being is that sustainable development, in moving from theory to practice, has been tethered to the principles of EM. As Keil (2007) says, through its relationship with EM, sustainability is "redefined as one of the possible routes for a neoliberal renewal of the capitalist accumulation process" (Keil, 2007: 46).

It is clear at this point why sustainability and EM principles are so appealing. At its core, EM is a theory of social change (Buttel, 2000), one that carries forward the positive view of modernization – modernization as progress – posited by functionalist scholars such as Talcott Parsons. 'Stronger' versions of EM are tied to the 'reflexive' modernization perspective that has gained prominence more recently, mainly in that key social actors must take a reflexive and vigilant approach to understanding environmental risks and their potential impacts (though without intruding too severely on corporate activity) (Beck, 1992). As Dryzek (2005) points out, what this means in practical terms is that EM and sustainability are both 'reassurance' discourses: "No tough choices need to be made between economic growth and environmental protection, or between the present and the long-term future" (Drzek, 2005: 172). To use Mol's words, EM has "created the theoretical basis for a growing confidence that environmental reform can no longer be viewed exclusively in apocalyptic terms" (Mol, 2003: 53).

To be sure, there are success stories pertaining to sustainability and EM. The concrete manifestations of sustainability range from bike paths to carbon reduction strategies to increased use of renewable energy sources and beyond (see Krueger and Gibbs, 2007: 6). As we will describe in upcoming chapters, the arrival of IPM in agriculture – and, as we will show, golf course management – has been regarded by some as a technology-aided, 'modern' environmental success story as well.

Given the centrality of EM to our analysis in this book, it is worth highlighting Mol's (2003) review of the five core features of EM-based environmental restructuring before outlining critiques of EM theory and practice. These features are as follows:

- A view that while science and technology are possible 'causes' of environmental deterioration in the sense that they have historical and contemporary associations with dirty forms of industrialization, they are also avenues towards resolving and even preventing environmental problems.
- Heightened emphasis on "economic and market dynamics and economic agents" as "social carriers of ecological restructuring, innovation and reform" (p. 61).
- A trend towards "decentralized, flexible and consensual styles of national governance, at the expense of top-down hierarchical command-and-control regulation" (p. 62) – and as such the emboldening of non-state actors such as corporations and NGOs.

- A more centralized role for environmental organizations and activists in government and, at times, in industry decision-making – a move that also brings the need for a less antagonistic and more conciliatory approach from environmentalists and environmental groups.
- A changed socio-political landscape that privileges economic and environmental compromise: "Intergenerational solidarity in the interest of preserving the sustenance base seems to have emerged as the undisputed core and common principle" (p. 62).

The language of 'undisputed' in this final passage positions EM as the only viable way forward.

Dark-green environmentalism: questioning 'super modernity'

Ecological modernization thus presents a compelling narrative. In later chapters we outline how an EM-inspired version of sustainability has taken hold in the golf industry. Paraphrasing Mol, this has effectively countered the view that golf's environmental future need be seen in apocalyptic terms. Yet EM still has its critics, as does golf. Lingering concerns about golf's environmental impacts to a great extent reflect 'darker-green' theoretical perspectives on the environment.

We can start in this regard from critiques of EM, or at least its key tenets. Some of the most compelling commentaries on this matter pertain to EM theory's emphasis on technological innovation as an economically friendly solution to environmental problems. Political scientist Thomas Homer-Dixon (2001), while not addressing EM specifically, offered criticism of this type in his book *The Ingenuity Gap*. Homer-Dixon's concerns lie with science and technology in general, as opposed to their application with respect to the environment alone. The main 'gap' Homer-Dixon identifies pertains to the potential for innovative problem-solving. He suggests that there is often a notable 'time lag' between the moment problems are identified and the point at which technologies can successfully be developed to resolve them. As Homer-Dixon writes:

> The products of science and technology – the treatments for antibiotic-resistant disease, the advanced computer models of Earth's changing climate, the bio-engineered grains that can grow in a water-scarce world – will not always be there, in the right forms, when and where we want them. History shows that

> just because we want a problem solved doesn't mean the problem will be solved. (Homer-Dixon, 2001: 255–256)

That oil continued to spill into the gulf coast at an alarming rate long after the British Petroleum Deepwater Horizon disaster first took place in 2010 is an excellent example of Homer-Dixon's point. There is also the problem of recognizing environmental issues in their full scope, as the passage of time can reveal certain environmental incidents or practices to be more damaging than first thought (Homer-Dixon, 2001). So too can technologies directed towards 'cleaner' environmental outcomes induce new, environmentally damaging problems of their own (Beck, 1992). We shall see practical manifestations of these concerns in our discussion of methods used to treat golf course turfgrass, even after the turn away from DDT.

We do not read Homer-Dixon's (2001) assessment of the contemporary 'ingenuity gap' as a denunciation of science and technology *tout court*, nor do we take such an approach in our own evaluation of golf. The criticism here is focused on the sometimes zealous faith in technological innovation as a dependable 'solver' of complex problems – in this case environmental ones. Davidson (2012) echoes Homer-Dixon's thoughtful scepticism over technological ingenuity, though his concerns are relayed specifically in relation to EM. The aforementioned distinction between weak and strong EM is relevant to this critique. For those advocating weak EM – that is, the variant taking a more market-oriented approach in keeping with neoliberal principles – the heightened rate of efficiency brought on by innovation is a key avenue towards improved environmental outcomes. But emphasizing efficiency often means downplaying *overall* consumption, something that can indeed rise higher even as production processes are made 'greener', given the growth imperative inherent to capitalism. This phenomenon, termed 'Jevons' paradox', is based on the finding of economist William Stanley Jevons in the mid-1800s that consumption of coal rose higher even as its uses became more efficient (see Davidson, 2012: 38; Wilson, 2012b). Davidson suggests that this same phenomenon was visible more recently as CO_2 emissions rose in the post-war years despite substantial improvements in carbon efficiency. At this point one might return to Mol's (2003) assertion that while early writing on EM heavily favoured technological solutions to emergent environmental concerns, later theorizing 'corrected' this through a heightened focus on the role of the state in guiding prevailing forms of production where necessary. Yet Davidson (2012) counters that the discrepancy between strong and weak variants of EM has been overstated. In his view, while strong and weak EM advocates may differ in their views on the extent to which governments should direct the economy in the name of achieving positive environmental outcomes, over-reliance on corporate-driven innovation remains a feature of both perspectives.

Foster (2012) argues that the empirical basis for EM is decidedly 'meagre', and as such employs the precise language used by EM advocate Arthur Mol (2003) to characterize the practical outputs of more radical environmental theories in the 1970s. Success stories tend to be highly specific and localized, EM critics point out. In keeping with the principles of Jevons' paradox, they often pertain to the *process* of 'greening' capitalism as opposed to improved outcomes. On a larger scale, EM is "largely silent on what to do on a global level" (Dryzek, 2005: 179). As Foster (2012) says:

> Ecological modernization theory stresses narrowly defined environmental improvement on a national level, principally in the rich countries of the Triad (the United States, Europe, and Japan), while generally ignoring the ways in which such improvements are shown by ecological footprint analysis to be dependent on greater resource extraction from the global South, and on the movement of polluting industries and toxic wastes abroad to poorer countries. (Foster 2012: 225–226).

This is a critique that resonates among those studying the global expansion of golf – a point we discuss in more detail in later sections of this book.

At the root of these concerns about EM, as well as sustainability, is a familiar point: that care for ecological limits holds little hope in the face of the capitalist growth imperative. To use the language of sustainable development, the 'triple bottom line' is moot if the *financial* bottom line overshadows its social and environmental analogues. As Gould, Pellow, and Schnaiberg (2004) say in reflecting on developments from 1976 to the time of their writing: "We could state boldly that increasing the return on *investment has displaced every other social and environmental goal in this period*" (Gould et al., 2004: 305, emphasis in original).

Limits to growth and the treadmill of production

Gould *et al*.'s (2004) arguments are aligned with theories that are commonly invoked to counter EM perspectives – namely, the limits to growth and treadmill of production perspectives. These theories emerged in the 1970s based largely on fears that the relationship between capitalism and the environment, as constructed to that point, was charting a path towards ecological collapse. As Dryzek and Schlosberg (2005) recount, this fear was not uncommon at the time, as environmental doom-saying was emerging from many directions. A number of texts stressing that mistreatment of the environment would engender the Earth's, and thus humankind's, demise circulated through academic and activist circles, and at times reached the mainstream. The fundamental argument underlying these dire synopses was straightforward enough: "modern economic life assumes that growth and expansion can go on without limits, while the planet is made up of systems of finite resources that are threatened and carrying capacities that we are in danger of overshooting" (Dryzek and Schlosberg, 2005: 7). Elsewhere, Dryzek (2005) notes that the 'limits' idea is tied to a discourse of 'survivalism'. That is to say, the environment question is deemed an existential one – survival hangs in the balance – and as such it mandates draconian interventions in the name of ensuring that ecological limits are not breached.

The book *The Limits to Growth* (Meadows *et al.*, 1972), authored by a research team from the Massachusetts Institute of Technology (MIT), remains the most famous text to enunciate the limits perspective. Informed by computer modeling, the problem these researchers outlined rested on the fundamental character of growth: it was not just that food production, industrialization, pollution, consumption, and population were increasing, they were increasing *exponentially*. With respect to the last element in this list, for example, Meadows and her colleagues highlighted both the rate of growth in the population over the past three centuries, and the rate of growth *in the rate of growth itself* (Dryzek and Schlosberg, 2005: 16). This was in fact 'super-exponential' growth; Meadows *et al.* predicted it would yield a world population of roughly seven billion by the turn of the century. The world's rate of industrial production since the 1930s followed a similar trajectory:

> Much of each year's output is consumable goods, such as textiles, automobiles, and houses, that leave the industrial system. But some fraction of the production is more capital – looms, steel mills, lathes – which is an investment to increase the capital stock. Here we have another positive feedback loop. More capital creates more output, some variable fraction of the output is investment, and more investment means more capital. (Dryzek and Schlosberg, 2005: 19)

Stated more simply, capitalism *inherently* sees no limits to expansion, "there is no amount of profit, no amount of wealth, and no amount of consumption that is either 'enough' or 'too much'" (Madgoff and Foster, 2011: 43).

The crux, at least for these purposes, is that all of this means more demand on capitalism's host: the natural environment. Writing in the early 1970s, Meadows *et al.* (1972) acknowledged the lingering uncertainty on the matter of the Earth's ability to absorb pollution. Nonetheless, they highlighted four key areas of concern in relation to the environment: (a) that pollution seemed to be growing exponentially (like population and industrial output); (b) that the upper limit of pollution growth curves was unknown; (c) that ecological processes could have delayed effects; and (d) that pollutants are often globally distributed (Meadows *et al.*, 1972: 69). Pesticides – which, as we shall see, had become crucial by this time to the golf industry – were cited in relation to all four points. For example, the computer model employed by the MIT team showed that even if the usage rate of the chemical DDT was gradually reduced to zero beginning in 1970, such were DDT's lingering effects in the environment that the level of DDT in fish would continue to rise for more than ten years (Meadows *et al.*, 1972: 82). They also noted, and expressed consternation over, the fact that DDT had been found in the body fat of humans "in every part of the globe" (Meadows *et al.*, 1972: 84).

At first glance, the 'treadmill of production' concept, introduced by environmental sociologist Alan Schnaiberg (1980), is near identical to the idea of limits to growth. The metaphor of the treadmill is, in essence, shorthand for the positive feedback loops described by Meadows and her colleagues. Investment yields profit, profit yields *re*investment, and the treadmill cycle turns over and over. Each round of investment puts greater demand on the Earth's ecosystem – for example, through heightened demand on natural resources.

But what Schnaiberg (1980) added in his initial writing on the treadmill, and what he and his colleagues have since stressed in their updated thinking on this concept, are the sociological underpinnings of capitalism's growth agenda. As Gould, Pellow, and Schnaiberg (2004) recount, the treadmill of production was mainly an 'economic change theory', meaning it was focused on the changing allocation of capital investment, and the changing relationship between capital and labour, in the period after the Second World War. "Essentially", they explain, "the major changes outlined by the theory were that more capital was becoming accumulated in Western economies, and this capital was being applied to replacing production labor with new technologies to increase profits" (Gould *et al.*, 2004: 296). These technologies could themselves require more energy and/or chemicals than labour-intensive production, thus upping the environmental ramifications of production processes. Furthermore, from the treadmill perspective, economic change also exacerbates the need for industrial expansion in the sense that technologies represent forms of 'sunk capital': their costs cannot be lessened as easily as, for example, cutting labour, and so profitability-via-expansion becomes all the more important. Gould and colleagues outline the treadmill's mode of operation in step-by-step fashion:

> The newer technologies [of the third quarter of the twentieth century] were inevitably more energy intensive and chemical intensive on one hand and less labor intensive on the other. Capital mobilization for these changes in production technology arose from a substantial postwar economic boom, which led to increased production and profits. Next, these profits were disproportionately used to develop and introduce new physical technologies. However, to amortize the fixed and operating costs of the new technology, production generally had to be substantially increased. In turn, this increased the demand for natural resources, both energy and other. Once in place, the expanded production of the new technologies substantially increased both the volume of production waste and the toxicity of wastes (due to increased use of chemicals). (Gould et al., 2004: 300)

The treadmill is thus Marxist in its inclination, with the idea that economic growth is a structuring logic – an *ideology*, as much as an outcome. Indeed, the appeal of economic growth extends beyond industry to governments and publics alike. As Meadows *et al.* (2004) say in their more recent writing on the limits to growth, governments see economic growth as a solution to problems such as employment and upward mobility; publics embrace it "because they believe growth will give them an ever increasing welfare" (Meadows *et al.*, 2004: 6). Furthermore, with its global expansion, the treadmill can be conceived as transnational in its scope.

All told, dark-green perspectives on the environment call into question the logic of the triple bottom line. If environmental sustainability is only valued *to the extent* it complies with economic goals, it is always at risk of being marginalized.

Sport and environmental discourse

How do these theoretical perspectives map on to sport? This is a question we explore throughout this book as it pertains to golf, though our analysis herein is not entirely without precedent. We noted in the previous chapter that sport's relationship with the environment has been studied previously (albeit limitedly), and that this includes initial work in the realm of critical golf studies. Here we can add that this literature in some ways reflects the debates outlined above.

We ourselves have argued previously that ecological modernization has become a powerful force in the realm of sport, even if EM often camouflages itself in the more accessible language of sustainability (Wilson, 2012a, 2012b; Wilson and Millington, 2013, 2015; also see Karamichas, 2013). An early and important contribution advancing the idea that environmentally and socially responsible sport is 'good for the business of sport' was Canadian environmentalist and consultant David Chernushenko's book *Greening Our Games* (Chernushenko, 1994; also see Chernushenko *et al.*, 2001). To be sure, Chernushenko is aware of the many problems associated with pursuing a sustainable development agenda in and through sport. Not least among these is the fact that such an agenda is easily corrupted by the privileging of economic development ahead of environmental or social goals and the fact that organizations driven by profit may be more committed to appearing green than actually carrying out a comprehensive and responsible green agenda. Even so, Chernushenko remains optimistic about the possibility of sustainability in its various dimensions. He sees great merit in reaching out to sport-related organizations and promoting the triple bottom line benefits of responsible corporate work.

Chernushenko, therefore, effectively voices a 'light-green' perspective – a point not lost on sociologist Helen Lenskyj (1998; also see Lenskyj, 2002) in her own foundational reflections on sport and the environment. But whereas Lenskyj is critical of this light-green sensibility, the optimistic spirit of *Greening Our Games* is now reflected in the practical sustainability initiatives of sport managers and organizers of various stripes. We suggested as much in our own assessment of what we have called 'a new breed of (corporate) environmentalist', what we termed the 'sport management environmentalist', or SME. We defined this archetype in the following way:

> The SME is a corporate or corporate-linked environmentalist – a manager, organizer, promoter or other that is often (though not always) affiliated with a sport mega-event. SMEs can also be major sport organizations (i.e. those hosting sport mega-events), corporations (e.g. Mizuno or General Electric), environmental NGOs (e.g. Greenpeace), or members of governments lobbying to host a sport mega-event. (Wilson and Millington, 2015: 366)

Our argument from there is that SMEs are now positioned across the sporting landscape, and that they have come to adopt EM principles in their attempts to organize and carry out sustainable sporting events – even if EM is never mentioned explicitly as being a guiding framework. In this sense, SMEs are effectively staking their claim as the 'new' environmentalists. They are often emboldened by new technologies such as carbon offsetting mechanisms or green forms of venue construction. Their work is furthermore bolstered by the welcoming hand of governments and, at times, environmental groups keen on using the power and appeal of sport 'for good'. Indeed, events such as the World Conference on Sport and the Environment – a biennial conference jointly hosted by the United Nations Environmental Programme (UNEP) and a local organizing committee for a sport mega-event – provide opportunities for showcasing sustainable sport and for collaborative dialogue between various stakeholders in sport-based environmental initiatives. It is telling in this regard that Arthur Mol (2010), noted above for his generally positive view of EM, has recently described sustainability as an 'attractor' that helps global 'flows' (e.g. of technology/technological ingenuity) 'settle' in particular places, and sporting mega-events as helpful contributors to this process. Mol gives the 2008 Beijing Olympic/Paralympic Games as a case in point. The environment, he writes, "permeated all Olympic processes – design and construction, refurbishment, marketing, procurement, logistics, accommodation, transport, office work, publicity and operational affairs" (Mol, 2010: 508).

The emergence of SMEs makes it hard to contest that stakeholders in sport are, in fact, concerned with the environment. Yet, as might be expected, even in a time of corporate responsibility, sport's relationship with the environment has still earned criticism. Indeed, for Lenskyj (1998), the light-green hue of Chernushenko's account needs be understood against a darker-green understanding of the environment that values nature intrinsically – and not simply when environmentalism aligns with capitalism. Without denouncing innovation in principle, we ourselves have taken a critical view of the prominent place of technological innovation in the recent work of SMEs. For example, we have noted limitations to the popular carbon credit system used to offset the impact of sporting mega-events:

> being 'carbon neutral' says little about how local ecosystems were potentially disrupted in the preparations for and holding of sport mega-events. For example, building a highway through an environmentally sensitive green space to an event venue still impacts that particular green space, even if the carbon emissions associated with that construction project are offset. Moreover, the criteria used for assessing what 'counts' as an emission associated with holding a sport event and what counts as an appropriate offset project are not straightforward either. (Wilson and Millington, 2015: 371)

In effect, the idea we are critiquing here – that through the balancing of economic and environmental 'costs and benefits', we can appropriately resolve environmental problems without compromises – is at the core of modernist thinking about what counts as progress. A related point in this regard is that EM, in making the triple bottom line unassailable, has shifted the ground on which sporting events are assessed. Questions under consideration generally pertain to *how* sustainable events might be organized, and not *whether* the environmental costs of hosting, say, the Olympic and Paralympic Games in the first place are unreasonably high, or whether holding a more modest event might be desirable even if it yields fewer economic benefits (Wilson, 2012a, 2012b). As we shall see in Chapter 7, there are questions here too about whether, in a time of market-based environmental solutions, governments are willing to hold industry to account in meaningful ways should they fail to adopt their pledged sustainability measures. Finally, in reference to golf specifically, Wheeler and Nauright (2006) suggest that heightened environmental awareness and improved practices (e.g. in the use of chemicals) have not been taken up evenly across the globe. This echoes the above-noted view that EM's benefits are highly contextualized.

How leadership is secured: sport, social change, and hegemony

Sport thus remains a site for environmental debate, though the work of SMEs shows that the logic of EM is now dominant. Sport in this sense reflects its wider conditions. The question remains as to *why* EM has become dominant in sport and beyond despite its many criticisms. We know why industries might embrace EM – it is conducive to economic growth. But why would others do so? Why would the public accept 'risky' environmental practices when it may not be in their own best interest to do so? EM advocates might say that EM's impeccable logic underpins its rise to prominence. In this section, however, we highlight sociological conceptions useful in understanding the processes by which certain ideas are accepted over others.

Sociologists have for some time taken interest in how particular groups establish leadership on important and potentially divisive issues. A key concept that is commonly used in this regard is hegemony, indebted especially to the work of Italian social theorist Antonio Gramsci. For Gramsci, power is most effectively maintained when subordinate groups come to accept the perspectives of those in authoritative positions (see Gramsci, 1971). Power is won, in other words, through a process of winning consent; in this regard, power is ideological more so than coercive. The work of influential French theorist Louis Althusser (1971) is also instructive in this sense. Althusser described how 'ideological state apparatuses' – meaning influential socializing institutions like education, mass media, and religion (and many have argued in the last several decades, sport) – could serve to reinforce the purportedly commonsensical nature of certain ideas, providing a structural dimension (apparatus) for their dissemination.

As we shall see in Chapter 4, media in particular has been important in golf's environmental 'story', as television images of tournament courses in the post-war years helped instil a common sense idea of how a golf course should in fact appear. Subsequent chapters explore the use of formal public relations (PR) campaigns in the golf industry's quest to explain golf's environmental compatibility. That said, and acknowledging that critics have highlighted corporations' enlistment of PR professionals to reframe activities considered environmentally unfriendly, Greenberg *et al.* (2011) also make the important point that *various* actors work with PR firms and use established PR techniques in their attempts to mobilize support for their preferred positions. In their own environment-related research, for example, Greenberg *et al.* consider how environmental NGOs and their corporate adversaries engaged in PR-enabled 'spin wars' when it came to framing climate change debates. Greenberg *et al.*'s (2011) 'agnostic' approach is helpful for our purposes in the sense that we are interested in how different actors have responded to golf-related environmental concerns. We are attentive to the impression management techniques used by golf industry members attempting to 'frame' and 'spin' their environment-related activities for key audiences, though we also consider how groups protesting golf course development projects or turf management practices strive to raise awareness about and generate support for their oppositional or counter-hegemonic positions.

By considering bigger picture theories (like those proposed by Gramsci and Althusser) that describe how consent is generated for particular viewpoints alongside research on the techniques and strategies used to sway opinions and perspectives, we can begin to develop a textured approach to understanding why particular forms of environmental decision-making become and remain dominant. Of course, there is more to this picture than just the PR activity of industry. Governments too have adopted EM – again, generally without naming it as such – as a viable way of addressing environmental concerns without invoking the spectre of demodernization. As suggested in our above discussion of the treadmill of production and limits to growth frameworks, governments generally take for granted the merits of economic growth, and so are naturally inclined towards EM's positive triple bottom line messaging (see Davidson and MacKendrick, 2004). John Hannigan's (2006) concept of 'environmental managerialism' helps in taking this point a step further. Hannigan sees governments as 'dually mandated' at present, inclined by mandate towards both economic growth, what with its positive implications for labour and capital, and environmental sustainability, what with its existential implications for humankind. The outcome of this Janus-faced predicament is often policies that gesture towards environmental solutions without impeding too much on industry. We shall explore environmental managerialism in relation to pesticide policy later in this book. For now, Hannigan's formulation is relevant to this discussion of hegemony in that it describes how, through the strategic and selective development of economic and environment-related legislation and policies, consent is generated or further cemented for particular responses to environmental concerns.

At this point it becomes clearer how a range of social actors – representatives of industry, government officials, sympathetic members of the public, and, at times, environmental groups – congregate around a particular (environmental) logic. There is one more 'character' to consider, however, in the fostering of consent: the environment itself. This may seem a curious inclusion. Yet authors such as Paul Robbins (2007) go a step beyond those who have used concepts like hegemony to describe how it is that practices such as the use of potentially harmful chemicals on golf courses are taken for granted by suggesting that non-humans can at times serve as 'active agents'. Here Robbins is drawing jointly on the writings of Bruno Latour and Louis Althusser in arguing that seemingly inanimate 'things' such as pristine turfgrass can ultimately compel people to act in certain ways. Robbins' (2007) own analysis centres on the treatment of personal lawns and the curious finding that 'lawn people' seem to be at the beck and call of their (highly manicured) grass. Lawn people are, according to Robbins, essentially 'turfgrass subjects' – compelled to use chemical applications *even though they generally accept that these chemicals are associated with negative health-related outcomes*. Of course, while the turf has agency in this seemingly bizarre relationship, this agency is itself derived from the wider context. The agency of the turf can be traced back to wider cultural norms and expectations about what a lawn *should* look like, how it can and should be treated, and what it means to have a blemished or unblemished lawn, among other factors. Mark Stoddart (2012) performed a similar analysis, in his case of sport, in assessing how non-human 'actants' on ski hills such as snow and animals 'direct' the activities of skiers and maintenance staff.

Thus, it is through the activity of multiple stakeholders – humans and non-humans alike – that we arrive at a situation whereby dominant ideas are established and alternative perspectives are made 'radical' or unrealistic. One interpretation here is that establishing a set of agreed upon principles, like those espoused by proponents of sustainability, is crucial for effective consensus building, and as such should be embraced. A more critical orientation, however, would point towards the grounds upon which consensuses *must* now be built. As Neo (2010) notes in his work on golf and the environment, and as we suggested in discussing sport and EM above, dialogue on *how* to deliver economically friendly sport events and spaces does not always include debates on *whether* such events or spaces should be offered or created in the first place. Said otherwise, the idea that economic and environmental issues can and should be dealt with simultaneously is never the subject of scrutiny.

Social theorist Slavoj Žižek (1999) calls these sorts of arrangements 'post-political' – meaning that only a narrow range of viewpoints and questions are considered viable – i.e. are heard or allowed – in forums where key issues are being debated. Post-politics differs from more open and inclusive forms of 'contentious' politics – i.e. political arrangements that leave room for myriad and perhaps 'radical' opinions. For example, under post-political conditions, the answer to potentially contentious questions such as 'how should we deal with the environment- and health-impacting behaviours of industry?' might begin from the consensus that economic growth should never be compromised. Dialogue then becomes about finding solutions that align with this already-established consensus – hence the post in 'post-political'. Indeed, the concept of post-politics takes the concept of hegemony a step further. This is not just a process of winning consent for certain ideas, but of acting from the premise that consent has already been won.

Theorizing golf and social change

Of course, even within post-political arrangements, still not everyone offers consent to the (environmental) solutions in question or their underlying premises. Counter-hegemony is still possible; contentious political positions are still alive (but are not always well). As the cultural theorist Raymond Williams (1977) posited, dominant ideas exist alongside other types of ideas. These include 'residual' ideas that were at one time dominant but are now marginal and, even more pertinent for our purposes (see Chapter 9), 'emergent' ideas that have come into existence but are not dominant and may never become so.

Informed by Williams' work, sociologists Jean Harvey, John Horne, and Parissa Safai (2009) devised a typology that depicted a range of sport-related responses to aspects of globalization and to related forms of neoliberal governance. In doing so, they distinguished between anti-globalization (or 'rejectionist') movements, alter-globalization movements (which include 'transformist' and 'reformist' movements), and pro-globalization or 'neoliberal' forms of globalization that value unimpeded trade. Harvey *et al.* (2009) depict these different responses as follows:

- Rejectionist (anti-globalization)
  - rejects all forms of globalization
  - privileges local/regional/national self-governing societies
- Transformist (alter-globalization)
  - resists neoliberal globalization
  - seeks new forms of globalization, opportunities for global movements
- Reformist (alter-globalization)
  - 'tamed' form of global capitalism
  - lobbies for better work conditions (e.g. in athletic apparel factories)
- Neoliberal
  - uninhibited, market-driven, limited regulation

Harvey *et al.*'s model is intriguing because it sheds light on the range of alternatives to the dominant neoliberal approach to globalization which sees the marketplace, above all else, as a driver of social 'good'. The model also highlights interesting and nuanced differences between these alternatives. For example, some alternative responses are intended to undermine fundamental features of globalization that are more closely aligned with neoliberalism, while others advocate for relatively minor tweaks to the current system. This model influenced our thinking about the sometimes stark and sometimes barely discernible distinctions that exist between the various responses to golf-related environmental problems that we identified through research of our own.

Our own strategy for arranging and visualizing responses to golf-related environmental issues was inspired by Harvey *et al.*'s theorizing. Yet our model also has several distinct features. Figure 1 maps out the pro-alter-anti-response (PAAR) continuum that we develop through the remainder of the book. The positions across the PAAR continuum each pertain to a set of responses to golf-related environmental problems. We have labelled the far left as 'pro-golf' to signify a position where golf course construction and maintenance takes place without inherent concern for environmental issues – a non-response if you will. It is also '*Promethean*' in the sense that it is human-centric – a point we elaborate on in upcoming chapters. Those taking this extreme position are concerned with consumer/golfer preferences, and effectively deny that golf need be any more environmentally friendly than it already is. As we shall see, actually

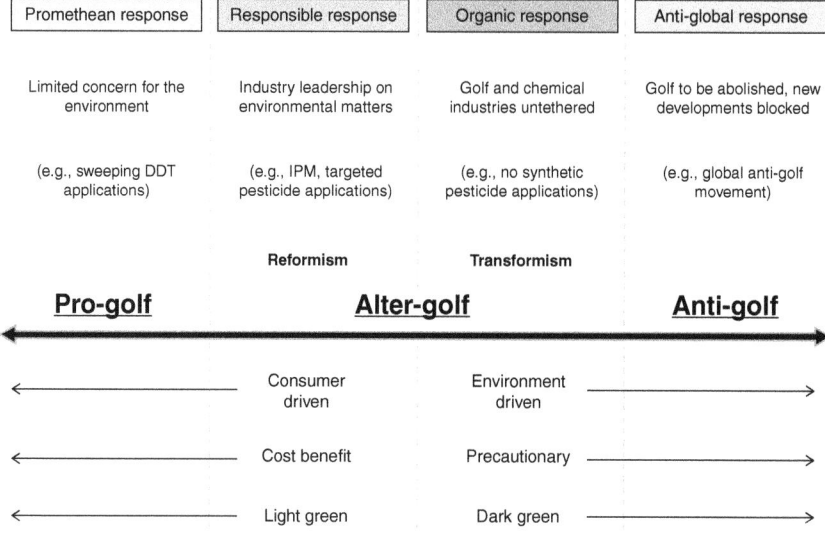

Figure 1 The pro-alter-anti-response (PAAR) continuum

taking this position – at least as a public stance on golf – is essentially untenable at the moment.

Across the middle of the continuum is a broader and more complex category of responses we call 'alter-golf'. This includes the reformist responses that come from many in the golf industry and many governments. This sub-category includes attempts at making existing course maintenance and construction practices greener without fundamentally interrupting key economic drivers in the process. Practically speaking, this means that pesticide use is still tolerated and that the growth of the golf industry and related tourist industry are still encouraged – the idea being that such growth can take place 'responsibly'. Such responses are open to critique from those who see responsible, industry-friendly activities as attempts to appear green without fundamentally changing environmental practices.

Alter-golf also includes transformational responses, such as 'organic golf' (see Chapter 9). The organic or 'chemical-free' response to concerns about pesticide use on golf courses is transformational in the sense that it demands that golf break from (or, at least, radically reimagine) the complex and lucrative supply chain that links the sport to the chemical industry. Organic golf also offers an alternative to the dominant and global trend towards pristine and predictable golf experiences that pro-golf is based on and that *reformist* versions of alter-golf seek to achieve by 'responsible' means. More generally, transformist alter-golf responses tend to recognize that golf courses should only be constructed and supported under certain circumstances. In the conclusion to this book, we further discuss and ultimately advocate for this way of thinking about golf and its environmental future.

Finally, on the far right of the continuum are those who reject golf altogether. Individuals and groups taking this extreme stance include members of the Global Anti-Golf Movement and those who, for various reasons, reject proposals for golf courses on a more local level (see Chapter 8).

We can think of the responses on the left side of the table as being the 'lightest-green' responses. Moving across the table to the right, responses become increasingly 'darker green'. The lighter-green responses are based on assumptions about the ability of humans to 'modernize' – to move society forward so that economic and environmental problems are overcome through managerial and technological innovations. The darker-green and more ecocentric responses attempt to unsettle the modernizing narrative that often goes unquestioned by those pushing forward with sustainability-driven environmental work. Across the following chapters, we look closer at these different responses, assessing their strengths, limitations, and contradictions. In the spirit of our above analysis of how, in theory, power relations are created and maintained, we also pay particular attention to why some approaches are dominant and others are marginal or residual.

At the outset of this chapter we noted that we encountered a wide range of perspectives in our research on golf, from those of the golf industry proper to those of community residents seeing merits in, for example, creating courses on old landfill sites to those that effectively see 'responsible golf' as an oxymoron. Now with a selection of theoretical concepts in hand, we can start to paint a more nuanced picture of golf's environmental past, present, and future.

PART II
Background and history

3

Waging a war on pests: golf comes to America

Having established our theoretical foundation, we begin this chapter in the early 1900s, at a time not long after golf had migrated to North America from the other side of the Atlantic. Golf's official history in North America begins in 1873 with the foundation of the Royal Montreal Golf Club in Montreal, Canada (The Royal Montreal Golf Club, 2011). Fifteen years later, the first American course was formed in Yonkers, New York (see PGA.com, 2013). The journey from Europe to Canada and the United States was surely not the first moment at which golf spiralled together with the forces of globalization. The Royal Calcutta Golf Club, for example, still considers itself "the home of golf in India", having been founded in 1829 and conferred the title 'Royal' at the start of the next century (The Royal Calcutta Golf Club., n.d.).

But our analysis in this chapter begins from the premise that golf's journey to North America, and especially the United States, is particularly important when considering the game's overall history – and its environmental impact. Although golf's origins are contested, Scotland is commonly presumed to be the birthplace of the game. Scotland is, if nothing else, the site of one of golf's more famous stories: King James II's attempt to ban golf on the grounds that it was distracting the masses from their archery practice (British Golf Museum, n.d.). This was an injunction destined to fail. In 1552, as Campbell (2002) recounts, "the citizens of the town of St Andrews [Scotland] were given, by charter right, the use of the links for 'golf, futball, shuteing at all times with other manners of pastime'" (Campbell, 2002: 15). St Andrews Links remains one of the most famous courses in the world; it brands itself as 'the home of golf' to this day (St Andrews Links, n.d.).

What is important to both our examination of golf in this chapter and to our claim that golf's voyage to North America has relevance to (current) thinking about environmental issues is the *form* that golf courses took before the sport arrived on North American shores. On this matter, Campbell's reflections on golf's foundational years in Scotland are instructive once again:

> The first golf courses were rudimentary indeed and very far from being anything like the courses of present day. There were no greens or tees as such and the hole was a crude affair cut roughly with a knife. It served not only as the ultimate resting place for the ball but as a supply of sand for teeing the ball for the next drive. (Campbell, 2002: 15)

The golf course was a mixed use terrain – a site, for example, for sheep grazing in addition to golf. So varied were the uses of golf course landscapes that golfers wore red coats to warn others than a golf ball might be headed in their direction (Golf Canada, n.d.).

This is not to say, of course, that there was no human modification of natural landscapes before golf arrived in North America. As Bale (1994) writes, golf spread through Scotland and England in the 1800s to the extent that "one observer noted that the resulting landscapes had no relationship with nature" (Bale, 1994: 54; cf., Lowerson, 1993: 134). Rather, it is to say that the game of golf, from its foundations to the twentieth century, was to a great extent subject to the natural whims of the land upon which it was played. We shall see how in later years this power dynamic was effectively reversed.

This review of golf's early history sets the stage for our main argument in this chapter – an argument that re-emerges in different forms throughout this book. The argument is this: to explain the emergence of chemical-intensive 'pro-golf', which reached a high point in the 1970s (the point where this chapter ends), it is crucial to examine how broader processes associated with modernization have impacted the sport. Specifically, and based mainly on our review of industry trade publications, we contend that golf's dominant storyline across the first three quarters of the 1900s in North America is one of modernization – that is, of finding ways to transcend an allegedly 'primitive' past, primarily through investment in science and technology. In this sense, golf came to reflect Latour's synopsis of the traditional view of what it means to be modern:

> The adjective 'modern' designates a new regime, an acceleration, a rupture, a revolution in time. When the word 'modern', 'modernization', or 'modernity' appears, we are defining, by contrast, an archaic and stable past. Furthermore, the word is always being thrown into the middle of a fight, in a quarrel where there are winners and losers, Ancients and Moderns. (Latour, 1993: 10)

In practical terms, what this means is that golf industry representatives were constantly on the lookout for devices that could 'tame' the golf course landscape and help wage 'battle' against unwanted 'pests'. With the arrival of the post-war years, superintendents, course developers, and other key figures in the golf industry could mark out distance from their industry forbears most of all by adopting highly potent synthetic pesticides. At this point in time, as we shall see, these same stakeholders in golf were entering a political landscape rife with critiques of modernization.

Modern warfare: golf in the early 1900s

In recounting golf's historical development, renowned golf architect Michael Hurdzan (1994) starts from the same point that we did above. "In the time of Old Tom Morris (mid-1800s to early 1900s)," he writes, "golf courses were laid out on the land with little or no modification to the ground except the clearing of brush or trees and seeding turfgrasses." Old Tom Morris was famous first as a golfer in the mid-1800s, though he is remembered in the golf industry as much for his contributions as a greenkeeper at the aforementioned St Andrew's Links course as he is for his playing accomplishments. Hurdzan continues: "Similarly, golf course maintenance was simple, requiring only that the greenkeeper occasionally mow the grass, topdress liberally, fertilize sparingly with natural fertilizer sources, and resod as needed. Golf had virtually no impact on the land" (Hurdzan, 1994: 191). The story was not all that different, Hurdzan suggests, from the early 1900s to the middle of the century. 'Crude' earthmoving equipment was adopted to help better shape the land; course maintenance became slightly more sophisticated, "but still relied heavily on mowing, topdressing, and natural chemicals" (Hurdzan, 1994: 189). Golf's environmental impacts were still muted – at least relative to later times.

Hurdzan's reflections are instructive, both for their historical perceptiveness and their implicit acknowledgement (which Hurdzan later renders explicit) that golf would eventually have much more significant environmental impacts. But the US publication *The Golf Course* – a regularly issued bulletin for discussing golf course construction and upkeep – suggests that golf course development and maintenance could be challenging even in the early 1900s, and that golf industry professionals at times saw themselves as breaking away from a preceding era. Indeed, *The Golf Course* has been described as a publication that hoped "to fill a growing technical information need" for key golf stakeholders (Turfgrass Information File, n.d.a). It was important in the sense in that it pre-dated the release of other influential publications (e.g. the *Bulletin of the Green Section of the US Golf Association*) and in that it provided a venue for discussing 'modern' construction- and maintenance-related practices.

The modernist sensibilities that informed *The Golf Course* were signalled in volume one, issue one of this publication. Readers of the bulletin could prepare themselves, the publishers wrote, for authoritative prescriptions from leading industry professionals. This much was needed as golf continued to evolve:

> In every section of the country new courses are being built and old courses reconstructed along scientific lines, which received but scant consideration about five years ago. Nowadays turf is produced and maintained to such a high degree of excellence that the early efforts are made to appear amateurish by comparison. Golfers everywhere are critical and fastidious, and no longer are they content with the primitive courses of early days. (Anon., 1916a: 2)

The Golf Course, then, set out to "present tested excellence in everything" (Anon., 1916a: 2). Subsequent issues would not fail in taking up this modernist theme. Most notable in this regard was the series termed 'Modern Golf Chats', penned by the well-regarded course architect A. W. Tillinghast. In one instalment of this series, Tillinghast wrote that early US golf courses – "with their featureless greens, mathematically correct and symmetrical bunkers and the ridiculous little bandbox teeing grounds" – had become a thing of the past. "The golf courses which we Americans are constructing to-day are very different, and so carefully are they built, after a thoughtful preparation of plans, that some of our productions are not surpassed even in the old home of golf" (Tillinghast, 1916a: 1). Presumably the 'old home' referred to here is Scotland, birthplace of Old Tom Morris.

Tillinghast's was not the only assessment of this kind. For example, an article from 1918 told of the uses of dynamite in course construction. Older methods of devising golf course landscapes could no longer be used, the author wrote: "Explosives are now included with horses, steam and gasoline as conservers of manual effort" (Anon., 1918: 53).

Yet while explosives were depicted as a time and labour-saving device for course developers, elsewhere in *The Golf Course* readers were told that maintaining already-developed courses could, in fact, demand ample energy expenditure. Take, for example, the following description of weeding from 1916:

> To free a lawn from tap-rooted weeds, divide the lawn into strips about 3 feet wide, take a basket to hold the weeds and a border fork with four flat prongs. Now, to remove the weed successfully, it is necessary to guess the depth of the root. Well grown dandelions and docks will go down over a foot, the smaller ones and the rib grass about 6 inches. In the first case, force the fork into the turf as deep as it will go and as far from the weed as the length of the prongs.

By depressing the handle of the fork the turf will be forced up like a mole hill. If the distance has been guessed correctly it will crack on either side of the weed, which can then be removed easily. In the case of the smaller weeds, force the fork into the soil about 6 inches from the weed and about 6 inches deep, and go on as before ... Always burn weeds, then you know for certain that they cannot give any more trouble. (Anon., 1916c: 81)

Here we see the pedagogical function of *The Golf Course* on full display. The aim, we can infer, was to create workable course maintenance norms for American greenkeepers. The 1920s would bring an initial 'boom' in course development in the United States (see Chapter 4) – in fact, even in 1916 we find reference to the "almost unbelievable number of new courses which have been built or are now in the state of construction" (Anon., 1916d: 114) – and there was an accompanying sentiment that courses need not disappoint. The image of a basket- and fork-wielding greenkeeper meticulously overseeing the land is one that would not stand the test of time. It can be read as proof, however, of the perception that the golf playing public would accept nothing less than the best course conditions possible.

Another article from 1916, in this case by Leonard Macomber, whom we presume to be the same Leonard Macomber who built many US golf courses near the turn of the century, gives further indication of the challenges faced by greenkeepers in the early 1900s. Macomber's was an even blunter assessment: "GREENKEEPING is no longer a peaceful occupation. It is a constant warfare throughout the entire season. The greenkeeper is always fighting against pests, grass diseases, weeds, bad drainage, etc." (Macomber, 1916: 27, emphasis in original). This contribution is worth highlighting for two reasons. First, while Macomber's language is indeed stark, it is clear too that it was not entirely out of step with what was being said and done in the wider context at the time – for example, in publications not concerned with golf per se. In 1922, for instance, renowned US entomologist Leland O. Howard penned an essay entitled 'The war against insects', a veritable call to arms for those involved in agricultural pursuits. This was a worldwide war, Howard argued, and one that, in the United States, had fomented research and interventionary measures at the state and federal levels. "All of this means that we are beginning to realize that insects are our most important rivals in nature and that we are beginning to develop our defense" (Howard, 2008: 20).

The second reason Macomber's essay is worth highlighting is for the view of science that underpinned his reflections on greenkeeping's 'constant warfare'. The idea that the golf industry's modernist turn was guided by science is suggested elsewhere in *The Golf Course* as well (e.g. see Anon., 1916e). For Macomber (1916), greenkeeping should be based on scientific principles. But here he provides a unique definition: "When applied to greenkeeping, science should be defined as organized common sense, and this is absolutely essential for success." Macomber continues: "For a greenkeeper to possess a comprehensive knowledge of agrostology, geology, botany, etc., is not necessary. *It is apt to prove very confusing*, and most always results in rule-of-thumb methods" (Macomber, 1916: 27, emphasis added). There is a risk, of course, in taking Macomber's words as the unquestionable truth of the greenkeeping experience. Other golf stakeholders may well have deemed botany (as one example) to be perfectly intelligible. Yet by virtue of their publication in *The Golf Course* it can be assumed that the publishers of this magazine saw at least some credibility in the notion that science was less a shared and systematic enterprise, and more the triumph of common sense. Other articles from this same source presented similar, if not quite as blunt, opinions on golf and modernity. In one of A. W. Tillinghast's 'Modern Golf Chats', for example, expertise was conceived as accumulated wisdom, rather than, say, the earning of credentials (Tillinghast, 1916b: 19).

The inter-war years: chemical solutions

As we shall see, Macomber's view that greenkeeping was 'warfare' would remain salient for years to come. His perspective on science was, however, far more fallible. In 1921, the United States Golf Association's (USGA's) *Green Section* publication emerged on the scene and took up the cause previously held by *The Golf Course*. Almost right away, a more systematic approach to turfgrass management than Macomber had imagined was emphasized.

Two of the key elements in the turn to 'responsible golf' that occupies our attention in Chapters 5, 6, and 7 are research and education. It seems that these were also prioritized in the early days of the *Green Section*. In 1921, for example, it was announced in this publication that Cornell University had established a course for golf course management training. "The original idea was that a two-year course to high school graduates should suffice", the article recounted, "but on further thought it was realized that to secure men skilled in such matters as soils, drainage, landscape architecture, turf growing, the use of machinery, the control of pests, etc., a more thorough training was necessary" (Anon., 1921: 141). In this same year, B. R. Leach from the United States Department of Agriculture explained that the Japanese Beetle had infested golf courses in

New Jersey and Pennsylvania. Leach was able to further comment on the implications of this development for golf thanks in large part to two years' worth of beetle-focused laboratory observations – in other words, thanks to research. More study was needed, though, to determine how the beetle might be eradicated without causing undue harm to the golf course itself (Leach, 1921).

Similar initiatives were evidently under way across the Atlantic. In 1929, the British Golf Unions formed the St Ives Research Station in Bingley, Yorkshire. Thereafter, their progress was reported on in the journal *Nature*. A report from 1930 highlights the rationale for this turn to empiricism:

> Greenkeeping problems have changed considerably in recent years, owing largely to such alterations in practice as the use of compost in place of the heavy roller, and by the introduction of mowers of improved design and numerous chemical fertilisers. Hitherto, agricultural methods have usually been employed, and too often the supposition that what is suitable for pasture is equally good for the golf green has proven a fallacy. A special type of turf is required for greens, free from coarse grasses, weeds, and worm casts. For this purpose the effect of various fertilizer treatments will be determined and a thorough, unbiased investigation of the so-called acid theory, which maintains that the type of turf required is obtained under acid soil conditions, will also be undertaken. (Anon., 1930: 30)

Worth noting in this passage is that greenkeeping is understood as having a kinship with other agricultural pursuits, but is ultimately seen as a unique activity. The specialized knowledge of those responsible for golf course management would in later years be mobilized in the face of criticisms of golf's environmental impacts.

The reference to chemical fertilizers in the above passage might be deemed conspicuous as well. As noted above, Hurdzan (1994) suggests that chemicals indeed found their way into the greenkeeping profession – albeit slowly – in the pre-Second World War period. To be sure, in the 1920s, chemicals were a 'tool' not hard to find if one looked to the world of agriculture in general. Returning to Leland O. Howard's anti-pest treatise from 1922, the thrust of his argument – beyond the demonizing of insect 'combatants' – was to champion the "the work of the chemist" (Howard, 2008: 21). The problem of pests was a pressing one, Howard wrote,

> That is why we are using a chemical means of warfare, by spraying our crops with chemical compounds and fumigating our citrus orchards and mills and warehouses with other chemical compounds, and are developing mechanical means both for utilizing these chemical means and for independent action. (Howard, 2008: 21)

Howard added that, even with these many uses, there were few effective insecticides in 1922. Diligence was needed in the years ahead to fortify the 'arsenal' that people would have at their disposal.

The value of the war metaphor to Howard's argument, just years after the First World War concluded, cannot be overstated: "there is a war, not among human beings, but between all humanity and certain forces that are arrayed against it" (Howard, 2008: 22). That said, it should not be assumed that chemicals were in all cases adopted with equal fervour. In the USGA's *Green Section*, for example, Albert A. Hansen wrote that chemicals have limited practical use on golf courses (something deemed through experimentation), though there are some situations where they might be usefully deployed. Dandelions, for instance, "may be killed by the application of gasoline, kerosene or carbon bisulphide to the individual plants" (Hansen, 1921: 129). This was especially true when gasoline was partnered with a tube and valve device that expedited the process of depositing the substance. Hansen's reflections take us further away from the basket and fork technique outlined in *The Golf Course*. The approach, though, was still *targeted*: "The method is too laborious to advocate except where the weeds are few in number and scattered over the turf" (Hansen, 1921: 129).

Yet Hansen also noted, almost in passing, the possibility of applying chemicals more broadly through sprayers. Four years later, Hugh I. Wilson (1925) of Merion Cricket Club in Pennsylvania took up this very cause. "There have been great difficulties in applying chemicals on golf courses," he wrote, "owing to the fact that either a hand pump had to be employed or else some larger and expensive spraying machine used" (Wilson, 1925: 33). Here Wilson is in almost direct conversation with Hansen. Importantly, however, he then described a 'proportioning machine' that allowed a green to be sprayed with a chemical solution in a matter of 15 minutes. The transition from targeted to broad-based pesticide applications was under way.

Another endorsement of the proportioning machine came from B. R. Leach (1925) of the United States Department of Agriculture. Leach followed his aforementioned synopsis from 1921 of Japanese Beetle infestations on golf courses in New Jersey and Pennsylvania with articles in subsequent years outlining the nature of the plague. By 1925, Leach was reflecting on the 'hysteria' of years past and how this frenzied discourse had largely subsided. The reason? The proportioning machine, working together with a carbon disulphide emulsion, made for the easy treatment of infested putting greens.

The point, then, is that chemicals were entering the greenkeeping profession at the same time that those managing golf courses – and presumably course owners overseeing their work – were seeking more efficient and modern methods of achieving their desired course aesthetic. It appears that at the same moment in time the search was on for cost-effective ways of maintaining a desirable golf course aesthetic in the UK as well. In an article in the journal *Nature* on the development of the St Ives Research Station, it was said that the most serious issue facing golf courses during the Station's first two decades was the prevention and eradication of weeds. Early work towards this end involved the use of ammonium sulphate and ammonium salts on the Station's many test turf patches. "Later, attention was turned to selective spraying with dilute solutions of arsenic acid" (Anon., 1950: 23). With the arrival of the post-war years, another product captured their interest: dichlorodiphenyltrichloroethane, better known as DDT.

The post-war years: 'the war on pests' intensifies

In 1936, the USGA's *Green Section* publication was fifteen years old. The greenkeeping profession was described at this time in laudatory terms: a 'fifteen-year miracle'. Since 1921, the 3,000 pages spent in USGA trade publications discussing turf management had "lifted greenkeeping out of the realm of mysticism, quackery, and humbug, and have revealed it as a science" (Anon., 1936a: 1). In 1936, the USGA also issued an index of key greenkeeping terms. The entry for 'chemicals' had an accompanying blurb:

> A large assortment of chemicals has been tested to determine their value for fertilizing turf and for controlling diseases, insects, and woods. Few important golf courses in this country are maintained without the use of some of the chemicals that have been tested by the Green Section. The testing of chemicals has supplied clubs with information as to their effectiveness for the purpose for which they are used as well as to the possibilities of harming the turf grasses. (Anon., 1936b: 4)

One might note here that it was turfgrass, and turfgrass alone, that was at risk of being harmed through the deployment of chemicals. The environment, as an integrated *system*, was evidently not a matter of concern.

But the challenge levied by science against 'mysticism' and 'quackery' in golf course management was only just beginning. In the post-war years, the technological inventiveness of the war period coalesced with the economic growth imperative of 'peaceful' consumer capitalism. Foster (2009) describes the period after 1945 as one characterized by a scientific-technical revolution that yielded substantial advances in five fields: steel, coal-petroleum, electricity, the internal combustion engine, and – most importantly for these purposes – chemicals (Foster, 2009: 4). This was especially true in the United States, where corporate research laboratories were devising new synthetic products that would eventually find their way to the marketplace. The aforementioned chemical DDT remains the most famous case in point along these lines.

The use of DDT as a powerful insecticide dates to 1939 and the Nobel Prize winning work of Paul Müller, employee at the Swiss chemical company Geigy AG (Kinkela, 2011: 7). The US public first came to know DDT through texts such as that penned by US Brigadier General James Stevens Simmons towards the conclusion of the Second World War. DDT was not new, Simmons wrote in the *Saturday Evening Post*, yet the knowledge of DDT as a safe and highly effective tool for eradicating insects was previously unknown. Moreover, the methods for its use had, by 1945, "been developed with phenomenal speed as a part of a streamlined program of wartime medical research" (Simmons, 2008: 32). Simmons showed little concern for the fanciful tales that warned of DDT's potentially deleterious impacts. Indeed, that ducks swimming on DDT-treated water could transport the chemical (unwittingly, of course) and in turn kill off mosquito larvae on *untreated* ponds was deemed a great boon to the human cause. Simmons (2008) expressed similar fondness over newly developed means for deploying this new product: "The most exciting development with DDT has been its experimental distribution from airplanes in the form of smokes and sprays to destroy mosquitoes in large inaccessible areas" (Simmons, 2008: 37). As entomologist Clay Lyle wrote in 1947:

> [At] no time in human history have the achievements of entomologists, working in collaboration with chemists and engineers, been of such universal value as to make in so short a time the name of an insecticide a common word in every household however humble or remote. (Lyle, 2008: 44)

DDT was thus re-territorializing the decades' old war on pests. Once hard-to-reach areas, whether within the household or far beyond, were now accessible thanks to a combination of modern chemistry and modern machinery. In historicizing DDT, Kinkela (2011) makes the case that the story of this chemical is a profoundly global one. In the most direct sense, DDT was deployed around the globe with the aim of eradicating illnesses – malaria especially – that had for ages plagued humankind. Yet DDT, Kinkela (2011) adds, was global in another way as well:

> Not only was it an effective pesticide, but it was mobile, persistent, and moved easily across borders and through the food chain. The hazards of DDT, therefore, were not bound by any one nation, but were, in fact, global. These environmental realities challenged prevailing notions of postwar development, highlighting the ecological interconnections between people, nations, and nature. (Kinkela, 2001: 6–7)

Foster's (2009) ruefulness about the post-war scientific-technical revolution can be read as an important add-on here: "Unfortunately, the progress in physics and chemistry [at this time] was not accompanied by an equally rapid expansion in the knowledge of how such substances might affect the environment" (Foster, 2009: 27).

'Chemical warfare' takes to the golf course

What of golf and the diligent greenkeeper in the face of these developments? Unsurprisingly, given the 'chemical turn' in golf in the 1920s and 1930s, the chemical innovations of the post-war years were also embraced by many in the golf industry.

It is perhaps not surprising that we find an initial mention of DDT in the USGA's family of trade publications in 1946 – that is, in the early days of DDT's non-military use. The reference in this case is notably cautious: DDT was described as a 'very promising' turf insecticide, and one that had helped control a range of pests both on the course and in the clubhouse. Yet it was also deemed dangerous if inhaled and "poisonous to cold-blooded animals, such as fish" (Anon., 1946: 3; also see Noer, 1946). A year later, in the greenkeeper publication *Golfdom*, DDT, along with other chemicals, was linked with the drive for efficiency among those responsible for golf course maintenance. Wrote Pennsylvania greenkeeper Joseph Valentine (1947): "Since World War II the trend toward greater thrift in maintenance is being advanced by the employment of more mechanized operations. The utilization of new chemical and mechanical developments does much to increase efficiency of golf course maintenance" (Valentine, 1947: 68). This is a familiar emplotment: innovation itself is deemed a time- and labour-saving device; the *embrace* of innovation is the shibboleth of the modern superintendent. At Valentine's course, DDT was applied with the help of a sixteen-foot wide dusting machine. He also mentioned the chemicals lead arsenate and 2,4-D in his reflections on technology and efficiency.

Indeed, according to industry trade publications, DDT was far from the lone pesticide used on golf courses in the post-war years. In 1967, for example, agronomist Lee Record opened his article in the USGA's *Green Section* by noting that fungicides, including those containing mercury, had become 'a must' in every golf superintendent's management programme. There were both broad spectrum and selective fungicides at the greenkeeper's disposal; either way, comprehensive knowledge of the land (e.g. as rendered through meticulous measurement) was needed before chemical deployment (Record, 1967).

In this same year, the Golf Course Superintendents Association of America (GCSAA)'s flagship publication, *The Golf Superintendent* (soon-to-be renamed *Golf Course Management*) featured an entry entitled 'Golf course chemical warfare takes to the air'. With tree spraying evidently a problem in managing the golf course landscape, a creative solution was suggested: "Low-volume applications of DDT sprayed by helicopter solved the tree spraying problem for many superintendents at a cost competitive with ground-based mist blowers or hydraulic sprayers" (Anon., 1967: 8). Even if this solution was not adopted en masse, the reference to ground-based mist blowers and hydraulic sprayers is suggestive that *broad-based* chemical applications were nonetheless valued at this time. Indeed, an ad from this same publication for the Shell Company's Vapona˙ insecticide from one year earlier showed a truck blanketing a tree line with an enormous fog cloud. The caption below read, "A Vapona˙ fog can reduce a mosquito problem to almost nothing in a matter of minutes" (Shell Vapona Insecticide, 1966: 29). Four decades earlier, greenkeepers were extolling the merits of course maintenance procedures whereby singular dandelions were injected one by one with pesticide solutions. The change from this earlier thinking, most evident by the mid-1960s, could not be more glaring.

To complement the above developments – and as suggested through the case of the Vapona˙ insecticide – in the post-war years pesticide advertisements were regularly appearing in publications like the GCSAA's *Golf Course Management*, as were ads for ever more sophisticated equipment such as mowers. Chemical suppliers at times used the opportunity to seize upon the modernist sensibilities of course management staff. For example, Hercules Turf and Horticultural Products advertised their 2,4-D pesticide through the image of 'Sitting Bull, the Sioux Chief' and the accompanying text "the professional knows better than to rely on hocus-pocus to build and maintain fine turf" (Hercules Turf and Horticultural Products, 1966: 9). Much the same was true in *Golf Course Management*'s Canadian analogue, *GreenMaster*. As one example, Killex Green Cross Products stressed the efficacy of their own chemical solution: "Killex combines 3 herbicides ... Mecoprop, 2,4-D and dicamba for safer, superior control of knotweed, dandelions, plantains, chick weeds, clovers, trefoil, creeping Charlie and dozens more of those problem weeds" (Green Cross Products, 1970: 7).

Two caveats are required in light of these developments. The first is that the relationship between the golf and chemical industries was, evidently, far from perfectly harmonious. In the 1960s and even into the 1970s we find articles in *Golf Course Management* warning the magazine's readership about the potentially nefarious commercial activity of pesticide salespeople. In April 1966, for example, the GCSAA published a letter entitled 'No Salesmen Allowed' in its regular 'The Thinking Superintendent' column (Sander, 1966: 40). Penned as a message for manufacturers and distributors of products such as fertilizers and fungicides, the letter expressed concern that salespeople were commonly uninformed and thus apt to waste a superintendent's time. In 1970, in both *Golf Course Management* and *GreenMaster*, we likewise find entries entitled 'Beware of Satchmo' – Satchmo being the conniving vendor with a "satchel [of] more gifts than a magic shop" (Powell, 1970a, 1970b; also see Cleaver, 1978a). With limited regulation in place, and with pesticide spraying emerging as the new, post-war 'normal', the superintendent's responsibilities had evidently grown to include deciphering the trustworthiness of chemical vendors.

The second caveat was that the golf industry was clearly aware in the immediate post-war years that pesticides such as DDT were potentially harmful. In 1966, for example, the GCSAA published an article entitled 'Poisons' in their flagship magazine. Therein, they listed a variety of chemicals alongside their toxicity levels, probable lethal dose, and symptoms of exposure (Anon., 1966). In a president's message in this same publication, also from 1966, pesticides were described as both part of the 'miracle of chemistry' and as having a Jekyll and Hyde-like quality. The Jekyll and Hyde metaphor referred to the consequences of pesticide mishandling; clear labelling was said to be the responsibility of the chemical industry, while ensuring labels are closely followed was the task of the superintendent (Roberts, 1966). To say this another way, 'harm' was indeed considered as it pertained to pesticides, though it generally meant potential harm to the golf course or to superintendent applicators themselves.

Silent Spring and the limits to growth

Of course, the arrival of potent synthetic chemicals at the marketplace in the post-war years was met with criticism as well. At the outset of this book, we saw the GCSAA's vehement, near-vituperative response to *Silent Spring*, the anti-chemical treatise authored by environmentalist and biologist Rachel Carson. Then-GCSAA Executive Director Gene C. Nutter decried the 'rumours' and 'distorted facts' (Nutter, 1964: 43) to which Carson had given legitimacy. Furthermore, he lamented the opportunity lost: "How much more useful Miss Carson would have been to mankind had she pointed out the great value of modern pesticides to the advance of civilization, and had she stressed the continued practice of precaution in use of all materials" (Nutter, 1964: 46). In a rhetorical move that perhaps hindered as much as helped his argument, Nutter acknowledged the existence of cases of unwise chemical use – and even that some deaths followed from this. "Do we limit the number of automobiles because of driver carelessness that kills thousands of people a year in the USA?" he asked rhetorically. "Certainly not! Why, then, pick on agricultural chemicals" (Nutter, 1964: 43).

Carson was not the first to 'pick on' pesticides in this way. In the decade preceding the release of *Silent Spring*, texts such as *Our Daily Poison* (1955) by American chemist Leonard Wickenden and *The Poisons in Your Food* (1960) by journalist William Longgood had similarly cast scrutiny on the mounting prevalence of synthetic chemicals in the United States (cf. Paull, 2013). Kinkela adds that in America, the military, government agencies, universities, and private institutions had all questioned the safety of DDT in the post-war years, yet without much tangible effect (Kinkela, 2005: 163). Meanwhile, across the Atlantic in London, Franklin Bicknell (1960) published *Chemicals in Food and in Farm Produce: Their Harmful Effects*, further weighting the 'critical' side of the pesticide scale (cf. Paull, 2013). In 1962, the world was also not far from the 'limits to growth' and 'treadmill of production' critiques of industrial development described in Chapter 2.

Yet Carson was the critic who captured the public's imagination, and who will forever be connected to the birth of the environmental movement, at least in America. It is noteworthy in this regard that Carson's prior publications were 'feel good' nature books more so than technical scientific texts (cf. Paull, 2013). She had, in other words, an accessible writing style, though in *Silent Spring* this was dotted with alarmist language. This alarmism was first exhibited in chapter titles such as 'Elixirs of death', 'Rivers of death', and 'Needless havoc'. It shone through as well in the prose that followed on from these macabre headings. The chapter 'Needless havoc', for example, begins as follows:

> As man proceeds toward his announced goal of conquest of nature, he has written a depressing record of destruction, directed not only against the earth he inhabits but against the life that shares it with him. The history of the recent centuries has its black passages – the slaughter of the buffalo on the western plains, the massacre of the shoebirds by the market gunners, the near-extermination of the egrets for their plumage. Now, to these and others like them, we are adding a new chapter and a new kind of havoc – the direct killing of birds, mammals, fishes, and indeed practically every form of wildlife by chemical insecticides indiscriminately sprayed on the land. (Carson, 2002: 87)

Indiscriminately sprayed on the land: it is not hard to imagine Carson writing this with helicopter-aided DDT spraying in mind.

Indeed, DDT was among Carson's primary foci. She was concerned with the proliferation of chemicals in the post-war years in general, and mentioned golf courses as one of the factors contributing to the 'astronomical' acreage that now 'needed' pesticide treatment (Carson, 2002: 68). We saw above how in 1945 US Brigadier General James Stevens Simmons imagined the transportable properties of DDT to be of great benefit: a duck could unwittingly do the pesticide applicator's work by transferring DDT on its feathers. Carson took the other side of this argument:

> One of the most sinister features of DDT and related chemicals is the way they are passed on from one organism to another through all the links of the food chains. For example, fields of alfalfa are dusted with DDT; meal is later prepared from the alfalfa and fed to hens; the hens lay eggs which contain DDT. Or the hay, containing residues of 7 to 8 parts per million, may be fed to cows. The DDT will turn up in the milk in the amount of about 3 parts per million, but in butter made from this milk the concentration may run to 65 parts per million. Through such a process of transfer, what started out as a very small amount of DDT may end as a heavy concentration. (Carson, 2002: 22–23)

Other chemicals deemed appropriate for golf courses (e.g. chlordane and 2,4-D) were similarly problematized in Carson's text. Yet even having outlined some of the precise consequences of pesticide exposure, Carson's greatest concern was perhaps the uncertainty wrought by the widespread adoption of synthetic chemicals. With products like DDT, "No one yet knows what the ultimate consequences may be" (Carson, 2002: 23). This is the same logic of caution in the face of scientific uncertainty that underpins the precautionary principle – now a guiding principle for many environmentalists.

In fairness, the 'story' of DDT is complex. As Kinkela (2005) documents, the fervour arising in relation to DDT in the 1960s and 1970s at times brought environmental and human ethics into direct conflict with one another. Proponents of DDT set out to stress the latter, emphasizing the health benefits of this product, especially in relation to fighting pest-borne diseases. For example, the World Health Organization claimed that their Global Malaria Eradication Campaign, started in 1955, had saved five million lives and had rescued millions of others from malaria's effects (this despite its inability to eliminate malaria-bearing mosquitoes and the emergence of pesticide-resistant insects – see Kinkela, 2005: 160). From this perspective, the question was whether it was fair for 'developed' countries to privilege environmental responsibility when human health was also at stake.

Such a view is certainly reflected in the golf industry's response to *Silent Spring*, and, more broadly, in its response to the alleged chemical 'panic' of the post-war years in general. Gene C. Nutter's view that Carson could have better served the cause of humankind had she only emphasized the merits of DDT and its kin is a case in point along these lines. Likewise, in 1970 the golf superintendent magazine *Golf Course Management* published an article entitled "A THREAT to the Turf Industry" (emphasis in original) written by a Turf Products representative. The titular 'threat' was posed by looming bans on mercury-based fumigants, DDT, and other chemicals that, in the author's estimation, protect grass, wildlife, and even people. "During, and immediately after World War II," he wrote, "DDT saved at least five million lives and prevented 100 million illnesses" (Kerr 1970: 28). In the USGA's *Green Section*, Professor of Biology Dr Robert White-Stevens – described by Kinkela as the chemical industry's lead spokesperson (Kinkela, 2005: 163) – argued that there was little point in debating pesticide bans until suitable replacement technologies had been found. "Great strides have been made by the 'Green Revolution' in producing food, clothing and shelter for billions of humans. Let's not negate these strides nor set an example for developing nations by hysterically restricting the use of pesticides" (White-Stevens, 1972: 21).

Let us pause for a moment on the word 'hysterically' in White-Stevens' synopsis. Kinkela (2010) recounts that the defence of DDT and other chemicals rested first on their merits – which is to say, their stunning effectiveness in eradicating pests. It was not long, however, before the focus turned to an aggressive anti-Carson campaign, with terms like 'emotional', 'hysterical', and 'unscientific' featuring prominently, and at times seen as part and parcel of her gender. Michael B. Smith (2001) highlights a particularly piercing account along these lines from 1962, the year of *Silent Spring*'s release. Published in *Chemical and Engineering News*, and written by William Darby of the Vanderbilt University School of Medicine, the piece adopted a forceful command – 'Silence, Miss Carson!' – as its title. As Smith (2001) writes:

> The title itself (which the journal later admitted was its own creation, not Darby's) expresses the prevailing attitude among many of Carson's critics that she was an uninformed woman who was speaking of that which she knew not. Worse, she was speaking in a man's world, the inner sanctum of masculine science in which, like the sanctuary of a strict Calvinist sect, female silence was expected. Darby began his review by lumping Carson with groups he considered to be antimodern 'freaks.' ... He then invoked a series of father-figure scientists who supported the use of pesticides and whom Carson supposedly ignored ... Francis Bacon would have been proud of such a manifesto advocating man's role as conqueror, master, and controller of nature. (Smith, 2001: 738)

In other words, the rejoinders to Carson's polemic were both gendered and decidedly *modernist*. To stand against chemicals was to irrationally stand against progress; to stand against progress was to fail in the task of carrying forward humankind's 'civilizing' tradition.

This depiction of pesticide critics as irrational anti-modernists did not escape the pages of golf industry trade publications. For Nutter – someone who, it is worth remembering, was the Executive Director of the GCSAA at the time – pesticide critics were 'crusaders' and 'opportunists', rather than, say, concerned citizens. They build rumours and distorted information, Nutter argued, then magnify these "to the point where the public becomes honestly concerned *out of all proportions of reason*" (Nutter, 1964: 43, emphasis added). In 1970, once again in the publication *Golf Course Management*, a similar sentiment emerged. In an article entitled 'Now is the time' – billed as the first in a series on the 'pollution-pesticide-environment-ecology controversy' – the author reflected on the 'tremendous' amount of literature devoted to pesticide pollution: "Our ears ring with radio messages telling us that birds are becoming extinct because of DDT poisoning ... [this] is pure, unadulterated and sensationalistic reporting. As such, it should be condemned by thinking people everywhere" (Alexander, 1970: 20). A year later, GCSAA President Richard C. Blake gave his President's Message the telling name 'Reason over emotion'. 'Myths' and 'half-truths' had been accepted as fact, he lamented, courtesy of a combination of the public's lacking scientific knowledge and the machinations of 'overzealous' and 'self-stylized crusaders' (Blake, 1971). We find a similar view in Canada in an article from 1971 entitled 'DDT: victim of incomplete facts': "Some people go so far as to demand that all pesticides be eliminated. Again, half turths [sic] and incomplete facts are leading to damaging legislation – legislation which weakens man's dominance in nature" (Van Buskirk, 1971: 9).

To be sure, counter-hegemonic views appeared on occasion in trade publications in the wake of *Silent Spring*'s release. In 1967, for example, agronomist Albert Neuberger wrote in the *Green Section* that while Carson had shown bias in her presentation of evidence, "unfortunately much of it is true" (Neuberger, 1967: 8). Neuberger's concern was mainly directed towards the *indiscriminate* spraying of chemicals. Insecticides were 'plastered' across golf course landscapes, he observed, with little concern for their proper use. Likewise, in 1973, the GCSAA gave space to a spokesperson from the EPA who praised *Silent Spring* and warned that an environmental crisis – the 'eleventh hour' – was nigh (Hoffman, 1973). Nonetheless, it is difficult to regard Carson and her sympathizers as anything but *personae non gratae* in the golf industry in the wake of *Silent Spring*'s release. The GCSAA, as said at the outset of this book, has in more recent years acknowledged the strong backlash she received (e.g. see Ostmeyer, 2001).

Prometheus on the tee

To make sense of these developments, it is useful to return to the theoretical concepts described in Chapter 2. As noted in that chapter, the 'treadmill of production' is, at its core, a theory of economic change. The story of golf in the early post-war years – and indeed, even before then – is one partially underpinned by a relationship between capital and labour expenditure. In the time of Leonard Macomber, A. W. Tillinghast, and their contemporaries, labour power, deployed together with mechanical tools, was relied upon to confront the 'pest problem' on North American golf courses. As Macomber observed, the greenkeeper had the benefit of accumulated common sense in the task of properly caring for the golf course landscape. But as Foster (2009) writes, what is important to capitalism – at least when it comes to its relationship with the environment – is not simply re-investment, but the *nature* of investment. The above-described 'proportioning machine' was an initial step towards the easier deployment of pesticides in the face of 'scourges' such as the Japanese Beetle. More importantly, whereas golf superintendents evidently experimented with varied chemical mixtures in the 1920s and 1930s, the scientific-technical revolution of the post-war years yielded new, highly potent synthetic chemicals, and thus new avenues for the investment of resources. Indeed, the aforementioned promotion of helicopter-aided DDT spraying in *Golf Course Management* in 1967 was deemed timely in that "superintendents are looking to labor-saving devices to stretch what man-hours they have to give the most efficient maintenance possible" (Anon., 1967: 9).

Of course, this is not strictly an economic matter. The quest for efficiencies in maintenance was directed as well by cultural values regarding how a golf course ultimately *should* appear to consumers – a point we explore in detail in the next chapter. For the time being, the point is that golf had come to rely to a great extent on chemical treatments; as such, the golf industry was swept up in the 'limits to growth' critique that problematized not simply the use of synthetic chemicals, but the growing pace at which they were being deployed. Even Carson was not against chemical insecticides *in principle*. The problems she described emerged "because of the sudden *rise and prodigious growth* of an industry for the production of man-made or synthetic chemicals with insecticidal properties" (Carson, 2002: 16, emphasis added).

In response, and with some noteworthy exceptions, the golf industry mounted what can be termed a 'Promethean' defence. As Dryzek (2005) recounts, the Promethean environmental discourse is one where humankind's dominant position in nature is merited, and unworthy of critical reflection. The name is derived from the story of Prometheus in Greek mythology: Prometheus stole fire from Zeus, and in doing so changed humankind's ability to manipulate the Earth. "Six Six have unlimited confidence in the ability of humans and their technologies to overcome any problems presented to them – including what can now be styled environmental problems" (Dryzek, 2005: 45). In 1971, GCSAA President Richard C. Blake offered a near-literal recounting of the myth of Prometheus:

> The truth of the matter is that civilization did not begin until man learned to use fire and other tools to modify his environment. In other words, the fate of the human race and the wildlife that has shared in its rise rests on man's ability to anticipate, modify, and control environmental *changes*. (Blake, 1971: 7, emphasis in original)

In Foster's (2012) terms, this is crude human-exemptionalism, whereby people hold the right to conquer nature.

Perhaps such a position could be expected. As Hoffman (2001) documents in his book *From Heresy to Dogma*, in the 1960s the chemical industry was taking a similar tack to that described above. This was evident in the industry's response to an incident in 1964 whereby the pesticide endrin was blamed for the death of over a million fish in the American Midwest. "In a move marked primarily by denial," Hoffman writes, "the CPI [chemical processing industry] maintained that there was no conclusive scientific evidence that pesticides damage the ecosystem and that its role in increasing food production was a proud example of its contribution to progress" (Hoffman, 2001: 52). The golf industry likewise decried the evidence put forth by 'opportunists' and 'crusaders'. Golf was on the side of reason; opponents were merely swayed by emotion.

Yet we might also expect this Promethean response in that the modernist sensibilities of those designing and caring for golf courses were far from new; they were years in the making, as the historical analysis undertaken in this chapter has shown. That is to say, the rhetorical flourishes in the pages of publications such as *Golf Course Management* against the 'anti-modernists' who questioned the safety of chemicals like DDT did not spring from nowhere. They originated, we argue, with the perception that golf needed to distance itself from its 'primitive' roots, and that greenkeepers needed to transcend the 'mysticism, quackery, and humbug' of their forbears in favour of a more scientific approach. From this perspective, DDT was merely the latest in a long line of innovations that made the superintendent's job easier, or at least more efficient, and gave superintendents themselves more control of nature. Modernization had reached its apotheosis. As we shall see, *ecological* modernization loomed.

4
Golf in consumer culture and the making of Augusta National syndrome

By the 1970s, then, chemicals had grown invaluable to the golf industry. The question of why this was the case is easily answerable on the surface. As recounted in Chapter 3, greenskeeper Joseph Valentine was not alone in thinking that the efficiency of pesticides was deeply appealing. Products such as DDT were the latest innovations in a lineage of time- and labour-saving devices – each contribution along these lines more remarkable than the last. Valentine's sentiments were confirmed more recently by James T. Snow, long-time director of the USGA's *Green Section*. Chlordane, a chemical banned in 1988 by the EPA, suitably exemplified the remarkable effectiveness of pesticides, as Snow averred: "All you had to do back in the 1960s was put chlordane on the greens and you wouldn't have an insect problem for 25 years" (Barton, 2008). There was surely a normative force driving the golf industry in North America towards the widespread adoption of sweeping chemical applications as well. Superintendent training was still establishing its footing at this time (as discussed in Chapter 6), and so trade publications were perhaps among the most proven sources of information for those managing golf course landscapes. The (generally) pro-chemical view offered by publications such as *Golf Course Management* can credibly be regarded as a driver of golf's 'chemical warfare' in the 1960s as well.

Yet our analysis of *The Golf Course* publication – that of the early 1900s – also points towards golfer expectations as a significant driving force in the quest to be modern. To be more precise, it points towards *industry's view* of golfer expectations – perceptions of perceptions – as potentially important in this regard. As said in Chapter 3, an early issue of *The Golf Course* publication depicted "golfers everywhere" as "critical and fastidious" … "no longer are they content with the primitive courses of early days" (Anon., 1916a: 2). If such a viewpoint indeed prevailed, it is no surprise that golf course owners, developers, and superintendents sought to leave the 'primitive' courses of yesteryear behind.

With this background, we spend this chapter exploring golf's pursuit of modernization – as well as the environmental ramifications arising from this pursuit – with a particular focus on the game's relationship to consumer culture. As will become evident, the 1960s are yet again an important period in our analysis. Although the decade of the 1960s was not the moment of golf's *entrée* into consumer culture, it was the time when golf found a new and tremendously powerful tool for its widespread dissemination: colour television. Over time, TV became invaluable to golf's commercial success. So too did it fortify an image of the golf course's 'proper' green and pristine aesthetic. At the same time, the golf industry also experienced a major course construction 'boom' in the 1960s. This took place especially in Canada and the United States, though, as we shall see, golf was entering a new stage of globalization as well. Thus, as the 1980s approached, golf courses were demanding on the environment in their own right, and were also demanding in their growing occupation of land. This helped set the stage for the 'light-greening' of golf described in Chapter 5.

Golf in consumer culture

Given its current prominence on television, it might be surprising to fans of the sport that golf was once thought unfit for TV broadcasts. For most of the first half of the 1900s, consumers relied on radio broadcasts and print media to stay abreast of developments in the sporting world. The equation changed, of course, with television: "Sport television brought moving images of the players and crowds, the atmospheric noises of the unique moment, and explanatory commentary … directly into the domestic environment" (Rowe, 2013: 65). In the United States, the first televised sport broadcast took place in 1939 when a single camera panned back and forth in filming a Columbia–Princeton university baseball game (Bryant and Holt, 2006; see Hitchcock, 1989). This same decade also brought the televising of events such as Wimbledon in the UK (Whannel, 1992).

More than simply adding pictures to words, however, the introduction of television to the sporting landscape further cemented an already-existing relationship between sport, media, and capitalism. This is a point emphasized by Sut Jhally (1984) in his writing on the 'sports/media complex'. For Jhally, the initial form of this complex manifested with television's predecessors. With both print and radio, media owners 'sold' their audiences – and more precisely the *attention* of their audiences – to advertisers. As Rowe puts it, "the time that [audience members] devote to viewing the advertising material around media texts constitutes a form of labor that produces surplus value to be expropriated by the owners of capital" (Rowe, 2013: 65). With television, this relationship was rendered all the more lucrative for both advertisers and media companies. This was signalled in perhaps a clearer way than ever before when the Gillette shaving company paid $100,000[1] to sponsor the 1939 baseball World Series in the United States, only to see a sales increase of 350 per cent during the event (cf. Johnson, 1971). More than a convenient relationship, from 1940 onwards, "advertising-dependent network television became so important that a fully-fledged, consolidated complex emerged of profound interdependency – or, more accurately perhaps, co-dependency" between sport and media (Rowe, 2013: 66).

And yet, as Barclay (1992) recounts, in the early post-war years, golf struggled to find its way into American households through the TV set. The problem was the game's expansive landscapes – they were far too vast for the camera technology of the time, and certainly differed from an enclosed tennis stadium or baseball field. Owen (2003) makes a similar point in his detailed history of the Masters tournament. The National Broadcasting Company (NBC) was close to airing the 1947 men's US Open golf tournament. When NBC opted not to, a local TV station stepped in, but chose to broadcast action on the final hole alone. "Golf was poorly suited to the TV technology of the day, since the game was played outdoors in unpredictable lighting, and the competitors roamed over an area that was hard to cover with stationary cameras" (Owen, 2003: 184). The first broadcast of the Masters tournament – perhaps the most famous of all golf competitions – would not come until 1956 on the Columbia Broadcasting System (CBS).

There was no question that golf was popular, and the game was entering an era of telegenic star male athletes such as Jack Nicklaus, Arnold Palmer, and Gary Player. As Barclay (1992) writes, by the mid-1960s, broadcasting had advanced substantially. In turn, the picture changed in both literal and figurative ways:

> From three fixed cameras and a handful of technicians, NBC and its competitors had gone to a dozen fixed cameras plus portables, mobile and stationary platforms, dozens of directors, and hundreds of technicians. More than six million homes were watching the Masters, the PGA, and the US Open, and about as many switched on to see Palmer, Nicklaus, and Player in an exhibition labelled the World Series of Golf. (Barclay, 1992: 451)

The popularizing of colour TV in the years that followed was a further benefit to golf's commercial prospects. The immaculate conditions of Augusta National, home of the Master's tournament, stood out in particular. As journalist Sharon Oosthoek commented, "starting in the late 1960s … colour broadcasts of the

Masters Tournament at the Augusta National Golf Club in Georgia showed the world a meticulously maintained course shimmering like an ethereal Emerald City. Golfers turned green with envy" (Oosthoek, 2012; see Millington and Wilson, 2014).

In retrospect, it is clear that televising the Masters in colour was hardly a fait accompli once colour broadcasting first became possible. Owen (2003) writes that the TV network CBS initially had a poor experience with colour television, and was thus reluctant to bring this technology to bear on its golf broadcasts. Yet key spokespeople from Augusta National differed in their opinion. In 1964, William Kerr, chairman of Augusta's television committee, wrote to William MacPhail of CBS on this matter: "I am deeply concerned that if we continue to stand still on this score it will be detrimental to the best interests of the Tournament, the sponsors, and CBS" (cited in Owen, 2003: 196).

Note the third key stakeholder mentioned alongside CBS and the Masters tournament in Kerr's expression of discontentment: sponsors. The first two Masters broadcasts failed to attract corporate sponsorship. In 1958, Augusta National itself found American Express as a sponsor – a role this company held until 1962. The insurance company Travelers became a sponsor at the end of the 1950s, as did Cadillac a decade later (Owen, 2003: 197). Sampson (1999) recounts that by the mid-1970s, one could encounter Oscar-winning actor Gregory Peck espousing the merits of Travelers in commercials shown during Masters telecasts.

Owen (2003) hastily points out that, under the direction of Augusta National Chairman Clifford Roberts, Masters organizers were careful not to be held to the whims of corporate advertising. Compared to other programming, few commercials were aired during the Masters, and Roberts stressed that those that did appear should comfortably overlap with the tournament's themes. Even today, the broadcasting and advertising arrangements at the Masters are unique, and indeed to some extent out of step with the principles of free market capitalism. Bloomberg Businessweek reported in 2013 that CBS organizers meet with Masters spokespeople annually to discuss the revenue needed to cover broadcasting costs and perhaps generate a small profit. "Augusta then acts as a broker, arranging for the tournament's three official sponsors – IBM, AT&T, and ExxonMobil – to cover those costs... CBS doesn't get to sell ad time on the open market" (Boudway, 2013).

Nonetheless, from the 1960s onward, delivering television audience attention to sponsors became part of the Masters equation – and certainly became important to the televising of golf in general. Golf was woven into the post-war 'sports/media complex'. To be sure, the Masters remains something of an outlier in terms of generating revenue through broadcast licensing. Elsewhere, and acknowledging that TV contracts are often shrouded in mystery, it was reported that the Fox network more than doubled the $37 million annual rights fee paid by competitors in recent years in acquiring rights to the men's US Open golf tournament (Sandomir, 2013). This is what truly embracing the free market can yield. Indeed, in the contemporary media landscape, the Masters and other golf events require audience attention *in the moment* – lest viewers miss out on a compelling back nine charge from Rory McIlroy or Tiger Woods.

Sport (and golf) is thus to some extent exempt from the contemporary trend whereby audiences record broadcasts and watch them at a later time, fast-forwarding through commercials in the process (Van Riper, 2012; also Hutchins and Rowe, 2012). The important point in the scope of this analysis is that television broadcasting, from the 1950s onwards, played an important role not just in golf's economic story, but in its environmental story as well.

Augusta National syndrome: the price of golf's Emerald City

In Rowe's (2013) retelling, Jhally's concept of the 'sports-media complex' speaks to important facets of the political economy of both sport and media. Sport, with its fantastical appeal, which itself lies in part in its 'live' unpredictability, is perhaps the perfect 'spectacle of (profit) accumulation'. Yet it should not be forgotten that television, among other media forms, is a *communication* technology in the last instance. Televised sport can accordingly serve as a 'spectacle of legitimation' as well – which is to say a platform for expressing and thus implicitly or explicitly legitimising particular ideologies (cf., MacNeill, 1996). For example, MacNeill (1996) draws on Jhally's framework in explaining how Canadian hockey telecasts for the 1988 Olympics in Calgary not only delivered audiences to advertisers, but crystallized a vision of what it means to be Canadian: rugged, hard-working, and certainly different from Canada's 'softer' competitors. This image was conveyed through both commentary and production techniques.

To ask which ideologies were (and are) reinscribed through golf telecasts is to ask a complicated question. Certainly, Augusta National, with its longstanding policies barring women and people of colour from membership, was presenting an image of exclusivity through Masters telecasts. From an environmental perspective, however, what was important was Augusta National's powerful image of how a golf course *should* appear.

Above we quoted journalist Sharon Oosthoek in saying that in the 1960s colour broadcasts of the Masters tournament had golfers themselves turning green with envy. Augusta National was developed in the early 1930s thanks to a partnership between Robert Trent Jones Jr., the famous course architect, and Clifford Roberts, Augusta's aforementioned owner and chairman. It became the site of the Masters in 1934, and it was not long before the course was celebrated for its perceived sublime beauty. In 1955, writing in the popular magazine *Sports Illustrated*, Herbert Warren Wind lavished praise on Augusta's "great green meadowland slopes" – the perfect site for an 'idyllic' golfing test. He went on to recount the story of Jones taking in Augusta's sweeping landscape from a raised vantage point ahead of the course's construction. A similar feeling was sure to befall anyone adopting the same point of view upon Augusta's completion:

> Each year the view from the hill, the view that instantly sold Jones, is breathed in by the thousands who journey to the Masters. There are few first-timers who, upon experiencing that view, do not exclaim either aloud or to themselves, "Yes, it's all it's cracked up to be and more." There are few 'repeaters' who, after hurrying to the brow of the hill, do not affirm to themselves, "It's just as lovely as I remember it. I hope it always stays the same because of what it personally means to me". (Wind, 1955)

To this day, portraits of this kind are not hard to find. Ahead of the 2014 Masters tournament, sports journalist Rob Hodgetts (2014) wrote that just the name Augusta calls to mind an iconic green image, "punctuated by explosions of colour from banks of azaleas and framed by towering pines, with grass so sumptuous you could make a suit out of it". The Golf Channel's John Hawkins (2014) made a similar point: "You only get to see the place for one week each year, and because it's so aesthetically stunning, it assumes a heaven-on-earth type of quality." Even the Masters' quaint customs – its cautious, controlling approach to commercialism, for example – arguably help convey an image of simple, bucolic splendour. Importantly, this manufactured image is not lost on television broadcasts. The music is serene, the Masters slogan – 'a tradition unlike any other' – hard to miss. CBS was even said to have added fake birdsongs to their broadcast one year, presumably to reinforce Augusta National's perfect alliance with nature (Shmavonian, 2011). The television viewer might too say, as Wind imagined, "It's just as lovely as I remember it. I hope it always stays the same because of what it personally means to me" upon watching the Masters on TV.

Yet for golfers to turn green with envy at the sight of Augusta was (and is) for superintendents, developers, and owners to face heightened expectations.

Maintaining the Masters standard requires tremendous care. For example, unlike many courses, Augusta National reportedly closes for much of the year, and needs only to appear 'perfect' for a short stretch in April (when the Masters is held) to fortify its image as a wondrous plot of land. Furthermore, its maintenance budget is believed to outstrip that of most courses (e.g. see Klein, 2012). Augusta National syndrome has therefore emerged as a term for describing the 'affliction' whereby consumers demand the 'perfect' golfing conditions that they see on TV. Golf writer Geoff Shackelford (2012) outlines this condition's symptomology:

> A pattern of symptoms that characterize or indicate a social condition in which golfers of all ages, races, religions and means demand a particular set of course conditions in the weeks, months and years following the annual Masters Tournament. Conditioning excesses requested include ultra-fast green speeds (regardless of long-term ramifications), lush green turf cut to absurdly low heights, snow-blindness-inducing bunker sand, artificially blue water hazards and on-course floral plantings no matter how expensive, unsustainable or excessive. (Shackelford, 2012)

Note the use of terms such as 'excessive', 'unsustainable', and even 'absurd', to describe Augusta National, in contrast to the flattering language noted above. Writing in *Golf Digest*, Whitten (2010) confirms that Augusta National syndrome arose with the televising of the Masters, and that it yielded 'expensive', 'misguided' attempts to emulate this famous course.

Thus, if the stunning effectiveness of 'modern' course maintenance practices can plausibly be deemed a first reason that the use of, say, DDT became popular in golf in the post-war years, and if advocacy of such practices in industry trade publications stands as a second exhortative force, the *mimetic* power lying in Augusta National syndrome can be considered important along these lines as well. In other words, ahead of the 1960s, there were already forces in place driving golf superintendents, among others, towards a highly manicured golf course aesthetic. Televised golf pushed the industry in the same direction, and spread the image of how a golf course might appear to an even wider audience.

Writing in 1993 in the USGA's *Green Section*, golfer, commentator, and designer Jerry Pate lamented the homogenizing force of Augusta National syndrome. Features like water hazards and island greens were 'everywhere', he wrote. He also problematized the environmental implications of television's idealizing force:

> Today there is a very misused practice in golf course maintenance, and that's the overwatering of our golf courses. I think television, no question, has played a part in reinforcing the misuse of irrigation systems. People want to see green

golf courses. When you go to major events, you have green tents, green cups, green observation stands, green hats, green jackets, green restroom facilities, green sandwich wrappers, and green pairing sheets. All we want to see is green. And as a player for many years on the tour, there's no question I like to see green, too. But there's no doubt, and you've heard this many times, that green is not always better. (Pate, 1993: 20–21)

Pate's comments foreshadow the topic of the next chapter, as his vision neatly articulates with the emergence of what we term 'responsible golf' as an industry-friendly 'alter-golf' environmental response in the 1980s and beyond.

The existence of Augusta National syndrome, we argue, shines sympathetic light on the plight of those working in the golf industry in the post-war years. Practices such as DDT spraying may well have been taken up (and often defended) by individual superintendents, among others. But individual superintendents were not – and, to this day, are not – working independently of the wider context in which they are situated. Indeed, in addition to Pate's contribution, in trade publications we occasionally encounter rueful meditations on the lofty standards that, by the 1960s, had come to reign in the golf industry. In a 1969 guest editorial in *Golf Course Management*, for example, golf superintendent Bill Brickell expressed concern that members of his profession were being asked to resign due to golfers' unrealized expectations. "Club members compare courses, condition-wise only. They do not compare budgets or location" (Brickell, 1969: 103). To be sure, this is more an *allusion* to Augusta National syndrome than a direct reference. As we explore in Chapter 6, however, there was indeed a deep concern among industry representatives at this time that the public did not know what an important and arduous job the golf superintendent faced. More recently, former golf superintendent Joel Jackson, writing in the pages of the superintendent publication *Golfdom*, asked rhetorically, "How many gray hairs and ulcers have been experienced by superintendents who have endured the apples and oranges comparisons from their members about Augusta National conditions or television golf in general?" (Jackson, 2000: 22). In the same publication, another superintendent wrote of the impossibility of meeting Augusta's 'perfect' televised standard. "For major tournaments, courses prepare for weeks in advance with hundreds of volunteers. It would be impossible to maintain those conditions years around" (Sharp, 2000: 20).

At the same time, there is a question here as to whether the demand for perfect courses is imposed upon the golf industry or is a product of the golf industry's will in itself. Robbins (2007) entertains a similar question in relation to the prototypical post-war suburban lawn. On the surface, the ideal lawn – lush, green, and weedless, much like the ideal golf course – is clearly the lawn owners' imperative. He or she demands it and follows the steps necessary to obtain it. But industry, Robbins argues, at the very least creates the conditions for demand – for example, by supplying and promoting pesticides in the first instance and by combatting legislation that would ban their use in the next. Here, the golf industry's active promotion of turfgrass chemicals through trade publications is relevant once again. As Robbins would have it, demand is impossible without this step. As we shall see in later chapters, the golf industry also took an active role as time passed in defending chemicals against regulation that would impede their use. Indeed, and as we saw in the introduction to Chapter 1, Gene C. Nutter worried not only about the alleged speciousness of *Silent Spring*, but also that it would incite legislation curtailing the use of pesticides.

Furthermore, golf industry representatives *themselves* have on occasion pointed to the golf industry as responsible in shaping golfer expectations. This was true of Pate's aforementioned account of Augusta National syndrome. A similar sentiment was voiced in 1997 by Denis Griffiths, President of the American Society of Golf Course Architects (ASGCA), in a letter published in the Canadian superintendent magazine *GreenMaster*. Golf's original courses in Scotland and England, Griffiths stated, were effectively designed by Mother Nature; the (human) course designer merely "discovered the routing". Golf's 'Americanization' (Griffith's term) instilled a perception that golf courses need be impeccable. "Television, golf magazines and the PGA Tour have all had a hand in furthering this perception, particularly in setting expectations that are often mistaken for standards" (Griffiths, 1997: 38). Superintendents, we would add, should not be fully immune from such a critique. In 1982, James A. Wyllie entitled his President's Message in *Golf Course Management*, 'The Masters, a visible standard'. Having lauded Augusta's beauty in a way reminiscent of Herbert Warren Wind's 1955 account in *Sports Illustrated*, Wyllie urged the magazine's readership to pursue the Augusta standard. "Some will always say that large budgets make this possible at Augusta and nowhere else … We should not fall into this trap" (Wyllie, 1982: 5).

The growth imperative: golf's booms and busts

The televising of golf in the 1960s was thus a major factor in golf's entry into the culture of consumerism that flourished in the post-war years. Yet television was not the only influence in this regard. Just as Augusta National was setting a new standard for courses across Canada and the United States, and just as modern 'weaponry' was made available to golf superintendents and others interested in a pristine golf course aesthetic, golf was also undergoing a 'boom' in course construction. In other words, courses themselves were changing and the *number* of courses at which golfers could ply their skills was changing too. Once again, this was a phenomenon not free of environmental implications.

Rewinding further, the 1960s golf course boom in Canada and the United States was not the first of its kind. To some extent we saw evidence of this in Chapter 3. Contributors to the superintendent publication *The Golf Course* at times remarked on the rapid pace at which courses were emerging around the United States especially. An article from 1916 noted the 'unbelievable' number of courses that had recently been built or were in the midst of construction in the first decades of the 1900s (Anon., 1916b). These were not wayward observations. From the unveiling of the first Canadian and US golf courses at the end of the nineteenth century to the onset of the Great Depression, over 5,600 courses were built in the United States alone (Strawn *et al.*, 2011: 1165). The 1920s saw the apex of this trend. As Hueber and Worzala (2010) recount in their writing on golf course real estate development in the USA, between 1923 and 1929, 600 new courses opened each year – a rate of nearly two per day (see Adams and Rooney, 1985).

Certainly the affluence of the 1920s played a role in these changes. Hueber and Worzala (2010) call the 1920s the 'Great Gatsby' era of course development, with 80 per cent of courses at this time existing as private clubs. Moss (2001) reports similar figures. He also adds, however, that US audiences could better relate to golf's post-First World War celebrities. The likes of Gene Sarazen and Walter Hagen came to replace the British-born stars that had previously dominated the game. Sarazen and Hagen in particular were from working-class backgrounds – something that, in Moss's (2001) view, fuelled golf's popularity among the public even with the relative shortage of public courses. Of course, golf remained deeply stratified in terms of who could participate at this time. Non-whites were generally barred from playing, including on the PGA Tour. In one of the more striking cases in point, in the early 1920s Joseph Bartholomew was denied access to Metairie Golf Club in New Orleans *even after serving as course architect* during construction (PGA.com, 2011).

In explaining the 1920s 'boom', there is overlap with Chapter 3 once again in the sense that new technologies were easing the process of manipulating the earth. Moreover, technological development was indirectly shaping course construction in the sense that advances in equipment were affecting how the game was played. In the late 1900s, a new, rubber core golf ball was patented in the United States; in the 1920s, steel-shafted clubs began to replace their hickory-shafted ancestors (Nauright, 2012a). Hueber and Worzala comment on the latter development: "This was significant because as golf equipment technology improved, golfers were able to hit the golf ball farther; so, it became necessary to lengthen the golf holes to preserve the score of par as being standard of golfing excellence" (Hueber and Worzala, 2010: 10). Golf was also colonizing land far and wide: "In 1916 there were four states with no courses and sixteen states with fewer than 10. In 1930 there was only one state with fewer than 10, and eighteen had between 10 and 400" (Moss, 2001: 114).

'Busts' are typically next off the tee after 'booms'. Such was the fate for golf in the 1930s and 1940s, when courses closed as a result of the Great Depression and Second World War. As noted, however, the 1960s brought a second high point in golf's expansion in the United States. The causes were much the same as they were for the previous peak. This was a time of affluence – at least compared to preceding decades – and one when golf's luminaries had more exposure than ever before thanks to television. Beditz (1994) notes that government funding for public golf courses increased around this time as well. This helped reshape the public/private split that for years had been weighted on the side of the latter. Beditz writes that by 1970, 55 per cent of facilities were publicly accessible – at least for those who could afford their fees (also see Readman, 2003). True to sport's modern spirit, equipment manufacturing only improved in the post-war years, yielding balls and clubs more resilient than ever and once again necessitating courses that could accommodate the technologically enhanced golf enthusiast.

One novel, and certainly important, development from the 1960s was that real estate developers came to see golf as an amenity for enhancing sales. Golf's bourgeois reputation was presumably not irrelevant in this regard. "So", write Hueber and Worzala, "the amount of acreage needed for the golf course development nearly doubled to an average of 150 acres in the 1960's [sic] allowing real estate developers to maximize their premium priced golf course frontage lots" (Hueber and Worzala, 2010: 11). This point, added to the fact that the number of golf courses doubled to a total of 10,200 by the onset of the 1970s, bore a fundamental environmental reality. Not only had chemical-intensive golf arrived, and not only was there pressure to match Augusta National's green aesthetic, golf courses were quite simply taking up more land in the United States than ever before.

The 1990s were a time for a third 'boom' in course development. Beditz (2000) suggests that the seeds for this growth actually began to sprout in the mid-1980s, as the golf participation rate grew to 13.5 per cent by 1990, roughly 5 per cent higher than in 1980. Public courses became even more prevalent. Yet in keeping with the tenets of neoliberalism, it was deregulation, rather than government investment, that largely spurred this growth. Deregulation in banking engendered savings and loans institutions keen on funding development activities; golf courses and golf-related real estate were two of the primary beneficiaries (Beditz, 2000).

Golf's growing public appeal might again inspire a sympathetic reading of these late century developments. *Why not* match consumer desire for new courses? But the question of whether demand in fact precedes supply is again relevant here. Indeed, in the late 1980s, with nearly two decades of stagnation in the rear-view mirror, the golf industry set out on an active campaign to promote its own growth. The Strategic Plan for the Growth of the Game, devised by the National Golf Foundation in conjunction with strategists at McKinsey and Company, specifically called for the development of a golf course a day across the 1990s. The slogan was literally 'A Course a Day', and was broadcast through public service announcements on TV. With the golf industry reaching 16,000 golf courses in the United States by the new millennium – 72 per cent of which were public – the campaign was certainly successful on its own terms (Hueber & Worzala, 2010). As Hueber and Worzala (2010) write, the golf industry had redefined itself as a *growth* industry through this late century campaign. As we show in the following chapter, an even more robust initiative was set in motion to spur the growth of golf as the 2000s arrived.

Augusta National goes global

A similar story to that described above unfolded in Canada in the post-war years, with substantial growth in the number of golf courses taking place during the 1960s (Barclay, 1992). And while we are interested mainly in this chapter in North America, and even more specifically the United States, the global growth of golf should not be overlooked.

Japan, for example, is commonly cited as a country in which golf witnessed tremendous growth in the post-war years. Exact figures vary, but it is believed that prior to the Second World War there were less than fifty courses in the entire country (Wheeler and Nauright, 2006). By the late 1950s, the industry had grown, but only modestly; Lockyer (2012) gives figures of 118 courses and 300,000 golfers for

1957. Yet the trend only intensified from there. Demand in subsequent years was spurred at least in part by the country's staging of the Canada Cup International tournament in 1957 – a televised event in which Japanese golfer Nakamura Torakichi thrived. By the mid-1970s, the 1,000 course milestone had been surpassed; by 1983 the number 1,500 was in sight. Lockyer writes: "Then things got out of hand ... In Japan", he continues, "irrational investment became outright speculation" (Lockyer, 2012: 295). This was fuelled by factors such as low interest rates, land privatization, and weakened regulation – all underpinned by a desire among policy makers to spur on the economy. Estimates in the mid-2000s put the number of golf courses in Japan at north of 3,000 (Wheeler and Nauright, 2006).

These developments evidently did not go unnoticed in other parts of the golfing world. In 1985, Walter Woods, links supervisor at the famed St Andrews golf course in Scotland, wrote in the Canadian publication *GreenMaster* of the resiliency of Japanese developers: "Using huge bulldozers and earth moving equipment they will move any amount of earth to achieve their aim – and money will never be an object" (Woods, 1985: 19). Woods too noted the role of television in propelling interest in golf among the Japanese public.

The mounting popularity of golf in Japan, among other places, further propelled an outward movement of golf tourists. Indeed, much as domestic markets for golf were growing in conjunction with the arrival of post-war affluence, so too were new courses springing up at rapid pace with the specific aim of attracting customers from afar. Palmer (2004) ties the growth of golf tourism, at least in 'developing' countries, to policy decisions in the 1960s based on the notion of 'comparative advantage'. This involves achieving economic growth by focusing on particular industries – namely, those for which a country is thought to be 'best suited'. In many cases, tourism fits this latter criterion, and the promotion of golf becomes one way of attracting affluent tourists above others. Palmer notes that there are other presumed benefits to such a strategy, apart from attracting consumers with spending power:

> A golf course can lengthen a destinations [sic] 'tourist season' by attracting golfers wishing to play when the weather is suitable in their own country. Degraded or derelict areas could be turned into golf courses thereby extending the utility of what would otherwise be difficult land to develop. A golf course can assist in diversifying the usual high season summer tourist product by offering additional recreational facilities and so enhance a country's competitiveness in the global tourism marketplace. There is also the potential for both direct and indirect job creation although putting exact figures on such a benefit is notoriously difficult. (Palmer, 2004: 123; see Cleverdon, 2000)

Richard Haass, president of the US Council on Foreign Relations, has suggested that golf has more recently become a bellwether for domestic development and openness to international relations – especially with the United States. "Countries that have numerous golf courses tend to be friendlier towards the United States. Governments closing golf courses tend to be the most anti-American of all. Think of it as the fairway theory of history" (Haass, 2009).

The growth of golf in Japan had knock-on effects in East Asia in particular. Golf infrastructure has arisen, for example, in Malaysia, Thailand, Indonesia, and the Philippines, though as we shall see in Chapter 8, this part of the world has given life to some of the fiercest opposition to golf as well (Palmer, 2004; Readman, 2003). China is also a growing site for development, while in Vietnam a range of luxury courses were recently built and given the label the Ho Chi Minh Golf Trail (The Futures Company, 2012). Mark Readman, in an instructive book chapter on golf tourism, adds that courses have been built in Central and South America recently for the 'sought-after reward' of the American dollar (Readman, 2003: 175). The company HSBC said in their recent report on golf's commercial prospects: "Even Cuba, which banned the game after the revolution in 1959, last year approved the construction of four large luxury golf resorts involving an investment of $1.5 billion" (The Futures Company, 2012: 38). The country's tourism minister has said that sixteen more courses could be built on the island.

In subsequent chapters we explore the politics of golf's global proliferation in detail, noting especially how resistance movements have crystallized around the cause of the environment, at least in part. For this chapter, what is noteworthy is not just that golf has been subject to the forces of globalization in a particularly intense fashion since roughly the 1960s; important too is *the way* in which golf has travelled the world.

First relevant here is the fact that golf has typically been tied to, and has often driven, larger development projects. In his writing on golf tourism, Readman (2003) describes four 'products' aimed at attracting the mobile golf enthusiast (see Priestly and Ashworth, 1995):

- 'Trophy courses', meaning those heightening their appeal by hosting a championship event. This type of development often comes in conjunction with the concerted efforts of, say, tourism authorities and local development agencies to promote golf in general. Spain, for example, followed this model in the 1990s, hosting the Ryder Cup in 1997 and quadrupling its stock of golf courses across the decade.

- 'Single integrated resorts' that act as self-contained, and often expansive, leisure complexes. In this case, other facilities – restaurants and places of accommodation, for example – are found on site, rendering moot the need for tourists to leave the facility. These are not uncommon, writes Readman (2003), in the United States, Australia, and the Caribbean. "In addition," he adds, "the recent development of golf in Asia has often followed this model, and in some cases large-scale golf 'leisurescapes' have been created, such as in Malaysia, Indonesia, and Thailand" (Readman, 2003: 178).
- 'Property-development-linked courses' attracting tourists who might buy a time-share property or second home. This type of development can have cascading benefits in the sense that tourists stay in the local community for longer, thus (ideally) spreading their spending dollars wider than they otherwise might. At the same time, and as suggested above, much more land is required in this style of development in that the golf course is one part of a larger real estate package.
- 'Course networks' that spread across entire regions, and are often accessed through package deals. Readman (2003) notes the Robert Trent Jones Trail in Alabama (USA) as an example along these lines. The aforementioned Ho Chi Minh Trail in Vietnam is likewise a case in point.

In the best case scenario, these forms of development stimulate local economies through the influx of new consumers. Perhaps the worst case – that which we explore in Chapter 8 – is that a form of 'tourism as imperialism' manifests (Palmer, 2004: 124; see Nash, 1989) whereby investors, operating perhaps from afar, promote a form of development unsympathetic to the needs of local residents and the environment.

On the matter of the environment, a second key point pertaining to golf's global expansion involves the nature of golf courses themselves *within* these development projects. Were golf's recent global expansion to have come at another time – say that of Old Tom Morris and the mid-1800s – one might imagine that that the less impactful 'links' style of course that was hegemonic in the past might have been disseminated around the globe as well. We think it fair to say, however, that the image of the 'ideal' course made salient in post-war America is that which has in fact shaped golf's movement around the globe. Said otherwise, Augusta National syndrome is not confined to America's borders; it holds ideological resonance on a wider scale.

Nauright (2012b) makes this point in suggesting that Augusta National syndrome has become a global problem, and not just a North American one.

Criticisms of golf emanating from Mexico, Scotland, Thailand, and beyond have rested largely on the environmental implications of 'American-style' courses – their use of pesticides and occupation of land, for instance. Notably, the international resonance of the 'ideal' aesthetic has been stressed *within* the golf industry as well. Writing in *Golf Course Management* in 1991, J. Michael Poellot of JMP Golf Design Group observed that "golf is now a worldwide game". He continued:

> With golfers from all countries now traveling all over the world to play, golf courses are no longer judged against those in the nearby local area. They are measured on the basis of the highest standards in the world. Every golf course is now in the worldwide market whether it wants to be or not. (Poellot, 1991: 7)

To be sure, this is at best an implicit reference to Augusta National syndrome. Nonetheless, the general point remains: golf, and the image of 'ideal' golf, knows no spatial boundaries. Poellot averred in 1991 that Japan was ten years behind the United States in its ability to understand and solve golf-related environmental problems. As we argue in the next section and upcoming chapters, however, golf was not without problematic environmental consequences even in America at this time.

'The beaver dams had been blown to bits': a 'pro-golf' response

Returning to the superintendent publication *Golf Course Management*, an article from the mid-1980s tells a story of the potential impacts of golf course development (Witteveen, 1986). Readers may have been surprised in encountering the image of an explosion set within a wooded area – a blast powerful enough to tower over the surrounding treeline – on the article's opening page. An accompanying caption explained that dynamite was used in reconfiguring the 'rocky, wooded, wet area' in Ottawa, Canada where Loch March Golf Club would eventually lie. As the article's author, golf superintendent (and consultant at Loch March) Gordon Witteveen, recounted, there were few open spaces among the trees before the course's development began. Other 'negative factors' potentially impeding Loch March's arrival were the rocks and swampland found on site. According to his own account, Witteveen presumed the realty team "would come to their senses and leave the swamps to the beavers" (Witteveen, 1986: 34).

Such was not the case. Returning to the course site at a later date, Witteveen found that construction was already under way: "The beaver dam had been blown to bits and a network of drainage channels had been dug through the swamp. As if by magic, the entire swampy area had become reasonably dry land" (Witteveen, 1986: 36). From there, a veritable 'armada' (Witteveen's term) of machinery – trucks and bulldozers, for example – were brought in for hauling earth "from morning 'til night" (Witteveen, 1986: 36). Returning to the image that first greeted the article's readers, he explained that 18,000 pounds of dynamite were used in levelling green and tee sites (p. 38). In the end, Ottawa-area golfers had a new course at which to pursue their hobby of choice.

Then again, perhaps the 'explosive' image at the start of Witteveen's article was not so striking. What we know from Chapter 3 is that, as the twentieth century unfolded, the golf industry in North America took advantage of modern 'weaponry' in the longstanding 'war' against turfgrass pests. This was a Promethean inclination to the extent that golf's representatives saw it as humankind's inherent right to manipulate the Earth. What we know from *this* chapter is that the culture of consumerism that reigned in the post-war years, and particularly the arrival of television into the 'sports/media complex', invigorated these existing trends. Augusta National syndrome made it *normal* to finely manipulate one's course in the pursuit of aesthetic perfection. And while the golf industry certainly bears some responsibility in 'infecting' consumers with this 'disease', individuals working within the industry can be forgiven for fearing their job security might be jeopardized should they disregard the presumption that golf courses can be perfectly manicured 'emerald cities'.

We of course do not presume that the environmentally destructive practices employed at Loch March in the mid-1980s are in fact characteristic of all development endeavours in the post-war years. In fact, as we shall see in the following chapter, practices such as 'blowing beaver dams to bits' – or, at least, the practice of reporting on such activity with Witteveen's candour – are misaligned with the tenets of 'responsible golf' that emerged near the onset of the 1980s. The point is that as time passed, the golf industry found it increasingly possible to manipulate the natural environment. A similar point is made by Strawn *et al.* (2011), who note that in the post-war years golf courses could be built anywhere from flat terrain to desert climates to rocky and steep alpine sites. These authors further emphasize how this constituted an important change from golf's early days:

> Horses and mules pulling scraper pans across aborning fairways were thus replaced by the steel and smoke of diesel engines driving heavy equipment, with

> blasting as common a procedure in building a golf course as it had become in a typical public works project. In fact, the expertise acquired in dam building, road building and other mass excavation projects was easily transferred to golf construction. (Strawn *et al.*, 2011: 1169)

Again, by the 1970s, the image of golf superintendents extracting weeds with mechanical tools was in the far distance of golf's rear-view mirror. Golfers sharing pastures with grazing sheep was even further behind.

In the broad scope of this book, what Chapters 3 and 4 point to is an age of 'pro-golf' in the early post-war years. Recalling our discussion of the pro-alter-anti-response ('PAAR') continuum from Chapter 2, the term pro-golf bespeaks a time of very limited concern for environmental issues (see Figure 1). It is 'pro', or 'for', golf first in that golf industry spokespeople support golf's expansion to new regions in North America and beyond. But it is also 'pro' in the sense of the 'Promethean' environmental discourse: recognizing that counter-hegemonic perspectives existed in the 1950s, 1960s, and early 1970s, practices such as DDT spraying were underpinned, we argue, by a dominant logic of human superiority. To be sure, and judging mainly from industry trade publications, the desire among key officials to expand the game and deploy chemicals, among other materials, in the name of modernizing the sport of golf was not entirely new at this time. The point is that in the early post-war years it was increasingly possible to *act* on this inclination. As we shall see in the following chapters, an emergent logic – a 'responsible', 'alter-golf' response – was lurking at this time as well.

Note

1 The currency symbol $ denotes US dollars, unless otherwise stated.

PART III

The light-greening of golf

5

The turn to responsible golf and the roots of golf's light-green movement

In Chapters 3 and 4 we described the sea change under way in the golf industry in the post-war years. By the mid-1960s, golf's landscapes had changed in a literal sense: thanks to a combination of powerful synthetic pesticides and powerful terrain-altering machinery, golf was making good on the modernist impulses held by its key spokespeople since it moved across the Atlantic. Yet the social and cultural landscapes surrounding golf were changing as well. On the one hand, television helped disseminate an arguably exaggerated version of what a golf course should look like – creating an aesthetic standard that was (and is) difficult to maintain across the industry as a whole. On the other hand, pesticide critics were assailing the widespread use of chemicals like DDT. In the eyes of some golf industry representatives, this latter development was tantamount to a 'crusade' against the cause of reason; it threatened humankind's Promethean right to manipulate the Earth. As we discuss in full later in the book, concerns about this 'threat' were not unfounded. For example, the early 1970s saw the formation of the EPA in the United States and a ban on the chemical DDT.

But our review of industry trade publications also gives reason to believe that golf industry members themselves were coming to see established practices as decidedly irresponsible. This was the view of agronomist Albert Neuberger, who in 1967 lamented in the *Green Section* that superintendents were 'plastering' their golf courses with pesticides. It is likewise the synopsis of some present-day representatives of the golf industry who admit that their forbears too easily took to chemicals like chlordane and DDT. To turn towards 'responsible golf' is to position golf industry representatives as conscientious stewards of the Earth. Or, said another way, it is to adopt a 'light-green' sensibility.

Our contention in this chapter is that the golf industry, facing an emboldened environmental movement, transitioned from a (mainly) Promethean position to a (mainly) ecological modernist one – what we term 'responsible golf' – beginning in the late 1970s. The main mechanism by which ecological modernization (EM) was achieved was the adoption of evermore sophisticated – which is to say, formalized and technology-aided – forms of course development and maintenance. Systems such as IPM were adopted from the agricultural sector as a way of addressing golf's purported dependence on chemical treatments. Precision irrigation also became de rigueur. In both cases, the golf industry could stress that changes were indeed taking place in defiance of its 'irresponsible' (recent) history. Moreover, these changes were underpinned by burgeoning research programmes led by organizations such as the USGA and the GCSAA. While recognizing its merits, we conclude this chapter by problematizing golf's 'responsible' turn in a manner that reflects existing criticisms of EM.

From shotgun to rifle shot: IPM and the targeting of golf course pests

The transition towards ecological modernization – and with it, responsible golf – that we are concerned with in this chapter is perhaps best shown by contrasting two articles focused on pesticides from the GCSAA publication *Golf Course Management*. The first was described in Chapter 3. Entitled 'Golf course chemical warfare takes to the air', this article from 1967 suggested that helicopter-aided DDT spraying might be a highly efficient way of tackling pest problems, and one that could replace mist blowers or hydraulic sprayers (Anon., 1967). This is presumably the type of initiative Albert Neuberger had in mind when reflecting on the 'plastering' of golf courses with synthetic chemicals. The second article came a decade later. Entitled 'Turf insect control programs changing from shotgun to rifle shot', the message was that superintendents could no longer indiscriminately spray their courses, despite their mandate to keep their golf courses green. "It comes down to better identification of the insect causing the problem, selection of the proper insecticide for its control and precise adherence to proper application standards to ensure control at the lowest cost" (Anon., 1977: 17). Pests, in other words, were to be dealt with as isolated problems, though notably the combat metaphor from decades past remained. The 'burden' of knowing how to accomplish this fell to the superintendent (Anon., 1977: 17).

In hindsight, we know that this contrast actually speaks to a wider transition under way in the North American golf industry when it comes to the use of pesticides: a transition towards the adoption of IPM as an industry 'best practice'. It is likely not surprising that golf took cues from other sectors in adopting IPM, considering how innovations in agriculture had informed golf course maintenance practices over time.

The history of IPM is traceable to the 1950s, and to the pragmatic concern of entomologists that, in one sense, pests were developing resistance to the chemicals designed for their elimination, and, in another, that non-targeted insects were suffering by way of too-liberal pesticide applications. Peshin *et al.* (2009) add that, by the early 1960s, "*Silent Spring* also got the attention of the scientific community on negative externalities of pesticide use" (Peshin *et al.*, 2009: 2). Entomologists thus turned their attention in the scientific literature at this time towards ways of redressing this chemical dependence. It is here that the notion of *integrated* control was popularized – integrated in the sense that chemical applications are brought together with other mechanisms that serve the cause of regulating pest populations. Kogan (1998) acknowledges that practical awareness of the multifaceted nature of pest management surely preceded these contributions to the literature. Hoskins *et al.* (1939), for example, argued that nature has its own biological means of controlling pests, and that chemical insecticides should accordingly be used as infrequently as possible (see Kogan, 1998: 244). Even Leland O. Howard's bombastic essay on 'The war against insects', highlighted in Chapter 3, stressed that biological controls could help in the fight against humankind's greatest foe. Nonetheless, in the post-war years pesticide dependency became a greater source of consternation.

Indeed, after debates in the 1960s as to whether 'integrated control' or 'pest management' was the best term for characterizing society's (changing) relationship with unwanted pests, in the 1970s the terms were brought together. The Council on Environmental Quality in the United States prepared a report in 1972 entitled *Integrated Pest Management*. By this point, Kogan (1998) recounts, there was fundamental agreement that:

> 1. 'integration' meant the harmonious use of multiple methods to control single pests as well as the impacts of multiple pests; 2. 'pests' were any organism detrimental to humans, including invertebrate and vertebrate animals, pathogens, and weeds; 3. IPM was a multidisciplinary endeavor; 4. 'management' referred to a set of decision rules based on ecological principles and economic and social considerations. (Kogan, 1998: 247–248)

These tenets have evidently stood the test of time, with the multi-method nature of IPM remaining perhaps its most important characteristic. In controlling pests, Boyd writes, "IPM combines biological pest control (introducing natural enemies or diseases of pest), cultural pest control (e.g. patterns of planting), genetic pest control (using pest-resistant varieties), and, as a last resort, chemical pest control (using the lowest quantity and toxicity possible)" (Boyd, 2003: 119). Manual or mechanical control, such as excising weeds by hand, can be considered an IPM tactic as well.

Whether chemicals are indeed a 'last resort', as Boyd describes, has been questioned in recent years, and is a point we return to below. Regardless, since the 1970s, IPM has built institutional support on its academic foundations. For example, in 1996 IPM was enshrined in the Food Quality Protection Act, which stated that "Federal agencies shall use integrated pest management techniques in carrying out pest management activities and shall promote integrated pest management through procurement and regulatory policies, and other activities" (cited in Beyond Pesticides, n.d.: 4). Most importantly for these purposes, IPM was also embraced by the golf industry in North America.

An early mention of IPM in the GCSAA publication *Golf Course Management* comes in 1979 in an article entitled 'IPM. An alternate approach to solving pest problems' (Bowen *et al.*, 1979). The title of this contribution is telling, as it signals through the qualifier 'alternate' that IPM was far from the hegemonic approach to course maintenance at the time. The text that followed suggested that IPM was nonetheless a worthwhile and timely endeavour:

> The phenomenal success of such chemicals as DDT, Lindane and Dieldrin in controlling the insect problems of turf led to their early adoption by professional turf managers and homeowners ... In recent years, the concerns of environmentalists and professional pest control specialists have led to stricter government regulations on the use of pesticides and to renewed interest in alternate pest control strategies. IPM is perceived by some as the proper alternate approach to solving pest problems. (Bowen *et al.*, 1979: 16)

The change in tone from articles in this same publication described in Chapter 3 is unmistakable: environmentalists are referred to in far less hostile terms than before. This same article also provided a definition of IPM that coincides with the multi-method approach described above.

In the Canadian superintendent publication *GreenMaster*, an early encounter with IPM's conceptual underpinnings comes in a 1977 article advocating the use of pesticide alternatives. This was deemed an 'environmentally clean' solution to pest problems, as well as one that was needed given that insects had starting "liking the pesticides" (Steklasa, 1977: 2). The year 1978 brought further support of IPM-like tactics – if not yet IPM itself. This was accompanied by a rather frank assessment:

protection of the environment is here to stay – and really in our hearts – can we truly justify the use of long lasting, stable pesticides for non crop production – in the proximity of heavily populated areas without really knowing what the long-term effect of those pesticides is going to be? (Pick, 1978: 4)

Indeed, with the arrival of the 1980s, the pro-IPM perspective was articulated with candid – at least by historical standards – reflections on the status quo in golf course maintenance. A 1981 article in *Golf Course Management* lamented the obsession in golf with 'pretty' courses, and the costs and consequences of maintaining this aesthetic (e.g. inadvertent chemical 'run-off' – Parascenzo, 1981). That this submission was called 'The times they are a-changing' is suggestive of a turn away from the standard set by the famed Augusta National course – or at least that such a turn was desirable. In 1983, the regular 'Thinking Superintendent' column in *Golf Course Management* was given the subheading 'Spray with restraint'. "There is a logical way of fighting pests with pesticides," the magazine's readership was told, "and that is to do so with some discretion" (Williams, 1983: 78). Again, consider the novelty of such an assertion against the image of helicopter-aided DDT spraying from years past. The April 1983 issue of this same publication offered yet another detailed, and discernibly *pedagogical*, review of IPM. The approach is not aimed at eliminating pesticides, it was made clear, but rather at flexibility: "[IPM] is a concept that uses more than one tactic to keep pest problems below levels that cause economic, aesthetic or functional turfgrass injury without creating a personal hazard to man, his environment or non-targeted forms of life" (Sherman *et al.*, 1983: 45).

IPM was therefore gathering steam, at least in terms of its promotion in trade publications. Following on from initial descriptions of its principles, the late 1980s and 1990s were a time for success stories in industry publications on golf's adoption of this integrated system. In 1988, agronomist John Foy historicized IPM in the pages of the *Green Section*. Before the Second World War he wrote, "Man was fighting a losing battle against weeds, diseases, and insects because brute force could not win over sheer numbers" (Foy, 1988: 9). Chemicals such as 2,4-D and DDT changed the equation, and by 1971 US producers were churning out 1.1 billion pounds of pesticide material annually. Yet while insisting that pesticides remained crucial in sustaining established standards of living, Foy also named Rachel Carson specifically in noting the rising fear over 'uncontrolled' chemical uses. The best response in turn was IPM – a systematic way of confronting pest concerns, and one successfully deployed at Sea Island Golf Club in the state of Georgia to cope with a longstanding mole cricket problem. Sea Island, in other words, bridged the gap between IPM theory and practice.

Further to the south, in 1995 the course Collier's Reserve was said in *Golf Course Management* to be "state-of-the-art from the start", in part because IPM (here referred to as integrated plant management) was thoroughly suffused through Collier's course maintenance philosophy (Anon., 1995a). It was not long before the GCSAA published a book-length overview of IPM and its relationship to golf (Schumann *et al.*, 2002). This included 'portraits' of regionally specific IPM practices. Florida superintendent Darren Davis wrote: "*All* of the pesticides applied at Olde Florida Golf Club are on a curative basis. Preventive application of herbicides, insecticides, nematicides, or fungicides are *not* done" (Davis, 2002: 223, emphasis in original).

Science, technology, and the new modern superintendent

The GCSAA's *IPM Handbook for Golf Courses* stressed that IPM is also a scientific enterprise. Indeed, as IPM became more prominent towards the end of the millennium, the golf industry was moving further and further away from Leonard Macomber's assessment from nearly a century earlier that botany, among other branches of science, is apt to prove highly confusing for golf superintendents – a view described in Chapter 3. A notable IPM 'success story' in *Golf Course Management* from 1987 on Sherman Hollow's golf course in Vermont noted the importance of measurement and monitoring to the successful implementation of an IPM system. In an inset to the article, penned by GCSAA Manager of Government Relations, Zachary Grant, superintendents were told they need to know, for example, the ratio of grubs to square footage on their courses so that they could, in turn, apply chemicals once an 'unacceptable' threshold had been crossed – and *only* once it had been crossed. Prior to that point, non-chemical means of control could be used. IPM was thus described as context-dependent: "As long as *you* know how many grubs can be allowed per square foot before treatment on your course, there is no need for an industry standard" (Grant, 1987b: 10, emphasis in original). In devising their own pesticide use plan, the Sherman Hollow management team consulted a number of authorities, including a hydrogeologist, toxicologist, agronomist, and environmental scientists. In a sign of how regulators would come to see pesticide usage on golf courses, the EPA was also enlisted to help with the operation of IPM (Grant, 1987a).

Apart from specific initiatives of this kind, the rise of IPM was accompanied by – and perhaps itself inspired – interest from golf industry members in bolstering their *organizational* research agenda. This is not to say the cause of research was new – for example, the GCSAA's Scholarship and Research Fund was founded in 1955 (GCSAA, n.d.a.). Instead, it is to say that research increasingly articulated with the perceived need for environmental responsibility. In the 1980s, the USGA and GCSAA combined forces to develop a formalized and robust Turfgrass Research Program. As written in the pages of *Golf Course Management* in 1985: "The objectives of the Turfgrass Research project are clear and simple to state: it is our goal to develop new grasses that will use 50 percent less water and require 50 percent less maintenance cost" (Anon., 1985: 19). By 1991, James T. Snow, National Director of the USGA *Green Section* publication, reflected fondly on what had been accomplished through this programme during its short history. He also described another initiative of this kind: the USGA's *Environmental* Research Program. Following a thorough review of the scientific literature in the early 1990s, this latter initiative was oriented around three key areas: the fate of pesticides and nutrients on golf courses; 'alternative' (which presumably meant non-chemical) methods of pest control; and the impacts of golf on people, wildlife, and the environment. Snow also noted that the USGA had allocated $2.8 million to fund environment-related research projects: "It is anticipated that this three-year study will produce a much greater understanding of the effects of golf course activities, including pesticide and fertilizer applications, on people, wildlife, and the environment" (Snow, 1991: 12).

The story was much the same in Canada. The Canadian Turfgrass Research Foundation (CTRF) was founded in 1967, and given charitable status by the federal government a decade later. It was administered by the Canadian Golf Superintendents Association (CGSA) until 1992, at which point control was passed to Golf Canada (CGSA, n.d.c). Regional organizations such as the Atlantic Turfgrass Research Foundation Inc. and the Ontario Turfgrass Research Foundation also emerged to complement the CTRF as time passed (AGSA, n.d.; Jiggens, n.d.). The main point here, however, is that the promotion of responsible golf, as in America, involved both touting IPM and professing the importance of research. In 1991, for example, IPM's multifaceted approach was compared to how a doctor might prescribe lifestyle, dietary, and medical remedies all at once (Fushtey, 1991). In the same year, *GreenMaster* reported CGSA President Ken Olsvik's view that, when it comes to the environment, "association policy and decisions have to be based on scientific data and that is why the CGSA is placing a high priority on promoting and supporting research" (Mellersh, 1991: 19).

Science, precision, responsibility: these were the new shibboleths of the golf industry as Rachel Carson's *Silent Spring* drifted further and further into the past. With the literature on EM in mind, it is not surprising that technologies grew evermore important in precision course management as well.

Computers are one case in point in this regard. In 1992, environmental scientist Kevin Franke described the Leaching Estimation and Chemistry Model (LEACHM), among other computer simulation programmes, as a useful development for golf course management. LEACHM alone would not produce an IPM plan, Franke wrote in the pages of the USGA's *Green Section*: "What LEACHM will provide is a determination of what, where, and when products can be expected to work efficiently and safely" (Franke, 1992: 19). Three years later, in an article entitled 'IPM, monitoring, and management plans', computer simulations were likewise discussed as useful in predicting the fate of pesticides in the environment. This in turn could help in selecting appropriate chemicals for use on the golf course (Peacock and Smart, 1995). In similar fashion, and with a new millennium nearing, *Golf Course Management* announced in 1999 the arrival of 'The computer age'. The magazine's readership was told that superintendents were increasingly adopting computer software programmes to help with everything from personnel files to fertilization scheduling to the irrigation of their courses (Goodman, 1999).

Indeed, as much as pesticides and pesticide backlash were concerns from the late 1970s onwards, so too did golf's demand on water supplies attract much attention in industry publications. In 1981, it was announced in *Golf Course Management* that the 1980s would be the 'water decade' (Rosillon, 1981: 35). A year later, the problem of overwatering turfgrass was described in the provocatively titled article, 'Does your irrigation system know there's a water crisis?' (Augustin, 1982). In this same year, the article 'Game plan for golf' came to similar conclusions about the pressing need to adopt a responsible approach with respect to course irrigation (Anon., 1982a). The outlook in this case, however, was also optimistic in the sense that science and technology could carve out a suitable – which is to say, *sustainable* – pathway forward. The Allied Associations of Golf, an organization that included, among others, the USGA, the GCSAA, and the American Society of Golf Course Architects, had settled on a multifaceted approach for the future:

> The priorities are, in order, reducing significantly the need for potable water on turfgrasses; developing grasses that will adapt to brackish, recycled or otherwise marginal-quality water; improving water utilization of turfgrasses; developing grasses that require minimal maintenance and are pest resistant, winter-hardy and traffic tolerant, and improving grass varieties through modern scientific methods. (Anon., 1982a: 71)

In a similar vein, the President's Message in the September/October 1988 issue of *GreenMaster* called attention to recent water shortages in Canada. "As turf managers," GCSA President Barry Britton urged, "we have to re-evaluate our watering methods and also update and fine-tune our irrigation systems so that our client, 'the golfer', has good golfing conditions available to him" (Britton, 1988: 6). In 1993, it was said that computerized irrigation both saves resources and cuts expenses. "Using the lack of water as a rallying cry, environmentalists have reasoned that golf course facilities waste water and shouldn't be built in arid regions, leaving developers out to dry." But, the article continued, "That scenario may be changing, thanks to computerized irrigation systems that save both water and energy" (McWhirter, 1993: 29).

Responsible golf in the new millennium

With the arrival of the new millennium, the trends described above showed no signs of abating. The 2000s brought increased discussion of another, even more robust turf management system: Best Management Practices (BMPs). In 2005, professor and turfgrass physiologist Robert N. Carrow was flanked by Ron R. Duncan, a retired professor and vice president of Turf Ecosystems LLC, and David Wienecke, a director of golf course maintenance at a course in California, in espousing the merits of BMPs. Indifference or inattention to environmental matters was no longer a viable option, the authors averred, for since the publication of *Silent Spring*, "societal pressures have increasingly moved toward national regulatory action to protect various aspects of the environment" (Carrow et al., 2005: 81). The two pathways remaining were those of 'rigid regulation' and 'holistic, science-based methods' – note the implication of mutual exclusivity. As might be expected, the authors favoured the latter. BMPs were positioned as similar to IPM in that they take an holistic, science-based approach to managing the golf course environment. The focus on BMPs, however, allows for a wider view, one considerate of, for example, water conservation alongside other environmental 'flashpoints' such as pesticides. Altogether, as Carrow and his colleagues explained, BMPs favour a scientific approach to environmental management whereby 'inputs' are applied to the golf course only as needed, and whereby new technologies are actively welcomed in the process of (re)imagining 'best practices'. This was deemed far more preferable than 'rigid regulations' based on politics rather than science: "The latest concepts and technology can be effectively applied to environmental problems, but political or personal beliefs that are not based on good science cannot" (Carrow et al., 2005: 82). As we shall in the next chapter, this was neither the first nor last time that golf's close relationship with science was emphasized in the context of discussing environmental policy.

Perhaps an even more important development for golf superintendents in the early 2000s came when the long-established research and education funding arm of the GCSAA changed its name to the Environmental Institute for Golf (EIFG). The integration of environmental awareness into the golf superintendent profession was by no means an overnight phenomenon, as we have seen. But with the arrival of the EIFG, golf's professed 'green' sensibilities were privileged more so than ever before. To be specific, golf's embrace of *sustainability* was emphasized with newfound intensity. The GCSAA now directly recounts the Brundtland Commission's definition of sustainable development on its website, while also situating itself as an organization that is indeed concerned with the 'triple bottom line':

> The US golf industry recognizes sustainability as the integration of environmental stewardship, social responsibility and economic viability as a critical and never-ending goal. The golf industry embraces sustainability as *"meeting the needs of the present without compromising the ability of future generations to meet their own needs"*. (GCSAA, n.d.b., emphasis in original)

In 2006, the EIFG set out on perhaps the most significant research endeavour in the GCSAA's history – one described as 'groundbreaking' by the organization itself (GCSAA, n.d.c.). The Golf Course Environmental Profile was designed to collect baseline data on environmental performance at golf courses across the country. It specifically featured five surveys, each with their own respective focus: (a) property profile and environmental stewardship of golf courses; (b) water use and conservation practices; (c) nutrient use and management; (d) energy use and conservation practices; and (e) pesticide use on US golf courses. The famed golfer and EIFG advisory council chair Greg Norman said in the foreword to the first report: "Thanks to a growing amount of data, the golf industry is able to state with even greater confidence that golf courses can be compatible with the environment" (GCSAA, 2007: 6).

Importantly, it is not the GCSAA alone that has devised and actively extolled the merits of such endeavours. The USGA's environmental research programme marches forward. Like the GCSAA, the USGA harbours the perspective that environmental sustainability and economic solvency are by no means incompatible (see USGA, 2009). For their part, the American Society of Golf Course Architects – allies of the GCSAA at least since the aforementioned Allied Associations of Golf was formed – shares many stories online of golf courses serving the cause of environmental sustainability. These often crystalize around the reconfiguration of environmentally damaging landscapes such as manufacturing plants and landfills to make them more in touch with nature (see American Society of Golf Course Architects, n.d.). Indeed, in Chapter 6 we explore the golf industry's simultaneous promotion of golf course management as a technological wonder and of golf courses *themselves* as pristine, natural spaces.

In Canada, IPM is still positioned by the CGSA as a 'sustainable approach', one "combining biological, cultural, physical, and chemical methods to manage pests so that the benefits of pest control and turf health are maximized and the health and environmental risks are minimized" (CGSA, 2007a; CGSA 2007b). The National Allied Golf Associations – an umbrella organization that includes Golf Canada, the CGSA, and the Canadian Professional Golfers Association, among others – has also emerged to actively profess golf's support of research in the interest of finding ever more effective products and management practices that go towards the reduction of environmental risks (see NAGA, 2009). And though we have not analysed the historical trajectory of environmental management in the UK to the same extent, key governing bodies across the Atlantic now advocate a similarly responsible position. As the R&A, a key UK-based governing body, tells golf industry representatives, "As a user of natural resources, you have a responsibility to operate in a manner which shows concern and awareness for environmental issues" (R&A, n.d.a.).[1] As in the USA and Canada, they too stress that water and pesticides need be used discriminately (e.g. with the help of precision technologies), and that water should be deployed in effluent form when possible (R&A, n.d.b.; R&A, n.d.c.). 'Spray with restraint' and, evidently, 'water with restraint' are now creeds on both sides of the Atlantic.

EM and its discontents: troubling 'responsible golf'

The aforementioned 'Game plan for golf' article appearing in *Golf Course Management* in 1982 is telling for more than just its description of looming technological and scientific endeavours. The changed *perception* of the environment in this submission compared to years' past is noteworthy as well. The opening lines of this article read as follows:

> Nothing on earth is permanent. Our world is in a constant state of change, and obsolescence results from an inability to adapt to that change. In fact, our survival is predicated on our ability to keep up with and adjust to the change going on around us. (Anon., 1982a: 71)

Compare this frank admission to GCSAA President Richard C. Blake's statement on a similar matter from just eleven years earlier:

> The truth of the matter is that civilization did not begin until man learned to use fire and other tools to modify his environment. In other words, the fate of the human race and the wildlife that has shared in its rise rests on man's ability to anticipate, modify, and control environmental *changes*. (Blake, 1971: 7, emphasis in original)

Ecological modernization, as said in Chapter 2, is as much dependent on a particular perception of humankind's relationship with the environment as it is the adoption of sustainability-driven technological initiatives. The comments in the second passage above are truly Promethean in both tone and content. Blake near-literally recounts the Promethean myth through reference to man's adoption of fire for the sake of environmental control. By contrast, the passage from 1982 admits that environmental change transcends humankind. It is undoubtedly humbler in this regard.

At the same time, however, rather than urging *demodernization* (e.g. the adoption of more precautionary course management techniques that are informed by a recognition of the limits of human-driven innovations, technologies, and the 'latest science') when confronting the realization that 'nothing on Earth is permanent', the solutions posited in the 'Game plan for golf' specifically, and in the pages of trade publications in general, in our view remain anthropocentric. That is to say, they see human-led scientific and technological endeavours – whether the development of more resilient turfgrass, precision irrigation, 'rifle shot' pesticide applications through IPM, or other, similar initiatives of this kind – as vehicles for manipulating the Earth, albeit with care.

Thus, after defensiveness in the immediate post-*Silent Spring* years, golf moved to a 'responsible', light-green approach to environmental management thereafter. With this change, the combat metaphor for managing pests was no longer applicable in the way it once was. A more apt metaphor was evinced by golf architect Mike Hurdzan in a recent interview in the publication *Golf Digest*. Hurdzan's response to the question, 'Do you think the pesticides used on golf courses today are safe?' was as follows:

> I do. They've got to be properly used. It's a very fine line between a medicine and a poison – we're trying to walk that line, to treat a pesticide as a medicine to get rid of these pests that are causing us a problem, but if we abuse them, then they can be poisons. The proper use of pesticides presents no problems at all. (Barton, 2008)

We saw above how IPM was compared in Canada to the way a doctor prescribes multiple remedies. The medical metaphor is a neat conduit for the principles the golf industry had come to stand for in the 1980s and beyond: efficiency, precision, erudition, and, above all, responsibility.

But while our above presentation of results suggests an easily discernible, linear narrative, and while proponents of responsible golf have recounted such a narrative as well, our findings on the North American golf industry's adoption of environmental responsibility are in fact more complex. That is to say, the narrative is disrupted by contradictions lying in golf's adoption of scientific research and technological ingenuity in developing their 'green(er)' sensibilities. Below we identify two particular issues related to the formalized systems associated with responsible golf. These issues reflect critiques of ecological modernization in general.

A first contradiction pertains to the certainty with which claims have been made – and continue to be made – by the golf industry about the risks associated with established golf course maintenance practices. Responsible golf rests on the premise that, while chemical uses should be reduced where possible, research has proven pesticides non-threatening and effective when applied according to label specifications. Indeed, this premise is *built in* to the principles of IPM. The response of pesticide critics has primarily been to stress that this organizational disposition is not precautionary enough. Pesticides, even when deployed in small quantities, might have toxic effects overlooked in research, might accumulate in the environment, or might have synergistic effects when encountering other chemicals (e.g. see Arya, 2005). Environmental activist Jay Feldman, director of the organization Beyond Pesticides, made many of these points in 2008 in the same *Golf Digest* article from which Hurdzan was quoted above:

> You'll hear golf course superintendents say, 'We're using such minuscule amounts of these chemicals.' But endocrine disruption can happen at really low exposures. We don't even have the testing protocol to assess this low dose ... With pesticides, we're not just dealing with what we do know, but also what we don't know. The risk-assessment protocol is filled with wrong assumptions. One example is the story of chlorpyrifos, whose trade name is Dursban, which was banned from household use in 2000 because of neurological effects. It had been widely used for insect control indoors and outdoors. But it's still used in golf. (Barton, 2008)

Criticisms of this kind tacitly implicate IPM, given that this integrated system ultimately allows for the continued use of pesticides at the applicator's discretion. It is perhaps unsurprising, then, that many environmental activist groups have urged that IPM is unsatisfactory as an environmental management system when it comes to the cosmetic (i.e. non-essential) use of pesticides. As the Canadian Cancer Society told the British Columbia provincial government in recent hearings over a potential cosmetic pesticide ban, IPM sounds reasonable on the surface, though in principle its tenets are vague and open to interpretation (Kaminsky and Seely, 2011; also see West Coast Environmental Law, 2011). A representative from the Canadian Association of Physicians for the Environment made a similar point in an interview for this research:

> We don't think IPM protects public health – I mean that's really the long and the short of it … I think IPM was essentially devised by industry to keep spraying. I mean at the end of the day, IPM allows you to keep spraying for non-essential purposes so we don't support IPM. (Personal interview, February 2012)

Yet, as noted, the first contradiction with which we are concerned pertains more to the *defence* of chemicals than their sustained use, though these are certainly related points. Specifically, what a historical analysis reveals is that the golf industry's present-day defence of chemicals is far from new. Some pesticides that are now widely discredited – at least when it comes to cosmetic uses – were once defended by industry representatives using familiar rhetorical techniques. For instance, in 1970 the publication *Golf Course Management* featured an article written by a representative of the turf industry suggesting that concerns about the negative impacts of chemicals such as DDT and mercury were ill-founded. Among the arguments made at this time was that the latest science was 'on the side' of continued pesticide use: "Scientists … who have been working with pesticides have concluded that there is no evidence that pesticides directly cause any disease" (Kerr, 1970: 28). In this same year, the GCSAA's Director of Education contended that concerns about DDT poisoning were tantamount to "pure, unadulterated and sensationalistic reporting." He added: "We need to work with facts and reason; not with protests and superficial knowledge" (Alexander, 1970: 20; also see Van Buskirk, 1971). In this way, golf was on the side of reason and logic, while pesticide critics were swayed by emotion.

DDT is not alone as a chemical for which the passage of time has not been entirely kind. In 1970, Gord Witteveen, then the newly elected president of the Canadian Golf Course Superintendents Association, supplied an unwelcoming assessment of a potential ban on mercuries and arsenicals: "I don't know how we can work without them … there are very few substitute chemicals available" (Marks, 1970: 45). In 1988, the GCSAA noted that their advocacy efforts engendered a legislative exemption for the use of cadmium fungicides on golf course greens, tees and aprons (Anon., 1987a). These two cases can be set against the more reflexive assessments of recent times. Golf course architect Mike Hurdzan said in the same *Golf Digest* article noted above: "Back in the mid-'50s we were using cadmium, lead, arsenic, mercury; we were using all these heavy metals. We were using farm-grade fertilizers. Well, those things are gone. We didn't know any better back then. Science has showed us a better way to do things" (Barton, 2008). In this same issue, superintendent Jeff Carlson, whom we mention again in later chapters for his work in organic golf, likewise recounted a story of his very negative experience with cadmium-based and mercury-based fungicides in the late 1970s (also see PMEP, n.d.). Another case in point here is the chemical 2,4,5-T, for which we find support in a 1984 *Golf Course Management* article saying this product is backed by an extensive safety record (though an editor's note clarified that this was the author's own opinion – Baskin, 1984). Not long after, use of 2,4,5-T was halted in both Canada and the United States.

Still another example lies in the case of the insecticide diazinon. As Wheeler and Nauright (2006) recount, it was banned from usage on golf courses in 1990, following a five-year legal dispute, and in light of evidence that it was poisoning birds. What our review of industry trade publications reveals is that Ciba-Geigy Corp., reported in the late 1980s to be the main supplier of diazinon-based products in the USA at the time, credited the support they received from the GCSAA – and, more specifically, the testimony of golf superintendents – in winning a 1988 legal decision to allow diazinon's sustained use (Anon., 1988d).

Of course, science improves and knowledge changes. Hurdzan makes this point. But a historical analysis suggests that, over time, the golf industry has in many cases effectively known the answer – pesticides pose no considerable threat – before the question is even asked. The fact that chemicals still used on golf courses such as 2,4-D remain a source of consternation for many researchers and activists, as discussed in our introductory chapter, stands out even more in light of this historical analysis. It is relevant here too that the depiction of pesticide criticism as based in emotion continued beyond the 1970s as well. In 1982 it was said in *Golf Course Management* that a small but vociferous group of activists were disregarding science in favour of anti-pesticide ideology and politics (Arnold, 1982: 45; also see Charters, 1989). And though relations with activists improved in the 1990s (as we discuss in the following chapter), concerns about emotional, rather than rational, anti-pesticide pleas did not disappear (e.g. see Langley, 1998).

The question of why a generally pro-pesticide perspective, as opposed to a more precautionary one, has remained in the age of responsible golf is a complex one. It is important to remember that Augusta National syndrome has yet to be 'cured', as discussed in Chapter 4, and so individual superintendents must still reckon with a lofty 'green' standard.

Yet if we return to the comments made by activist Jay Feldman in *Golf Digest*, the close affiliation between the golf and chemical industries should also be taken into account. In Chapter 3 we noted the concern occasionally expressed in trade publications in the 1960s and 1970s over 'Satchmo', the pesticide vendor with a satchel of magical (read: untrustworthy) elixirs. But, as Feldman notes, over time chemical suppliers have formed a bond with golf course chemical applicators, at least at an organizational level. In one sense, therefore, trade publications such as *GreenMaster* and *Golf Course Management* have served as venues for chemical companies to advertise their products, thus allowing direct communication on the merits of pesticides with those who might use them. In another, perhaps even more significant sense, chemical companies have also become leading donors to the aforementioned Environmental Institute for Golf (EIFG) – a matter for which, to their credit, the GCSAA is clearly transparent. The chemical company Syngenta, for example, is in the 'Victory Club' of donors, having pledged over $1 million towards matters like research, educational initiatives, and scholarships. Bayer Environmental Science, another pesticide supplier, is listed in the 'Star Club' ($500,000–$999,999) while other, similar companies such as Dow AgroSciences and the Monsanto Company have pledged support as well (GCSAA, n.d.d). In Feldman's words: "The chemical companies always have their hand in the trade associations ... And because of this, it becomes a pro-pesticide industry" (Barton, 2008). Indeed, our point here is not that EIFG-sponsored research is necessarily invalidated by these affiliations; it is instead that with this 'golf-chemical complex' in place, it is unsurprising that the golf industry has arrived at a position whereby chemicals can *at best* be reduced, and are defended almost as a matter of principle.

A second contradiction emerging through our historical analysis pertains to the golf industry's quest for efficiency through the tenets of ecological modernization and its simultaneous pursuit of economic growth through both the popularizing of golf and the development of new courses. The 1990s may well have been a time when 'responsible golf' truly began to flourish. But, as noted in earlier chapters, this decade also brought another 'boom' in course development. The supply of golf courses in the United States grew by roughly 20 per cent in the 1990s, while demand (gauged by rounds played) increased by roughly 15 per cent (Hueber and Worzala, 2010). It is important to say that this substantial uptick in development was not simply the result of individual entrepreneurialism; as noted in Chapter 4, in the late 1980s, the National Golf Foundation (NGF) devised a Strategic Plan for the Growth of the Game calling for the development of 'A course a day' in the following decade (Hueber and Worzala, 2010). Hueber and Worzala (2010) note that the 1990s 'boom' also brought the 'marriage' of golf and real estate development, with 60 per cent of courses tied to real estate projects in the United States. The common result, they argue, were courses that brought a high degree of difficulty for players, a manicured aesthetic, and, ultimately, the subsuming of environmental concerns under the maximizing of profit.

The 1990s 'boom' came to an end as the new millennium arrived: the number of rounds played per eighteen-hole equivalent decreased by 9 per cent from 2001 to 2008, yielding "an unhealthy imbalance between supply and demand" (Hueber and Worzala, 2010: 7; also see NGF, 2009). The response, then, might have been to 'purge' golf courses – and in doing so, much of their environmental impact – in the interest of aligning supply and demand. Indeed, Hueber and Worzala quote Joe Beditz, president and CEO of the NGF, as saying, "the problem of oversupply will fix itself once the industry loses some 1,500 to 2,000 golf courses" (Hueber and Worzala, 2010: 8). Yet the golf industry has evidently chosen the opposite tactic: to reinvigorate the popularity of the game through a formal PR programme. In 2000, 'Golf 20/20' was launched by a group of allied golf organizations and stakeholders for this very purpose. Within its remit are initiatives targeting specific demographic groups – for example, youth and women – as well as programmes aiming to change the perception of golf in the view of lawmakers and the public in general (a matter we explore further in the following chapter). Organizations such as the GCSAA have also stressed the merits of Golf 20/20 for its membership, including the development of new courses. As said in *Golf Course Management* (GCM) shortly after this programme's unveiling:

> because the goal of Golf 20/20 is to encourage rapid growth of the game's popularity and numbers of participants, superintendents would likely see more job opportunities, both on alternative courses designed for teaching new players, as well as on new, full-size golf courses built to meet rising demand as those players gain enough confidence to take their games to a higher level. (GCM Staff, 2001: 13)

As said in Chapter 3, demand is shown in this case to be an industry construction at least as much as a natural market force.

From an environmental perspective, the optimistic (that is, ecological modernist) view of this ongoing emphasis on economic growth is that it can be offset by heightened efficiencies in, for example, the use of pesticides and water. But the opposite view is equally compelling: that the efficiencies so celebrated by the golf industry are easily counteracted by increases in the amount of terrain requiring 'treatment' as golf courses are built at a frantic pace (at least in the 1990s). To be sure, it is no surprise to find any given industry actively supporting its own economic well-being. Yet when this same industry is ostensibly driven towards environmental responsibility, a contradiction emerges in the style of Jevon's paradox (described in Chapter 2). That is to say, the pursuit environmental efficiencies exist in a wider context where the need for overall expansion goes unquestioned. Moreover, our critique here does not yet account for the *global* growth of golf – a point we explore in examining the 'dark-greening' of golf in Chapters 8 and 9.

Taken together, these contradictions unsettle the linear narrative commonly evinced by golf industry representatives in present times – that is, the view that golf has unquestionably moved beyond its brief irresponsible turn in the early post-war years, and has arrived instead at a deeply responsible place. Scientific research and technological innovation are crucial to this light-green disposition: it is effectively an article of faith that science and technology can deliver properly 'green' outcomes while also allowing the golf industry to thrive financially. Said otherwise, whereas the golf industry in North America spent the first three quarters of the twentieth century modernizing its approach to service provision, the last quarter was directed towards a slightly different end: *ecological* modernization.

But scientific research and technological innovation do not stand alone as articles of faith. A historical analysis suggests that they have been deployed in a context that takes for granted other principles as well: namely, that pesticides cannot be eradicated *tout court* and that the golf industry must unfailingly grow larger. The point in highlighting these contradictions is not to suggest that science and technology are irrelevant to the pursuit of environmental solutions. In keeping with critiques of ecological modernization, it is to say that there are excellent reasons to be sceptical about situations where science and technology-oriented solutions are presented as *the only solutions* to environment-related problems. Our own scepticism about unfettered faith in these sorts of solutions becomes quite pronounced as we came to learn about how science and technology were mobilized in defence of practices that history has ultimately deemed 'irresponsible'. As shown in the following chapters, the golf industry has gone to great lengths to stress the value of their responsible practices to lawmakers and the public both.

Note

1 The name R&A refers to and derives from, but is separate and distinct from, The Royal and Ancient Golf Club of St Andrews (for details, see http://www.randa.org/en/RandA.aspx).

6

Environmentalism incorporated: professionalization and post-politics in the time of responsible golf

A key theme of our analysis so far is that managing a golf course is a difficult job, and became ever more so as golf adopted its 'modern' sensibilities. At present, the Canadian Golf Superintendents Association (CGSA) describes the duties of the golf superintendent as follows:

> The Superintendent must know and understand the complexities and interrelationships of soils, irrigation, plant pathology, entomology, plant fertility and drainage hydrology. Superintendents must have a thorough understanding of the safe use of agricultural pharmaceuticals such as insecticides, herbicides and fungicides – plus a general understanding of various tools and equipment ranging from hand tools to complex, hydraulically operated machinery. The Superintendent must also have the knowledge required to deal with problems related to roadways, trees, flowers, buildings, tennis courts, skeet ranges, swimming pools, golf car fleets and other facilities related to golf. (CGSA, n.d.a)

All of this comes in addition to the skills required for personnel management, communications, and financial management. A sound understanding of the game of golf itself is said to be important too. Altogether: a complicated profession indeed.

It is noteworthy that the above passage falls under the heading 'Education Required' on the CGSA's website. Whereas in Chapter 5 we examined the evolution of course management systems in the golf profession (e.g. IPM and BMPs) in this chapter we turn our focus to a related matter: professionalization, and in particular education and impression management. As described below, our reason for selecting these two specific realms, and for connecting them to the broader idea of 'professionalization', stems from the fact that, over time, individuals within the golf industry themselves deemed improvements in education and external communication (i.e. impression management) as central to the goal of becoming recognized and respected professionals. To advocate for golf's 'responsible', 'light-green' disposition in the time of 'responsible golf' requires systems for both training golf superintendents (among others) and for outwardly professing that superintendents possess the above-described skills.

In other words, our main contention in this chapter is that educational and impression management mechanisms were formalized over time within organizations like the GCSAA with the goal of professionalization in mind. The upshot of this was that golf superintendents could deliver, and could be seen to deliver, a more responsible 'product' – meaning a safe but still picturesque and enticing golf course environment.

We pursue this argument by exploring the evolution of environment-related professionalization practices from the late 1960s onwards. The urge to professionalize, we suggest, surely stems in part from a sincere desire to ensure that members of the golf industry are doing their jobs in a proper and compliant way. In the final section of this chapter, however, we also provide a more critical assessment of the professionalization strategies described herein. We reflect especially on professionalization's *ideological* function at this time: in positioning golf industry representatives as leaders in the environmental movement, professionalization tactics have served to elevate golf's *version* of environmentalism to a 'leading' (i.e. hegemonic) position as well. We employ the aforementioned notion of 'post-politics' to help make sense of this development. Furthermore, we 'trouble' professionalization by noting the disjuncture that has arisen at times between the golf industry's external and internal communication tactics. For example, golf's outward messaging on the readiness of superintendents to tackle environmental issues has not always aligned with internal communication on the pressing need for environmental education. The urge to professionalize, therefore, may indeed be genuine, but professionalization is a matter of politics and power as well.

Stepping stone or stumbling block? Education and the golf course superintendent

That professionalization in general and education in particular were matters of concern in the golf industry in the time of 'pro-golf' is best evidenced in a 1969 submission to *Golf Course Management* entitled 'How professional are we …?' Therein, Colorado golf course superintendent Stanley E. Metsker outlined steps that his colleagues might take towards professionalization. Included in these steps was "prolonged political agitation" (Metsker, 1969: 34) – a point we return to in discussing impression management below. What Metsker appeared most concerned with, however, was the dearth of opportunities for superintendent training at the time:

> There is a wide knowledge of specialized technique that should be known by each golf superintendent. However, there is no way at the present time to tell who knows what. Because there is no formal recruiting program, no schools or curriculum required, and no registration, certification, or license, there is no way to judge this criterion in a man, except perhaps by past performance. (Metsker, 1969: 32)

Metsker was envisioning a scenario whereby the means of proffering idyllic golf course conditions could better be explained. Until it was known 'who knows what' in the golf industry, the answer to the question 'How professional are we?' was evidently 'not very'.

Metsker's was not the only contribution of this kind in the pages of *GCM*. Norman W. Kramer's President's Message from June 1970 in the same publication was given the title 'Certification – stepping stone or stumbling block?' (Kramer, 1970a). Kramer was himself a proponent of the GCSAA's emerging certification programme, but the title of his essay, and specifically the notion that certification might cause superintendents to 'stumble', is suggestive of the uncertainty that surrounded this form of professionalization in the early 1970s. Indeed, Kramer wrote in the style of a Q&A, responding to some of the questions he was frequently asked on this topic. Among them: "Isn't Certification really just a 'club' for college type superintendents?" (Kramer's answer: "No"); and, "If I choose not to apply for Certification, will I be branded as a 'second-class' superintendent?" ("No" again) (Kramer, 1970a: 9). A follow-up article from a year later noted that recent writing on certification had inspired a heavy response from GCSAA members. In one pro-certification letter, Michigan superintendent Roger O'Connell (1971) likened certification to a 'yardstick' for measuring professional capability.

Despite its apparent contentiousness, the GCSAA indeed unveiled a certification programme in the early 1970s. But what did certification comprise? GCSAA Secretary-Treasurer Clifford A. Wagoner (1971), writing in the USGA's *Green Section* publication, explained that the Association's certification programme was in fact nearly three years in the making, and was urgently needed at a time when golf superintendents had to stay abreast of developments in various realms: turfgrass science, new equipment, and the business side of golf course management especially. The process of obtaining certification would evidently test the breadth of knowledge of the GCSAA's membership:

> The written examination is divided into six major categories. Each segment covers important points of knowledge and skills needed by top superintendents. Among them are turf culture procedures, plant protectant chemicals, business administration, management, rules and game of golf, and understanding of the GCSAA. (Wagoner, 1971: 6)

Moreover, certification was tied together with education in the sense that: (a) re-examination was required five years after becoming certified; and (b) superintendents needed to complete one GCSAA-approved workshop or correspondence course per year.

Wagoner (1974) returned to the same publication three years later to say that 157 golf superintendents had, by that time, earned the title 'certified golf course superintendent'. By 1976, the number had reached 245 (Olivar, 1976). Carol Olivar (1976), under the title of 'Advertising Manager', described in *Golf Course Management* the point system that would be used for future processes of re-certification. Two points were given, for example, for GCSAA seminar attendance, while a half point was awarded for attending the Association's annual conference (Olivar, 1976: 41). The latter event was of particular importance for many golf superintendents, whether certified or not – something evidenced by the fact that discussion of the conference occupied substantial space in the *Golf Course Management* publication each year. Palmer Maples Jr. was both a certified golf course superintendent and GCSAA President in 1976. His presidential message from January of that year depicted the Association's annual International Turfgrass Conference and Show as an event not to be missed:

> The individual who participates in the conference has much to benefit from the program, industry exhibits, association meetings and the opportunity to confer with people from around the world who share a common interest. (Maples, 1976: 7)

Like Olivar, Maples noted too that the number of certified golf superintendents was growing rapidly. He highlighted that the GCSAA's general membership (different from certification) was also expanding, and by 1976 had surpassed 4,000 members. GCSAA members receiving their regular copy of *Golf Course*

Management likely considered this publication an educational device in itself. Features such as 'Questions from the floor', for example, offered expert guidance on key issues related to course management.

Towards environmental education

As seen in the preceding chapter, the 1980s brought responsible golf to the forefront as a reformative, 'alter-golf' response in the golf industry. Responsible golf was and remains both a sensibility and an articulated set of best practices (e.g. IPM). What can now be added to our discussion is that new educational initiatives – including environmentally focused ones – eventually became an important part of this mix. That is to say, as new, purportedly environmentally friendly construction and management tactics were emerging, so too was training on ways of properly adopting these now-available tactics.

Indeed, in the first edition of *Golf Course Management* from the year 1980, certified golf course superintendent Gary Bethune implored his colleagues to take to the classroom:

> Apathy and complacency are the greatest threats to our profession. One of the most important tasks we have as managers is maintaining a high degree of expertise and interest in each segment of our responsibilities. This ability and interest level is directly proportional to the amount of effort we devote to acquiring knowledge relating to our profession. So, if we want to grow professionally, we must be willing to learn. (Bethune, 1980: 46)

The backdrop for Bethune's comments was the changing environmental policy landscape of the day (discussed further below). As such, Bethune did not fail to portray environmental matters as among those in which superintendents needed to be fluent. The theme of the GCSAA's 1980 International Turfgrass Conference and Show – 'Conservation ... our key to the future' – sat nicely alongside Bethune's take on education (Anon., 1980). Incoming GCSAA President Melvin B. Lucas Jr. also impressed the virtues of education and certification as the decade began (Marquis, 1980). With respect to the latter, by 1980 there were 512 superintendents with the designation Certified Golf Course Superintendent (Lucas, 1980).

Seven years on, GCSAA President Donald E. Hearn (1987a) echoed the sentiment of his predecessor. In his April 1987 message to *GCM*'s readership, however, Hearn addressed 'The need to listen and learn' on the matter of *pesticides* specifically. Pesticide critics were often misinformed, Hearn stated. Still, the subtitle of his text – "The time is at hand to recognize the dimensions of everyone's responsibility for professional self-education" – suggested that superintendents still needed to develop a knowledge base of their own, and a robust one at that. "To say, 'I didn't know ...' carries little weight when confronted by a regulatory agency or your employer" (Hearn, 1987a: 5).

What lurked around the corner from Hearn's words of encouragement was a formal system for providing the type of environmental education he seemed to value so highly. To be sure, by the late 1980s the GCSAA had arranged for workshops on environmental themes for some years. But just as IPM and BMPs were adopted as *formalized* procedures for golf course management, as described in Chapter 5, the Environmental Management Program (EMP) of the early 1990s was devised as a formal mechanism for environmental training. GCSAA Education Manager Claudia G. Larkin described the certificate programme as follows:

> When fully implemented, the [Environmental Management Program] will offer six distinct certificate programs. Each program will consist of a curriculum developed by superintendents, experts in particular fields of study and GCSAA curriculum specialists. This will enable participants to develop their expertise in chosen areas of specialization. Superintendents may choose to complete one or more of these specializations. (Larkin 1992: 58)

According to Larkin, one of the first areas of specialization made available was IPM.

At roughly the same time, Mark Dufresne (1993), President of the CGSA, noted that education programming would be ratcheted upwards in Canada as well in the face of growing environmental concerns. In general, golf superintendents further north seemed to have walked a similar trajectory to their American counterparts as the post-war years unfolded. For example, there was recognition in the early 1970s that a superintendent's job description was growing increasingly complex. "[The superintendent] is no longer a simple lawn mower," wrote Camil Labelle in his August, 1971 President's Message, "but a technician" (Labelle, 1971a: 2). Sound knowledge of agronomy, entomology, chemistry, agriculture engineering, mechanics, horticulture, and other disciplines was therefore required. And although Labelle (1971b) used the same platform months later to implore *GreenMaster*'s readership to take advantage of the many agricultural-themed programmes at Canadian educational institutions, there was evidently still a need – as in the United States – to repudiate the idea that certification is meaningless (e.g. see Finn, 1971).

Nonetheless, through the 1970s and 1980s the CGSA offered educational opportunities through seminars, its own annual Turfgrass Conference and Show, and features in its flagship publication, *GreenMaster*. It was 1987 when the Association introduced their own accreditation programme – one recognizing experienced and qualified candidates as 'master superintendents' (see Gurney, 1987; and CGSA, n.d.b). With the arrival of the 1990s, CGSA President Mark Dufresne was not alone in stressing the need for enhanced training specifically on environmental management. In the same issue of *GreenMaster*, for example, CGSA Executive Director R. Vince Gillis emphasized the Association's support of environmental education and reflected on the matter of public perception: the challenge facing superintendents, Gillis wrote, was to simultaneously *be* environmentally responsible and to *be seen* as environmentally responsible from an external perspective (Gillis, 1993). Professionalization among golf industry stakeholders was a core concern across North America.

Golf is in good hands: managing impressions

With Gillis' comments on golf's public image in mind, it is useful to circle back yet again to the late 1960s and early 1970s – the time of 'pro-golf'. While educational opportunities were evidently in short supply at that time (at least compared to later years), so too was there a sentiment that golf was not doing enough when it came to impression management. As noted in the previous section, Stanley Metsker (1969) saw 'political agitation' as central to professionalization. One year earlier, GCSAA President James W. Brandt (1968) also reflected on the matter of external communication – though his message centred on other 'audiences' of note. Brandt commented:

> For too long we have neglected the responsibility of informing our 'publics' – the golfer and would-be golfer, the club official and owner, and all the other professionals involved with us in the operation of today's golf courses – of the problems we face. (Brandt, 1968: 7)

Brandt acknowledged that some within the profession might see an enhanced communication strategy as an excuse for making superintendents into 'glamour boys'. He insisted that this was not the case.

What we find in analysing trade publications like *Golf Course Management* and *GreenMaster* is that government officials and members of the public were indeed primary 'target' audiences for the golf industry over time – and grew increasingly so as chemical-intensive golf gave way to its 'responsible' successor. This makes sense. On the one hand, and as we have seen, the tide of public sentiment was turning against many of the golf industry's common practices in the wake of Rachel Carson's *Silent Spring*. On the other hand, and as previously mentioned, the environmental policy landscape was changing too. In the United States, the EPA was formed in 1970 and was soon helping to enact regulations that took important 'tools' from the golf course manager's toolkit. Most uses of DDT were banned in the early 1970s. The passage of the Pest Control Products Act (PCPA) in Canada in 1969 and the related PCP Regulations three years later were likewise a step towards greater stringency (see Millington and Wilson, in press). We shall look closer at environmental policy and its impacts on golf in the next chapter.

Returning to impression management, the point is not that golf associations never sought to sway the public or policy makers before the 1980s. In 1970, for example, GCSAA President Norman W. Kramer expressed consternation that "hippies and yippies" – presumably a euphemism for environmentalists – might influence the young people they encounter. Superintendents, in turn, could not be "shrinking violets":

> you, as a professional man in your own right, must stand up and make your club officials know that YOU are the man that is responsible, YOU are the man that has professional training and integrity to meet the problems and answer the questions related to the maintenance of a golf course and grounds. (Kramer, 1970b: 9, emphasis in original)

The message was therefore on the importance of engaging the public. Indeed, even two years before this clarion call, the GCSAA had embarked on a PR programme around two high profile golf tournaments aimed, in part, at explaining that the golf superintendent was a "greatly experienced and capable man" (Anon., 1968: 24).

The point instead is that impression management grew to be much more formal – *professional* – and environmentally focused as time passed. By our reading, the key messages for publics and/or policy makers were as follows:

Key message 1: Golf is in good hands

That golf superintendents were 'greatly experienced and capable' was in fact a common refrain as organizations like the GCSAA enhanced their PR programmes. As the 1980s drew nearer, GCSAA President George W. Cleaver was still lamenting that superintendents stood as 'gardeners', 'farmers', or 'greenskeepers', rather than respected professionals, in the public imagination (Cleaver, 1978b: 9). By the middle of the next decade, though, the Association had devised 'TV spots' of thirty and sixty seconds to help redress this problem. For instance, the spot entitled 'Without them' contrasted the factual scenario of golfers on a well-manicured course with the fictional one of golfers looking for their balls in what was effectively a wilderness setting. The latter would be a reality if not for the golf superintendent. Meanwhile, the script for the spot 'Unseen partner' unfolded in part as follows:

> When you take to the golf course ... there's someone with you that you may never see ... but who's with you on every shot. Someone with the education from leading universities ... in business management ... and in the science of turfgrass management. (Anon., 1986: 68, ellipses in original)

That 'someone', of course, was again the skilled but 'hidden' superintendent.

Roughly a decade later, the GCSAA pursued an even more noteworthy endeavour of this kind – and one connected more intimately to the Association's professed environmental sensibilities. 'Par for the course' was the name given to the GCSAA's official television programme, to be aired on the American sports channel ESPN on Sunday mornings. As said in *Golf Course Management*: "The program highlights golf from a course management point of view and provides an important platform for positive environmental messages that will benefit the entire golf industry" (Anon., 1995b: 142). Interestingly, it was also noted that the show was about "managing golfers' expectations of fantastic conditions on less-than-fantastic budgets" (Anon., 1995b: 144) – an apparent allusion to Augusta National syndrome. GCSAA Director of Communications Pat Jones also signalled the 'golf is in good hands' trope by noting that superintendent professionalism was an underlying theme for the show.

Perhaps 'Par for the course' was seen by lawmakers in addition to the (green fee paying) public. Regardless, a more direct mechanism for reaching government officials was devised as the GCSAA was making its way onto TV: the Association's Government Relations Program. This was an initiative with many stated aims. Communication was to flow in two directions, with the GCSAA's government relations staff (inclusive of a Government Relations Manager) sharing information on superintendent practices 'upwards' to the EPA and updates on environmental policies 'downwards' to the Association's membership (Anon., 1987b; Hearn, 1987b).

It seems clear too, however, that the GCSAA was especially keen to express their level of expertise to key government officials where possible. An article entitled 'Government relations in practice' in *Golf Course Management*, for example, reported on the testimony given by GCSAA Secretary-Treasurer William R. Roberts to the US Senate Subcommittee on Toxic Substances in March 1990. Roberts made clear that more than 1,100 superintendents had at that point successfully passed through the Association's certification programme. "In order to achieve this level of professional recognition," he added, "a superintendent must meet stringent educational requirements, complete a six-hour examination and subject his or her golf course to a formal review by a team of certified peers" (Anon., 1990a: 56). Roberts furthermore noted the steady promotion of IPM within the industry. Golf, as a result, was clearly in good hands.

Key message 2: Golf is a boon to the environment

More than this, though, the messaging emanating from key golf spokespeople was that golf *itself* is a public good. If one of the (still lasting) concerns about golf is that it occupies an inordinate amount of space, and that there is an environmental 'opportunity cost' in that the same land might be a forest or wetland (concerns we explore further in examining the 'dark-greening' of golf in later chapters) – it makes sense that golf proponents would aim to make golf's purported environmental benefits known as widely as possible.

Certainly, golf industry representatives had for some time suggested that golf could be a boon to the environment. Once again, though, in the 1980s and beyond this notion found its way into formal impression management campaigns. One of the best cases in point comes with the adoption of a new logo for the American golf industry in 1982. In a context marked by concern over waning water supplies – a January, 1982 article in *Golf Course Management* was titled 'Water. Will it become as precious as oil?' (Goldsmith, 1982) – the GCSAA teamed together with the PGA tour, the USGA, the Ladies Professional Golf Association (LPGA), the American Society of Golf Course Architects, and other major golf associations to devise 'A logo with a message' (Anon., 1982b). In front of a black, circular backdrop was drawn a white water droplet, itself containing a putting green and flagstick in the foreground and a mountain range and sun in behind. Around the circumference of the circle were the words 'Golf Courses', 'Recycle Water', and 'Part of the Solution' – all connected together through arrows reminiscent of the now-famous recycling symbol. The logo on the whole was described in *GCM* as a key step towards heightened public awareness of golf's role in water maintenance at a crucial time. Indeed, the subheading of the article introducing the logo to *GCM*'s readership – 'Golf is one of the good guys!' – left little room for an alternative interpretation (Anon., 1982b).

Furthermore, according to trade publications, golf's environmental benefits did not end with the use of recycled water. Readers of Canada's *GreenMaster* magazine were told in 1991 that "greenspace managers have a strong public benefits story to tell" (Anon., 1991a: 21). The Green Care Horticulture Association, in which the CGSA held membership, had recently delivered a brief at a Federal Pesticide Registration Review hearing. The value of greenspace – and by extension, golf courses – was said to include, among other things: its role in water and energy conservation; soil erosion control; heat dissipation and temperature moderation; and the conversion of carbon dioxide emissions. In the same vein, the Executive Summary of a *Golf Course Management* article from one year earlier went so far as to say that turfgrass, with benefits like oxygen production and temperature modification in tow, was 'An environmental hero' (Anon., 1990b). The important point again for these purposes was that this type of messaging was deemed ripe for external communication. For example, the GCSAA embarked on a print advertising campaign in the early 1990s emphasizing golf's 'hidden benefits'. One ad showed cartoonish animals huddled beside a putting green with the caption "Golfers aren't the only ones who love golf courses". Another showed a golf course with the simple heading "Air conditioner" (GCSAA staff, 1991).

With this last point in mind, the agency of the golf course manifests yet again. In this case, it is not so much that the immaculate golf course is 'hailing' the golfer (and, for that matter, the golf course owner, superintendent, TV executive, etc.) as with Augusta National syndrome (see Chapter 4), but that the golf course allegedly takes on a 'heroic' quality in its ability to yield environmental benefits. An important caveat here, however, is that human agency does not disappear. In the eyes of the golf industry, it is *properly cared for* courses that yield these benefits. The text accompanying the GCSAA's environmentally themed print advertisements from the early 1990s made this clear:

> Each ad concludes with the question, 'Who's in charge of keeping these amazing ecosystems in harmony with nature?' The ad wraps up by underscoring the fact that today's golf course superintendent is more than the person who keeps golf green, but a business manager, scientist, troubleshooter and 'all environmentalist' rolled into one. (GCSAA Staff, 1991: 91)

Thus, this is still a Promethean inclination in the end. The golf course has agency – amazing ecosystem as it is – but the human superintendent remains 'in charge'.

Key message 3: ... and a boon to the economy as well

That golf is a boon to the environment – point 2 – was likewise professed in a *GCM* article entitled 'GCSAA responds to report from New York'. The report in question was published by the State Attorney General's office for New York State. Following a survey of fifty-two golf courses on Long Island, NY, it was found that golf courses used seven times more pesticides per acre than food crops. The GCSAA's first claim in response was that the report was baseless. In communicating with state officials and media afterwards, the Association added that properly maintained golf courses benefit entire communities – for example by preventing erosion, cooling the atmosphere, and providing 'green space' in urban settings. Added GCSAA President Stephen G. Cadenelli: "Modern emphasis and education is on using pesticides 'curatively,' as a doctor would use a specific medicine to treat a specific problem" (Anon., 1991b: 98). Again, the medical metaphor arises in place of the combat metaphor of times' past.

Importantly, though, according to *GCM*'s post hoc analysis, GCSAA representatives also stressed the economic merits of golf courses: "They provide thousands of jobs and millions of dollars in property taxes" (Anon., 1991b: 98). This, in fact, appears not to be an aberrant view. If golf's environmental benefits did not go far enough in managing impressions on the sport, the game's economic dividends could be highlighted as well.

Take another *GCM* entry, in this case from 1981 – just one year before the golf industry in the United States released its 'water friendly' logo. The topic matter in this case was how golf industry representatives might deal with pressure and even legislation requiring their water usage to be significantly curtailed during water crises. It was acknowledged that under such circumstances everyone would surely be required to do their part. But golf's 'bottom line' was an important consideration too:

> Figures should be collected concerning the cost of renovating the course after it has gone without water and the cost to the club facility in terms of employees, purchases, membership, reputation and tax and revenue loss. The complete picture should also include the impact on suppliers, hotel patrons, area businesses and the long-term effect on the area's reputation for quality golf. (Goldsmith, 1981: 17)

Such figures were not to be a 'hammer' in negotiations with key officials, said then-GCSAA Director of Education (and past President) Palmer Maples Jr., but rather "a base to seek changes in any unreasonable situation" (Goldsmith, 1981: 17).

A similar view on golf's benefits arose in the case golf industry representatives put forth to a 'task force' in one US county towards the end of the same decade. Among other benefits, the forty-eight golf clubs in the region were said to generate nearly US $6 million in annual tax revenue. This was in addition to golf's many environmental benefits – that golf courses can act as de facto air conditioners, for example (Anon., 1988a). Likewise, in 1994, *GreenMaster* provided its Canadian readership with a series of 'tips' – presented in the style of a Q&A – on explaining golf's relationship with the environment to 'non-expert' members of the public and media. The response to the first question – "Why do golf courses use pesticides?" – included commentary on how pesticides can selectively limit damage to turf, trees, and other living things. It also included a common refrain:

> Golf courses are tremendous economic assets as well as vital green spaces for communities. They employ thousands of people, enhance local economies through tax revenues and tourism and provide many ecological benefits. (Anon., 1994: 16)

Golf's 'agency' thus extends to its economic benefits as well.

Key message 4: Golf representatives are leaders in the environmental movement

Taken together, these first three points lead towards a fourth and final one: that the golf industry was adopting a *proactive* position in the quest for sustainability. That is to say, in expertly providing services (message 1) that are environmentally (message 2) and economically (message 3) beneficial, golf was positioned as neither an enemy of, nor a bystander in, the environmental movement. Golf representatives were in fact environmental leaders.

Perhaps the best case in point in this regard involves the golf industry's environmental leadership awards. In 1991, the GCSAA unveiled its President's Award for Environmental Leadership, given first to four courses participating in a study of pesticides and local groundwater (Anon., 1991c). The Environmental Steward Awards – then funded by Ciba-Geigy and Rain Bird, chemical and equipment companies, respectively – were unveiled the following year, and were deemed an opportunity for superintendents to gain public recognition for their devotion to environmental management. Indeed, upon announcement of the Environmental Steward Awards in *Golf Course Management*, success in PR was portrayed as both an outcome of *and* an avenue towards success in the awards competition. Judges would be looking for submissions that showed a course's environmental value – for example, through the use of computer-controlled irrigation, the presence of native or endangered vegetation, "or even efforts by the superintendent to communicate ecological information about the course to golfers or the public" (Anon., 1992: 94). The CGSA eventually devised their own industry-sponsored environmental awards as well (e.g. see Anon., 2000).

Furthermore, 'leadership' in the time of responsible golf also came to mean *policing* one's self with environmental sustainability in mind. The adoption of best practices such as IPM, as described earlier, can be interpreted as a form of self-policing, or self-regulation: in IPM theory, pesticides are to be used only if absolutely necessary. Indeed, in 1997, golf superintendent Mark Clark went so far as to say that golf's adoption of BMPs was evidence that golf superintendents had become the 'true environmentalists' (Clark, 1997: 105).

Yet as time passed, the task of making inroads with governments was further helped by the fact that the golf industry was also adopting strategies that privileged autonomy in assessing a course's environmental strengths and limitations. A primary example here involves the provision of self-auditing kits for superintendents – something made possible in the late 1980s through the GCSAA's partnership with Hall-Kimbrell Environmental Services. In short, with a self-auditing kit in hand, the superintendent completed a lengthy questionnaire on matters ranging from pesticide usage to water quality to hazardous waste and beyond. Hall-Kimbrell then assessed the questionnaire responses before providing a detailed compliance appraisal (Jones, 1989). The upshot in the first instance was regulatory compliance – the GCSAA's desire to achieve this should not be overlooked. For their part, the EPA was actively encouraging self-audits of this kind, while also urging that self-auditing should remain voluntary (Anon., 1988b). Furthermore, self-auditing was said to yield benefits in terms of public perception:

> The superintendent who thoroughly examines his management practices and develops standards that go *beyond* the existing regulatory requirements can also be assured of maintaining a positive public perception about his course and his profession. (Anon., 1988c: 52, emphasis in original)

Golf was thus in a leadership position, not just in the expertise of golf superintendents or in the game's environmental and economic merits. Formal mechanisms were available for checking golf's environmental impacts and for championing superintendents as environmental leaders.

Professionalization in the new millennium

Interestingly enough, in 1990 Stanley Metsker – presumably the same Stanley Metsker who had two decades earlier lamented the state of professionalization among golf superintendents – commented on professionalization in the golf industry yet again:

> It is clear that GCSAA is well on the road to professionalization for golf course superintendents and recognition for its members. It is not a process that can happen overnight, but the prospects are bright for our profession moving up the ladder of success. (Metsker, 1990: 9)

This seems a fair assessment. In the time since Metsker penned his 1969 article, 'How professional are we …?', golf superintendents, often working together with those in other facets of the industry, took major steps towards developing both robust educational curricula and formal mechanisms for liaising with governments and the public. There are clear links as well between our analysis of scientific and technological developments in the golf industry, as described in Chapter 5, and the emergence of environmental training and PR campaigning, as described above. For example, IPM, a key scientific development, was an area of specialization in the GCSAA's certificate-based Environmental Management Program from the early 1990s. With the advent of environmental awards, it also became commonplace for winning superintendents to state their allegiance to an IPM programme in their daily management activities (e.g. see Berndt, 1996). Professionalization and ecological modernization are closely linked in this case, as becoming a qualified superintendent requires faithful commitment to IPM's science and technology-reliant narrative for managing golf-related environmental problems.

These trends that began in the 1980s with the arrival of responsible golf only continued as the 1990s came to a close and the 2000s arrived. Consider that the Environmental Institute for Golf (EIFG) – the GCSAA's research-focused philanthropic arm, as discussed in Chapter 5 – notes that both education and advocacy form key components of its work. For example, as the GCSAA reoriented its educational offerings around a set of core principles – agronomy, business management, communication, environmental management and leadership – the EIFG deployed resources to ensure that the environment was properly included on this list (GCSAA, n.d.e). When it comes to advocacy, the Institute continues to stress golf's economic, environmental, and social/recreational benefits. It evidently does so through multiple platforms: "Publications including daily newspapers and magazines, television, radio, digital platforms and social media are now flooding the market place with the advances being made in the golf industry" (GCSAA, n.d.f).

More broadly, the GCSAA has teamed together with an array of partners from both within the golf industry (e.g. the PGA Tour, the National Course Owners Association, the USGA, the Golf Channel, the manufacturer Ping®) and beyond (e.g. Chevron, Yamaha) to form the coalition 'We Are Golf'. Their messaging is thorough, if predictable to those familiar with golf's responsible turn: golf yields invaluable economic impacts; its charitable side is commendable; it has benefits in terms of environmental sustainability; and – perhaps most debatably of all, given golf's associated costs – golf is 'a game for all' (We Are Golf, n.d.a). It is with these benefits in tow that We Are Golf claims to advocate on the golf industry's behalf on a daily basis to Congressional leaders (We Are Golf, n.d.b). The coalition in these ways is not unlike Canada's National Allied Golf Association (NAGA) – itself made up of constituent organizations such as Golf Canada, the Canadian Golf Superintendent Association, and the National Golf Course Owners Association Canada.

Furthermore, in the spirit of Hall-Kimbrell's environmental auditing kit, there are now ample independent parties to whom golf industry members can turn for environmental assistance. The most notable of these in the North American context is Audubon International – an organization that certifies qualifying golf courses as Audubon Cooperative Sanctuaries (and one that is in fact distinct from the more famous National Audubon Society). Indeed, articles urging golf superintendents to obtain the 'sanctuary' designation date back more than two decades in golf industry trade publications. In 1993, the Sanctuary Program was deemed a valuable, albeit strictly voluntary, PR opportunity in the pages of *GreenMaster*. That certification was awarded by an independent body was deemed a source of credibility (Anon., 1993a). In this same year, Audubon was awarded the GCSAA President's Award for Environmental Leadership (Anon., 1993b).

Achieving Audubon designation is certainly far from a PR endeavour alone. Audubon International provides educational materials in six areas – environmental planning; wildlife and habitat management; chemical-use reduction and safety; water conservation; water quality management; and outreach and education – while also performing a site assessment that goes towards a customized environmental management plan. From there, integrating and documenting environmental practices is the step that leads towards certification (Audubon International, n.d.).

The Golf Environment Organization (GEO) – a group known especially for its work with recent Ryder Cup hosts – provides a similar certification programme, and has carried out work in more than forty countries to date. As with Audubon certification, obtaining the 'ecolabel' 'GEO Certified golf club' requires both engagement with educational materials and an on-site visit. GEO Certified, again like Audubon certification, is depicted as a way of achieving 'real results' – water efficiency, lowered electricity use, protection of wildlife, and so forth – and enhancing communication with the public at large (e.g. see Golf Environment Organization, n.d.a). GEO's action plan more broadly is to devise "a new modern sustainability system" inclusive of a set of clearly defined Voluntary Sustainability Standards for Golf (Golf Environment Organization, n.d.b). Now 45 years from Stanley Metsker's exhortations towards the development of formal educational systems and the pursuit of political agitation, one might indeed observe how professional golf superintendents had become.

The (post-)politics of professionalization

All told, a rather straightforward narrative again seems to be in place. In Chapter 5 we saw how the golf industry moved towards heightened sophistication in their course management practices as time passed. From the above discussion, heightened *professionalism* seems to have been a high priority as well – something achievable specifically through enhanced educational opportunities and improved interfacing with governments and publics both. Indeed, from a place where relatively few educational opportunities existed in the late 1960s (at least according to the likes of Stanley Metsker), formal training programmes proliferated in subsequent decades. The GCSAA, for example, developed a thorough certification programme, offered educational services through its trade magazine and annual conference, and eventually devised a certification system around environmental issues specifically. In the time of responsible golf, organizations such as Audubon International have lent credibility to the golf industry's professed environmental stewardship in that certification can be allocated by an independent party.

On the impression management front, the golf industry went from fretting over public misconceptions of golf and the work of golf superintendents to the development of polished materials for swaying public opinion. And whereas there was great concern in the late 1960s over the threat of government regulation, initiatives such as the GCSAA's Government Relations Program made for formal systems for liaising with policy makers. As GCSAA president Joseph Baidy said in 1994, "our ongoing contacts with government officials allow us to help shape realistic regulations, responsibly minimizing the burden of compliance where possible" (Baidy, 1994: 7). The GCSAA's interest in engaging policy makers is perhaps best shown by the Association's unveiling of Excellence in Government Relations Awards in the early 2000s, devised with the goal of honouring both advocacy and regulatory compliance (e.g. see McKeel, 2003).

The pursuit of education and enhanced external communication are, in the abstract, and to a great extent in practice, commendable. As said previously, we do not doubt the sincerity of golf industry representatives when it comes to their environmental stewardship. Yet, when we looked more closely at the range of industry-driven and environment-related developments that emerged over time (i.e. the developments in education and impression management outlined in this chapter) some key concerns and contradictions emerged. We outline some of these here.

In one sense, there is a concern that, in their haste to externally convey the golf industry's proactivity and responsibility on environmental matters, golf spokespeople seemed to overstate the extent to which golf is in fact 'in good hands' across the board. This point came from our observation that, on the one hand, superintendent training and formal systems like IPM were relatively slow to develop over time – and that, on the other hand, impression management campaigns that describe and highlight industry progress and leadership on environmental issues were strikingly candid. Put simply, it seemed at times that industry portrayals of its activities did not obviously match-up with what was happening in practice.

Indeed, dating back to the time of 'pro-golf', we find assertions that superintendents need not be 'shrinking violets' in the public domain due to their 'professional training' (Kramer, 1970b) and that superintendents are 'proven experts' not unlike medical professionals (Blake, 1971). These points were made, however, at roughly the same moment at which Stanley Metsker was observing that there was no way "to tell who knows what" among golf superintendents (Metsker, 1969: 32). A decade on in the mid-1980s, at a time when the GCSAA's TV spots implied that superintendents were necessarily schooled in turfgrass science, Association

President Donald E. Hearn was urging superintendents to recognize the need for professional self-education (Hearn, 1987a). To be sure, it is fair for contributors to *GCM* and similar publications to have different views on the state of professionalization in the industry. Even more recently, though, the Association has recognized problems in their history of external communication. Said GCSAA President Timothy O'Neill as the Association embarked on its multiyear Golf Course Environmental Profile project in the mid-2000s: "Existing environmental data is limited and not complete, uniform or centralized. *Information provided to the media, government and industry often is inaccurate or misleading*. This is not a healthy state of affairs" (O'Neill, 2006: 13, emphasis added).

A related point in this regard is that the professionalization mechanisms described in this chapter are in many cases voluntary, and that volunteerism is not an ironclad mechanism for ensuring uptake. For example, although Audubon certification has become part of golf's environmental leadership profile, in 2001 Ron Dodson, president and CEO of Audubon International, observed that only 247 of the roughly 16,000 courses in the United States had earned the designation 'Certified Audubon Cooperative Sanctuary' (2,500 courses were Audubon members) (Dodson, 2001). Seven years later, *GCM* senior staff writer Terry Ostmeyer noted that participation in Audubon's programme had "all but stagnated" (Ostmeyer, 2008: 18). According to reports, the GCSAA's certification programme – central to PR over time – has likewise struggled with uptake in recent years (Jones, 2012; Kauffman, 1999).

In another sense, there is a deeper issue at play with the developments described in this chapter. Professionalization need be understood as part of a wider context in which golf representatives have obdurately stressed the need for pesticides – including those eventually found to be far more problematic than originally imagined, as per Chapter 5. It is a context too where the golf industry's sustained growth, and thus its growing occupation of land, is commonly taken for granted also. To put the golf industry in a leading position is, by extension, to put *these ideas* in a leading position as well.

To say this another way, the developments described above do *ideological work* in sustaining a particular interpretation of 'what's best' for golf and 'what's best' for the environment. Here we return to the aforementioned concept of 'post-politics', described first in Chapter 2. 'Post-politics' bespeaks a situation whereby dissenting opinions on the status quo are foreclosed under the weight of a seemingly irreproachable consensus. Subjective political views, often codified as irrational, are to a great extent replaced with technocratic knowledge; contentious politics are left behind, hence the concept's name. As Žižek explains, "Post-politics thus emphasizes the need to leave old ideological divisions behind and confront new issues, armed with the necessary expert knowledge and free deliberation that takes people's concrete needs and demands into account" (Žižek, 1999: 198).

As noted in Chapter 2, geographer Harvey Neo (2010) has convincingly applied the post-politics concept to the study of golf and the environment. His focus laid specifically with the provision of new golf courses in Singapore. While there was room in planning discussions between stakeholders in Singapore – activists, industry, and government officials among them – for consideration of modifications that might be made to new courses in the interest of environmental sustainability, the underlying assumption and consensus from which these stakeholders were working was such that new courses would in fact be built in the end. Said otherwise, the alternative of *not* developing new courses – for example, because their environmental impacts would be too severe – was foreclosed. Indeed, Eric Swyngedouw argues that neoliberal capitalism, with its focus on sustained growth, effectively draws boundaries around the possibilities for consensus under conditions of post-politics. The 'environmental question', he further argues, is not simply representative but is *constitutive* of the process of post-politicization in contemporary times. It is around environmental matters, as much as any others, whereby antagonisms are displaced "on to the terrain of consensually manageable problems, expert knowledge and interest intermediation" (Swyngedouw, 2010: 225).

It is through the lens of post-politics that we can better understand the golf industry's professed environmental leadership. In February 1997, GCSAA President Bruce R. Williams titled his message to *Golf Course Management*'s readership, 'We've come a long way'. Whereas once, he said, the issue was presented as golf versus the environment, the combination of science and superintendent dedication had led to a situation whereby golf and the environment had been rendered compatible. Williams continued:

> Today, the collaboration of golf course architects, superintendents, developers, legislators and environmental groups has become an outstanding force for positive change. We have proven that we can accomplish a great deal by working together, rather than working against one another. We know that we can work together for the growth of golf, and we can anticipate continuing growth with continuing environmental sensitivity. (Williams, 1997: 7)

We shall explore the matter of legislation further in the following chapter. We have already seen, however, how the EPA took kindly to the golf industry's interest in self-auditing from the late 1980s onwards. As per Williams' comments, the golf industry's different branches indeed rallied together frequently in the age of responsible golf – for instance, in devising a new logo pertaining to golf's water friendliness or in forming organizations like We Are Golf and NAGA. Environmental groups such as Audubon International have played a role in providing educational resources and certifying golf's environmental stewardship as well.

Consensus is not inherently problematic, and we would do well to stress yet again that organizations such as the GCSAA have urged environmental compliance as much as advocacy over time. The point is that golf's environmental leadership is tied to a specific vision of environmentalism – a 'light-green' one in which chemicals are 'medicine for the earth' and, as Williams says, continued growth should be anticipated. We would argue here that the emphasis on economics that is often inserted strategically into dialogue on environmental sustainability corroborates the 'consensus' put forward in the time of responsible golf. To depict golf as an environmental *and* economic boon fortifies ecological modernization as the 'consensus' way forward.

Thus, by situating themselves as the 'true environmentalists', golf representatives also situate the responsible use of chemicals, natural resources, and land as the 'true' form of environmental*ism*. In the following chapter we consider in detail the extent to which governments have accepted this consensus view.

7

Light-green regulation? Environmental managerialism and golf's conspicuous exemption

"Our generation has taken to the cosmetic use of pesticides and I think, perhaps unwittingly, not fully understanding the dangers it represents to ourselves and, most importantly, to our children" (Campbell, 2009).

This was the pronouncement of Ontario Premier Dalton McGuinty – fittingly delivered on Earth Day, 2008 – as he prepared the public for his provincial government's new environmental initiative. McGuinty's view of pesticide risks may ring familiar: it is not unlike the frank admissions of many in the golf industry in recent decades that an irresponsible past in the realm of environmental sustainability needed to give way to a responsible present and future. Whereas the golf industry in turn adopted measures such as IPM in response to the perceived 'dangers' of chemicals, McGuinty's Liberal government unveiled the Cosmetic Pesticides Ban Act.

To this point in *The greening of golf*, we have focused mainly on the activities of the golf industry itself. Although examining these activities is crucial for reasons that should be obvious by now, we think that studying and appraising responses by governments to questions about golf's relationship with the environment is equally and perhaps even more important. We say this because golf industry members are, in our view, acting in mostly predictable ways – ways intended to ultimately preserve golf's economic viability. By contrast, governments are typically compelled by a number of different causes (including, in theory, the cause of protecting the environment and public health) and hold the authority to dictate industry behaviour through legislation. In other words, then, industry leadership on environmental issues might be accepted *or* rendered moot depending on the decisions made by those working at different levels of government.

Ontario's Cosmetic Pesticides Ban Act presents an interesting case in this regard. Surely to no one's surprise, the governing Liberal Party in Ontario championed the merits of this Act – and especially its stringency – before and after its unveiling. Most notably, the government stressed that the law was the product of consultation with health experts such as the Canadian Cancer Society, and that it followed from the 'convincing case' they had heard for protecting against pesticide exposure (Ontario Ministry of the Environment, 2013). In turn, the Act was championed by health and environmental organizations as well. Environmentalist David Suzuki's eponymously named Foundation suggested that, "the new ban has the potential to meaningfully protect human health and the environment from an unnecessary source of chemical exposures" (David Suzuki Foundation, n.d.). Peter Goodhand, CEO of the Ontario Division of the Canadian Cancer Society remarked: "This is a significant success in our efforts to further our mission to eradicate cancer" (CNW Group Ltd., 2009).

As its name suggests, the Cosmetic Pesticides Ban Act pertains to *cosmetic* pesticide uses, as opposed to non-cosmetic applications in, for example, agriculture. It therefore prohibited the use of pesticides for cosmetic reasons on lawns, vegetable/ornamental gardens, patios, driveways, cemeteries, and in parks and schoolyards across the province. The Act went on to ban more than 250 pesticides for sale and outlawed over ninety-five pesticide ingredients for cosmetic uses (Ontario Ministry of the Environment, 2009). The stringency of the law was also marked by a shortage of 'excepted' uses, or loopholes. For our purposes, however, one excepted use stood out: *pesticides could still be deployed on the province's golf courses*. In a curious wrinkle, a law banning pesticides earned support from the pesticide-reliant golf industry.

To fully understand the Cosmetic Pesticides Ban Act and golf's positioning within it, it is necessary to turn first to Canada's evolving system of environmental (and especially pesticide) regulation. This, as we shall see, is an exercise in accounting for nuance: environmental regulation has in many ways become more stringent over the years in Canada while at the same time becoming more susceptible to industry influence. The argument we present in this chapter is that golf's positioning in the Cosmetic Pesticides Ban Act is telling of environmental policy in general: it is representative of the turn to voluntarism in contemporary environmental regulatory systems, and of governments' reliance on the 'responsibility' programmes that various industries have so carefully crafted. In other words, the light-greening of golf has been forged in a policy context open to light-green solutions.

Having also considered the intersections of golf, voluntarism, and regulation in the United States, we conclude this chapter with reflections on government-industry relations and the aforementioned concept of 'post-politics'. We also situate our analysis of the arrival of responsible golf from Chapters 5, 6, and 7 along the PAAR continuum, thus placing it within the wider narrative of *The greening of golf*.

The exception in context: pesticide regulation in Canada

The Cosmetic Pesticides Ban Act was introduced into a Canadian regulatory system already laden with stipulations pertaining to the testing and approval of chemicals. These regulations can be divided into two broad categories for our purposes. One category includes 'pre-market' regulations that pertain to the fate of pesticides before they reach the applicator's hands. This form of oversight falls within the remit of the country's federal government. The second category includes 'post-market' regulations that pertain to the actual use of chemicals once in the applicator's possession. Post-market regulation is for municipal and provincial governments to decide.

As Ivo Krupka (2000) recounts, the federal government's involvement in (pre-market) pesticide legislation stretches as far back as the 1927 Act to Regulate the Sale and Inspection of Agricultural and Economic Poisons. The focus in this initial Act, however, was on combatting fraudulent claims regarding a pesticide's purported merits. It was not until the post-war years, and specifically the 1969 PCPA, that legislative attention turned towards safeguarding both the environment and the Canadian citizenry.

As readers will have gleaned by this point, the timing in this regard was not coincidental. Apart from the 'chemophobia' inspired by *Silent Spring* and the general DDT fallout, the legislative imperative of the 1960s was one of reining in 'big business'. This constituted a corrective to the liberal economic climate that preceded the Great Depression; in hindsight, it also makes for a stark historical contrast to the deregulatory turn in the decades that followed. Douglas MacDonald (2007) lists some key exemplars of the turn to *dirigisme* in the 1960s: restrictions on cigarette sales, heightened attention to automobile design, tightening of food and drug regulations, and efforts to control pollution, to name a few. Canada's 1969 Pest Control Products Act stands as a key contribution along these lines. In combination with the PCP Regulations that passed three years later, the Act set out that pesticides could not be imported or sold in Canada without registration and sufficient labelling. Successful registration required (industry-supplied) data on a 'control' product's environmental and health-related risks, as well as information on its value and efficacy (Hughes, 2000). A theme was thus instituted that would remain in place to this day: that federal pesticide legislation should account for economics and health at the same time.

This does not mean, however, that pesticide regulation at the federal level was impervious to change. The most significant modifications came in the mid-1990s with the formation of the Pest Management Regulatory Agency (PMRA), and in the early- to mid-2000s with the rewriting of the PCPA. As David Boyd recounts, there were many perceived problems with the old PCPA at this time:

> The PCPA and its regulations were criticized for not considering multiple sources of exposure, total exposure, or cumulative effects; not assessing formulants (chemicals mixed with the active ingredients); not considering impacts on vulnerable groups, particularly infants and children; not requiring regular review and reevaluation or postregistration monitoring; not providing opportunities for public involvement; lacking a national compliance strategy; not requiring companies to report the results of new research indicating adverse effects; not including pest reduction as a goal; and not requiring the availability of less harmful substitutes to be considered in registration decisions. (Boyd 2003, 120–121)

The Canadian system was furthermore seen to be lacking in comparison to those of other countries, and to be opaque when it came to sharing information with the public.

The new PCPA took aim at many of these problems. For example, in the government's eyes it supported risk reduction "by ensuring that only pesticides that make a useful contribution to pest management are registered and by expediting the registration of lower-risk products" (Health Canada, 2006). Among other measures, it was also established that 'pest control products' would be re-evaluated on a fifteen-year cycle, meaning new science could pick up on problems overlooked in times' past. The opacity question was addressed through public consultations and a public registry (Health Canada, 2006). In short, and as Boyd wrote around the time this new framework was being crafted, "The new PCPA creates a modern system for the evaluation, registration, labelling, import, and export of pesticides" (Boyd, 2003: 120).

At the heart of the revised regulatory system was, and remains, the PMRA, a body situated within the wider agency Health Canada. Created in 1995, the PMRA is responsible for administering the PCPA. By way of Health Canada's own description, the PMRA's role is "to determine if proposed pesticides can be used safely when label directions are followed and will be effective for their intended use" (Health Canada, 2013). Thus, the PMRA evaluates industry-supplied science in order to assess the toxicity of a given pesticide (i.e. a 'risk assessment') as well as its potential utility (a 'value assessment' – see Parliament of Canada,

2000, Chapter 1). The agency thus retains the dual focus in pesticide regulation on economics and health that began with the formation of the PCPA in the 1960s. These twin priorities are further codified in the PMRA's advisory bodies: the Economic Management Advisory Committee, housing representatives from industry; and the Pest Management Advisory Council, replete with spokespeople from health, environmental, and consumer groups, and from industry as well. As we shall see, this dual focus has not come without controversy.

From pre- to post-market: municipal and provincial oversight

Canada's pre-market regulatory system is therefore built around a host of important actors: the Health Minister (working within Health Canada), the PMRA, advisory bodies, scientists reviewing pesticide studies, and of course industry, who supply research in support of their products. The question remains: what of the fate of chemicals once in the possession of applicators such as golf course superintendents? The post-market use of chemicals, as noted, is a matter for provincial and municipal governments. It is also where Ontario's 2009 Cosmetic Pesticides Ban Act becomes relevant.

The basic principle by which provinces and municipalities must abide is that legislation may further restrict, but never relax, the permitted uses of a product according to federal regulators. As Boyd writes, "All provinces have laws governing the sale, use, transportation, storage, and disposal of pesticides, as well as emergencies such as spills" (Boyd, 2003: 123). He adds that for industrial uses, sellers and applicators are often required to obtain certificates and permits, and in some cases education and training as well. Historically, consumers have been mostly unencumbered in their quest to obtain chemicals for deployment on private property. This has changed, however, in the wake of recent legislation.

Perhaps the most significant event in the history of post-market pesticide regulation in Canada came in 1991, when the small town of Hudson, Quebec passed legislation stopping the use of non-essential chemicals within its boundaries. If such a decision in a town of less than 5,000 people at first glance seems inconsequential, for chemical producers and applicators it was evidently an unsettling precedent in the making. The protracted legal battle that followed was one that mobilized both pro- and anti-chemical antagonists from far afield (McAllister, 2004: 122). The outcome of the case, not settled until 2001, was a 9-0 decision from the Supreme Court of Canada in favour of the municipality. The non-essential use of pesticides was outlawed.

Hudson's fate was therefore settled, yet there were broader ramifications still. Most significantly, Hudson indeed set a precedent, for in the wake of the Hudson verdict municipalities across Canada devised similar laws. A noteworthy case along these lines came in the mid-2000s when Toronto, Canada's largest city, enacted a municipal ban on cosmetic pesticides. As in Hudson, supporters and opponents of the ban prepared for a confrontation. On one side, the Toronto Environmental Alliance fervently advocated for new legislation, at first by canvassing the city for support from the public (Porter, 2013), and later by defending the ban in court. In carrying out the latter act they were flanked by other health and environmental groups, such as the Canadian Environmental Law Association, Environmental Defence, and the Ontario College of Family Physicians. On the other side stood CropLife Canada, a trade association representing the manufacturers, developers and distributors of 'plant science technologies' such as 'pest control products' (CropLife Canada, 2013a), and one motivated to challenge the by-law in Canada's Supreme Court. CropLife's President commented: "Municipal regulation that restricts the use of registered pest control products works at cross-purposes to the federal regulatory regime for pest control products and deprives the public access to beneficial products" (CropLife Canada, 2013b). In CropLife Canada's view, the above-described pre-market regulatory system was stringent enough (see Sandberg and Foster, 2005).

Nonetheless, Toronto's by-law survived *CropLife Canada v. City of Toronto*. And in that the precautionary principle was called forth in both the Hudson and Toronto cases – that is, the notion of striving for harm prevention *even in the absence* of final evidence about, for example, a pesticide's capacity to inflict harm (e.g. see Boyd, 2003: 125; Canadian Environmental Law Association, 2012a) – an interventionary regulatory climate was ostensibly taking hold.

Yet if we zoom out from the municipal to the provincial level, the picture in the mid-2000s was one of a regulatory patchwork: municipalities were acting on their own accord, and not in harmony. The partial effect of the Cosmetic Pesticides Ban Act was to overlay Ontario with blanket legislation. To be sure, environmental groups persisted in calling for further intervention (i.e. beyond changes in the federal PCPA). Writing in the *Canadian Journal of Public Health*, Neil Arya (2005) recounted common pesticide-related concerns: continued exposure to pesticides on the part of 'vulnerable' groups such as children and pregnant women; the possibility for multiple and/or chronic exposures; uncertainty surrounding pesticides' endocrine effects; and the PMRA's reliance on industry-supplied data in chemical reviews. Public health officials, Arya concluded, must therefore be heard: "Their voice should be measured, credible, allowing uncertainty as to the precise magnitude of effects, but they certainly must support a ban on any and every non-essential pesticide use" (Arya, 2005: 92).

In 2008, a collection of well-known health and environmental organizations released a joint statement in support of province-wide legislation. In doing so, groups such as the David Suzuki Foundation, the Canadian Cancer Society, the Ontario College of Family Physicians, and the Canadian Association of Physicians for the Environment reported survey evidence that 71 per cent of Ontarians are in favour of province-wide restrictions on pesticides and that environmental protection is the top priority for those living within Ontario's boundaries (Canadian Environmental Law Association, 2012b).

Representatives of the chemical industry voiced their perspectives on the implications of province-wide pesticide legislation as well. For example, spokespeople for MREP Communications – who themselves represent applicators of synthetic and organic products – and, once again, CropLife Canada, expressed their views to a provincial Standing Committee on Social Policy in June 2008 (many of the above-noted health/environmental groups did the same; see Legislative Assembly of Ontario, 2008). CropLife Canada also made their policy submissions pertaining to the Bill available online, expressing therein (among other things) the already stringent nature of Canada's regulatory system and their support for exemptions for a variety of stakeholders – the golf industry among them. Pesticides, they stressed, were being unfairly stigmatised, while the legislative climate risked stifling innovation (CropLife Canada, 2009). More broadly, CropLife Canada has positioned itself as an environmental caretaker, much as health and environmental groups have over the years. This includes listing on their website precise ways in which the plant science industry is "protecting people and the planet" (CropLife Canada, 2013c).

Ultimately, the Cosmetic Pesticides Ban Act would not be impeded. As noted, the government named the Canadian Cancer Society specifically in claiming they had followed medical expertise (Ontario Ministry of the Environment, 2013).

A conspicuous exemption: golf and Ontario's new law

It might be expected that the golf industry too would mount a defence against Ontario's new law. Even with the 'greening' of golf, the industry had not abandoned pesticides. As we have seen, so too had golf industry representatives spoken out against government intervention in the past.

Yet in the time before the Cosmetic Pesticides Ban Act became law, golf associations of various stripes outwardly supported it. As Ken Cousineau (2008), Executive Director of the Canadian Golf Superintendents' Association (CGSA), explained, the support of groups such as the CGSA, the National Golf Course Owners Association, and the Royal Canadian Golf Association was based on two factors. First, the passage of municipal anti-pesticide bylaws in recent years in their view made for 'piecemeal' legislation, and in turn engendered regional inconsistencies and forced "the golf industry to utilize a significant volume of resources lobbying municipalities" (Cousineau, 2008: 45). Overarching provincial legislation was deemed a remedy for this problem. Second, and presumably more important, golf was to be exempted.

To be specific, golf courses were and are *conditionally* exempted from the Cosmetic Pesticides Ban Act, provided they follow what the McGuinty government described as "tough new rules" (Ontario Ministry of the Environment, 2009). Golf courses were required to prepare an annual report on their pesticide usage and convey this to the public at an annual newspaper-advertised meeting. More significantly, by 2012 golf courses were required to obtain accreditation in IPM, the turf management system described in preceding chapters that urges reduced chemical usage through a combination of targeted spraying and, where possible, non-chemical alternatives. The gambit, then, on the part of the provincial government, was not to deny the golf industry pesticides registered through federal regulation, but to leverage industry's scientific expertise in the realm of course management. Indeed, IPM, as we have seen, has been key to the golf industry's ecological modernization project. In the view of the IPM Council of Canada – the body responsible for administering IPM accreditation – "science has shown IPM ensures environmental sustainability and minimizes the requirement for pesticides" (IPM Council of Canada, 2013a).

As MacDonald (2007) notes, it is difficult to ascertain with complete certainty whether and the extent to which policy makers are swayed by lobbyists. Nevertheless, it is noteworthy that the IPM provision was one clearly favoured by industry in the prelude to the Cosmetic Pesticides Ban Act. As CGSA Director Ken Cousineau wrote in 2008, the CGSA, Royal Canadian Golf Association, National Golf Course Owners Association, and two Ontario-based turfgrass groups offered responses to the government's initial proposals on the law. One shared element across their replies was that municipalities indeed be prohibited from adopting more stringent laws – a caveat that was ultimately adopted (see Ontario Ministry of the Environment, 2013). The other response, wrote

Cousineau, was that "IPM certification be the requirement established by the legislation and the standard to which all golf facilities in Ontario should be held in order to have full access to the use of approved products" (Cousineau, 2008: 45). After all, in the preceding decades, IPM had already become an established 'best practice' in environmental management. In that these recommendations were ultimately adopted, the long arc of golf's professionalization was paying dividends.

Managing the environment in a time of 'environmental managerialism'

How can we make sense of golf's conspicuous exemption from the Cosmetic Pesticides Ban Act? The 'light-greening' of golf that we have described in previous chapters – the fact that golf industry members pursued ecological modernization (EM) in order to position themselves as responsible environmental stewards – is no doubt important. The McGuinty government was not dealing with just any industry, but rather one that was keen to profess its environmental credentials.

But this, we argue, only accounts for part of the story. The sensibilities of governments, and indeed their sometimes-competing responsibilities, are equally important. Industry stewardship, if it is to exist at all, requires a welcoming hand.

We can turn to both theory and empiricism in explaining the policy side of golf's place in the Cosmetic Pesticides Ban Act. Theoretically, John Hannigan (2006) uses the term 'environmental managerialism' to point to the perceived need among governments in contemporary times to balance economic and environmental concerns. That is to say, governments now inherently face a 'dual mandate': there are simultaneous pressures towards *dirigisme* in the name of environmental protection and *deregulation* in the name of private sector growth. The result, in Hannigan's view, are policies that gesture towards environmentalism while ensuring, to the greatest extent possible, that growth is indeed realized. In Hannigan's words:

> [G]overnments often engage in a process of 'environmental managerialism' in which they attempt to legislate a limited degree of protection sufficient to deflect criticism [e.g. about environmental concerns] but not significant enough to derail the engine of economic growth. By enacting environmental policies that are complex, ambiguous and open to exploitation ... the state reaffirms its commitments to strategies for promoting economic development. (Hannigan, 2006: 21; see Redclift, 1986)

Hannigan's observations hark back to the criticism that EM – and particularly its 'weak' variant – is overly trusting of corporate responsibility. EM is, after all, typically reliant on a decentralized governance style, which is to say one that mobilizes industry proactivity as a solution to environmental problems (Berger et al., 2001).

Empirically, while a credible case can be made that Canada's pesticide regulatory system has moved along a progressive, linear trajectory in the post-war years (a case we have made above), there are complexities that also need be considered. Most of all, scholars such as Boyd (2003), MacDonald (2007), and McKenzie (2002) highlight the mounting use of voluntarism as a policy instrument when it comes to environmental regulation in Canada *in general* – as well as the often negative effects of voluntarism on Canada's system of environmental oversight.

In the most direct sense, voluntarism has meant embracing voluntary environmental programmes. Boyd writes, "For example, instead of passing laws or regulations to govern greenhouse gas emission, reduce smog, increase motor vehicle fuel efficiency, or require energy-efficient buildings, the federal government made voluntary agreements with industry" (Boyd, 2003: 243). A programme instituted at the national level in 1995 entitled The Climate Change Voluntary Challenge and Registry Program is a case in point (Government of Canada, n.d.) – one that Boyd characterized eight years later as deeply unproductive. MacDonald lists several potential causes for the transition to voluntarism in Canadian governance that took hold especially in the 1990s, including the perception that law-based regulation was not working to, for example, curb pollution, the wider deregulatory climate of the day, and, most difficult to discern with complete certainty, the lobbying pressure of business groups. Whatever their cause, MacDonald is in turn critical of voluntarism's effectiveness: "While some new regulatory initiatives were put in place, for the most part governments were unable or unwilling to do more than ask politely for voluntary improvements in environmental performance" (MacDonald, 2007: 172).

These observations hint at the second side of voluntarism: budgetary cutbacks. With a federal election looming in 1993, both the incumbent Conservatives and soon-to-be governing Liberals appeared ready to act on the environmental side of their 'dual mandate', to borrow from Hannigan's description of environmental managerialism. What followed, however, was an 'unprecedented downsizing' of environmental departments, including a 30 per cent cut to Environment Canada's budget by 1998 (Boyd, 2003: 239). Cutbacks have come again more recently under the aegis of Stephen Harper's Conservative government (see Leahy, 2011; May, 2012). All told, McKenzie (2002) labels the post-1996 era one of 'deregulation, destaffing, defunding, and voluntary compliance' when it comes to environmental policy. Of course, Hannigan's description of environmental managerialism and the empirical turn to voluntarism across the past two decades are interrelated: voluntarism is a mechanism to assuage the tensions inhered in governments' dual economic/environmental mandate.

The most direct interpretation of how these critical assessments of Canadian environmental policy pertain to the Cosmetic Pesticides Ban Act is one that sees golf's exemption as a case of voluntarism at work. In one sense, the IPM Accreditation Program (IPMAP) in which golf courses must now enrol, is built (as the name suggests) on IPM: a system with no definitive guidelines on how much or what kind of chemicals should be utilized, but rather one that suggests the use of chemicals when necessary, which in theory means when other tactics (e.g. biological or cultural control) have proven ineffective. In another sense, IPMAP *itself* began as an industry-led programme (IPM Council of Canada, 2013b). The IPM Council of Canada, which oversees IPMAP, is composed of representatives from various turf-related industries – including representatives from the golf industry and from CropLife Canada (IPM Council of Canada, 2013a). The latter organization, you may recall, was noted above for their staunch opposition to recent pesticide legislation. *In other words, the opponents of pesticide legislation have themselves become regulatory agents.*

The point here is not to speculate on the precise decisions that members of the IPM Council make regarding golf course accreditation. Though intuitively it makes sense for individuals from groups such as CropLife Canada to favour the ongoing use of chemicals on golf courses, it is at least possible that in their role on the IPM Board they act precisely as any other observer would. The point is not even to criticize these groups; it is to be expected that they would desire influence in the pesticide regulatory system. The point is that the principles of voluntarism have found their way into the process of regulating pesticides on golf courses in Ontario, much as they have infiltrated other aspects of environmental regulation in Canada in recent years (MacDonald, 2007). Thus, whereas Premier Dalton McGuinty stressed that his government listened to medical experts in devising the Cosmetic Pesticides Ban Act, the Liberal Party evidently overlooked the recommendation of the Canadian Cancer Society, among other health and environmental organizations, to ban pesticides on golf courses too (Canadian Cancer Society, 2013; also see Bachand and Gue, 2011). Moreover, the Canadian Cancer Society does not support integrated pest management in cases of cosmetic applications – recognizing as it does that IPM pledges only to reduce, and not eliminate, pesticide usage. Society representatives have stated, clearly and unequivocally, that "in practice [IPM] does not work as its principles are vague and open to interpretation" (Kaminsky and Seely, 2011).

Of course, golf course pesticides are still regulated; post-market restrictions operate alongside the federal government's pre-market regulatory apparatus. This point is not without merit when made by groups opposing pesticide legislation. But this analysis has another layer. The *federal* system of pesticide regulation has also faced criticism, and indeed from a noteworthy source.

Standing Committee on Environment and Sustainable Development

Specifically, in 2000, a Standing Committee on Environment and Sustainable Development in the Canadian House of Commons released a report on federal pesticide oversight. The committee made a number of recommendations, some of which were indeed reflected in the aforementioned revisions to the PCPA in the mid-2000s – for example, for heightened transparency in the chemical review process. But the Standing Committee's main point was a radical one: it was to problematize the *very existence* of the PMRA, the agency in Health Canada administering the federal PCPA. The Committee chair made this clear in his preface to the report:

> We looked at the current system of regulating pesticides in Canada and we asked ourselves whether it is possible for one agency, the Pest Management Regulatory Agency (PMRA), to perform two virtually conflicting tasks, namely that of approving chemical pesticides as requested by industry while at the same time regulating them in order to protect human health. We asked ourselves whether it is possible to strike a balance between economic and health protection goals. (Parliament of Canada, 2000: Chair's preface to the report)

The answer in the Committee's estimation was evidently "no" – it was not possible to strike a satisfactory balance in this way. Ultimately, the PMRA's Economic Management Advisory Committee – composed as it was of industry representatives and tasked with advising on efficiency, cost-effectiveness and competitiveness – "unduly tilts the balance in favour of trade and economics" according to the report (Parliament of Canada, 2000: Chapter 15, Institutional changes). Put simply, in the view of the Committee's government officials, "the PMRA should not be in the business of supporting industry competitiveness" (Parliament of

Canada, 2000: Chapter 2, The need for new legislation). As such, they ultimately recommended *the dissolution of the Economic Management Advisory Committee in the interest of public health* (Parliament of Canada, 2000: Recommendations). It is hard to imagine a clearer description of environmental managerialism, the idea that governments face a dual and oftentimes conflicting mandate on health and economics.

In the end, radically restructuring the PMRA was not adopted as a course of action. At the time of this writing, the Economic Management Advisory Committee evidently remains in place and flush with representatives from companies such as Syngenta, Monsanto Nufarm, and DuPont Canada (Health Canada, 2012). It is of course possible that, behind the scenes, the authority of this Advisory Committee has been hindered. But the point made in the government review speaks to an apparent conflict of interest lying in the Economic Management Advisory Committee's *very existence*. This is in addition to the smaller-scale conflict – also noted by the Standing Committee – lying in the PMRA's exclusive reliance on industry-supplied science in the registration process. There are also reports that voluntarism's other arm – funding cuts – have reached the PMRA as well. For example, the Canadian Centre for Policy Alternatives recently reported that a hundred PMRA jobs belonging mainly to biologists had been affected by budgetary cutbacks (Nelson, 2014; also see Krupka, 2000: 255).

Canada's regulatory framework for pesticides is thus suffused with complexity. It should not be forgotten that Ontario's Cosmetic Pesticides Ban Act was widely lauded. But golf's exemption from this act tells an important story. It tells a story of a regulatory context that has grown more thorough in the policing of chemicals in some ways and more open to self-policing on the part of businesses in others. In addition it tells a story about golf itself: golf's adoption of greener practices makes sense in a context where governments are indeed searching for responsible partners upon which to download regulatory responsibility. Golf's exceptional status in Ontario's cosmetic pesticide law is in fact *unexceptional* once contextualized in this way.

(Voluntary) regulation beyond Ontario

Ontario's Cosmetic Pesticides Ban Act is not without compare. Outside Canada's largest province, golf has earned conditional exemptions in provincial pesticide bans in Quebec, Alberta, New Brunswick, Prince Edward Island, Nova Scotia, and Newfoundland and Labrador (Legislative Assembly of British Columbia,

2012). Legislation similar to Ontario's was also under consideration recently by a committee in British Columbia composed of members of the provincial Legislative Assembly.

Ahead of the British Columbia committee's verdict, Canada's National Allied Golf Association (NAGA) urged that golf should once again receive special status. Their reasoning at this point might be predicted; it included, for example, information on golf's adoption of IPM, on the obtainment of Audubon certification by some courses, and on golf's substantial economic impact (NAGA, 2011). The idea of exempting golf specifically was ultimately rendered moot: the committee recommended against any province-wide ban on cosmetic pesticides, whether on golf courses or not (CBC News, 2012). It did, however, make a golf-related recommendation: "Ask the golf industry to develop a province-wide certification process, or to modify an existing one, that will ensure a high standard of pesticide use by all golf courses in BC, including the use of IPM principles" (Legislative Assembly of British Columbia, 2012: 52). The language of 'ask' and 'certification', and the promotion of IPM are all consonant with the principles of voluntarism.

Moreover, the legislative landscape surrounding golf is not entirely dissimilar in the American context. In one sense, both federal and state governments are involved in regulating chemicals:

> [The Environmental Protection Agency, or EPA] and the states (usually that state's agriculture office) register or license pesticides for use in the United States. EPA receives its authority to register pesticides under the Federal Insecticide, Fungicide, and Rodenticide Act (FIFRA). States are authorized to regulate pesticides under FIFRA and under state pesticide laws. States may place more restrictive requirements on pesticides than EPA. Pesticides must be registered both by EPA and the state before distribution. (EPA, 2014b)

The EPA was originally formed in 1970 at the behest of Republican President Richard Nixon. As David Kinkela (2011) recounts, Nixon was moved by the great success of Earth Day in 1970, and by the political potential of acting on the environmental concerns of the time. FIFRA, similar to Canada's Pest Control Products Act, came about in the early 1970s as well, mainly in response to the lingering DDT controversy (Schroeder, 2011: 262).

In another sense, environmental regulation in the United States has been subject to the whims of 'pendulum politics' (Andrews, 2006), much as it has moved between stringency and leniency-through-voluntarism in Canada over time. The making of the EPA swung the pendulum in one direction in the 1970s, though in the early 1980s President Ronald Reagan mounted what Richard Andrews characterizes as a campaign against environmental regulation. Acting in the spirit of Reagan's small government ideology, Reagan's budget director, David Stockman, mobilized a policy of deregulation, defunding, and devolution:

> *Deregulation* meant not simply regulatory reform or consolidation, but halting outright the growth of federal regulations, and relaxing existing ones that were targeted as especially burdensome by the regulated industries. *Defunding* meant drastic cuts in the regulatory agencies' budgets, along with large tax cuts to prevent future spending. *Devolution* meant turning over as many functions as possible to state and local governments, or to voluntary action if state and local governments were unwilling to accept them. (Andrews, 2006: 257; emphasis in original)

The pendulum would swing yet again in the mid-1980s as part of the backlash to these measures – for example, Congress passed a range of environmental laws and amendments while the EPA increasingly sought harsh penalties for environmental infractions (p. 256).

Yet even as the pendulum 'swung back' towards governmental authority – sometimes termed 'command-and-control' environmental politics – a movement was afoot, as in Canada, to find environmental solutions that could leverage industry expertise. In Aseem Prakash and Matthew Potoski's assessment, a shift was under way in the 1980s and 1990s from reliance on centralized governance, technology specification, and the enforcement of complex laws, "to finding incentives to induce firms voluntarily to undertake environmentally progressive action" (Prakash and Potoski, 2006: 11). The Pollution Prevention Act of 1990, for example, ultimately left the implementation of pollution prevention in the hands of industry and voluntarily enacted initiatives (Andrews, 2006: 265).

Moving from environmental regulation in general to pesticide regulation in particular, the latter has not escaped the politics of voluntarism in the United States either. Perhaps the best case in point in this regard is the Pesticide Environmental Stewardship Program (PESP), established in 1994. As explained by the EPA:

> PESP is a voluntary membership and grants program that works with the nation's pesticide-user community to reduce human health and environmental risks associated with pesticide use. PESP and its sub-initiatives promote the adoption of innovative, alternative pest control practices such as IPM. PESP is guided by the principle that voluntary programs complement the standards and decisions established by regulatory and registration actions. The informed actions of

pesticide users can further reduce the risks from pests and pesticides by playing a major role in ensuring human health and environmental safety. (EPA, 2013a)

PESP is in fact part of a family of voluntary and grant-giving pesticide-themed programmes offered by the EPA. The GCSAA joined in this programme in 1995. In 2002, the GCSAA was named a PESP champion: "GCSAA was selected as a Champion for providing education and information to its members that enable them to effectively utilize pesticides as one tool in IPM programs for golf course maintenance" (Anon., 2003: 17). The GCSAA currently holds a 'Gold' membership with PESP – a designation that recognizes 'outstanding' environmental stewardship (and specifically, once again, the successful use of IPM – see EPA, 2012). The USGA holds 'Silver' membership for its 'higher' environmental achievements (EPA, 2013b).

Once again, the point is not that voluntary programmes are the sole means for controlling pesticides on golf courses and beyond. The point is that in a context where governments must show a commitment to environmentalism without unduly constraining industry, and where industries seek profits while needing to profess their green sensibilities, voluntary environmental programmes emerge as palatable options on both sides.

Of course, golf's environmental impacts extend beyond pesticides specifically, and include matters such as land and water usage as well. The EPA has thus at times shown concern for golf in general – the best example being the formation of a document entitled 'Environmental principles for golf courses in the United States' in the mid-1990s. The principles were in fact endorsed by a wide range of interested parties: the EPA, USGA, GCSAA, and environmental groups such as Audubon International and the National Wildlife Federation, among other organizations. They pertained to matters from planning and siting to designing and constructing to maintaining and operating a golf course in the interest of the environment. Sound maintenance, for example, involved employing IPM and using "native, naturalized or specialized drought-tolerant plant materials wherever possible" (USGA, n.d.). Good design involved, among other measures, striking a balance between accommodating environmentally sensitive areas, playability, and aesthetics. Perhaps unsurprisingly, these principles were explicitly said to be voluntary:

> The principles are meant to be used as a guide to making good decisions relative to the planning and siting, design, construction, maintenance and operation of a golf course. They are voluntary, and should be interpreted as representing a whole philosophy of good environmental design and management rather than

specific dictates, each of which must be met in all cases. It is hoped that the principles will be widely adopted and used to improve the level of environmental awareness, practice, dialogue, and quality achieved within the game of golf. (USGA, n.d.)

Conclusion: the light-greening of golf, complete

The thread that runs through the different initiatives described in this chapter is the adoption of self-governance mechanisms on the part of industries with a contentious environmental past. As noted above, voluntarism has been spurred by a number of factors. It has also had many advocates.

In the face of potential regulatory alternatives – for example, banning pesticides outright or severely restricting their use by outlining specific conditions and quantities in which they can be deployed – the golf industry might offer the plausible rejoinder that golf courses are different from one another, and thus have differing maintenance needs. Industry representatives might add that the public continues to expect idyllic golfing conditions in exchange for their green fees (remember Augusta National syndrome). Andrews (1998) notes that apart from potential environmental benefits, self-regulation can have financial merits – for example, in leading to reduced waste and energy costs. Coverage in the trade publication *Golf Course Management* of the GCSAA's involvement in the EPA's PESP moreover offers what some might see as a heartening vision of industry and government officials constructively discussing environmental best practices with equal authority. As the article concluded, having already described a process of reciprocal industry-government dialogue, "GCSAA will continue to work to strengthen its relationship with the agency and provide data and information the EPA needs to make sound decisions on golf course products" (Riordan, 2003: 32).

Yet the political instrumentation of voluntarism has engendered criticism as well. A concern in principle about voluntary environmental programmes is their potential toothlessness. As Jill Harrison argues in her analysis of pesticide drift in the United States, voluntarism typically offers little by way of punitive recourse: "incorporating sanctions would undermine the 'voluntary' and industry-friendly quality that compels firms to participate in [self-regulation] programs in the first place" (Harrison, 2011: 57). There is a concern too that 'success stories' can draw undue attention. MacDonald (2007) points to an EPA initiative that began in 1988 called 33/50, which invited 7,500 companies to reduce the release and transfer of seventeen priority chemicals (e.g. mercury and mercury compounds) by 33 per cent by 1992 and 50 per cent by 1995 (also see EPA, 1999). The EPA hailed the programme as a success in the end; indeed, two thirds of the 500 largest invited companies ultimately participated. MacDonald takes a less optimistic view, noting that a full third of large firms faced *no regulatory pressure at all* (MacDonald, 2007: 144; also see Webb and Clarke, 2004). There is a concern as well that the positioning of financial benefits as extra incentive on top of environmental ones calls to light the possibility that environmental action will be viewed through a cost-benefit lens, and that businesses can thus make *rational* choices by eschewing environmental best practices (e.g. see Leiss, 2003). This tension between profits and environmental stewardship was not lost on the aforementioned Parliamentary Standing Committee in Canada that recommended abolishing the PMRA's economic focus at the beginning of the 2000s.

In golf, the effectiveness of regulatory mechanisms such as the Ontario Cosmetic Pesticides Ban Act remains to be seen. Yet groups that have sought more stringent pesticide legislation such as the American organization Beyond Pesticides have also pointed to recent legislation in Denmark that calls for specific 'impact ceilings' when it comes to the usage of different pesticides (see R&A, 2013). What is most noteworthy in the context of this discussion is that this recent legislative imperative follows on the heels of a voluntary agreement, initiated in 2005, in which Danish golf courses were urged to reduce their pesticide usage to 0.1 kg of active substance per hectare. The measured figure in 2009 was in fact 0.24 kg of active substance per hectare, and so the voluntary arrangement was found unsuccessful. As Beyond Pesticides (2011) notes, a stricter long-term plan for phasing out pesticides was thus deemed necessary.

Yet beyond these debates over voluntarism, our analysis in this chapter reveals a broader point: the completion of golf's post-politicization when it comes to the environment. Post-politics, as described in previous chapters, involves the displacement of contentious politics in favour of multi-stakeholder consensuses. This requires, in one direction, those historically placed in a defensive position on environmental issues to adopt a proactive environmental stance – to effectively say, 'we are not the cause of environmental harm, but rather a source of environmental protection'. In the other direction, it requires policy makers to accept a populist notion of imminent environmental danger; in Hannigan's (2006) terms, it requires that governments adopt an environmental mandate in addition to their existing economic one. But, as Eric Swyngedouw writes in his discussion of post-politics and the environment, the latter mandate not only accompanies, but also typically sets boundaries for the former:

The architecture of populist governing takes the form of stakeholder participation or forms of participatory governance that operates beyond the state and permits a form of self-management, self-organization and controlled self-disciplining (see Dean, 1999; Lemke, 1999), *under the aegis of a non-disputed liberal-capitalist order.* (Swyngedouw, 2010: 223 emphasis added)

For example, that new golf courses might be built in Ontario in the name of economic expansion, and thus affect the *overall* use of pesticides in the province, falls outside the boundaries of the Ontario Cosmetic Pesticides Ban Act.

In his 1964 response to Rachel Carson's *Silent Spring*, Gene C. Nutter, writing as executive director of the GCSAA, fretted over heightened governmental control: "the threat of increased governmental controls is a threat to greater freedom of action in our country and to the necessary use of essential agricultural tools" (Nutter, 1964: 50). In the subsequent decades, the golf industry would adopt: (a) measures for building and treating golf courses in a 'sustainable' fashion; (b) measures for expressing to the public their progress in this regard; and (c) measures for engaging governments proactively and directly. Governments, for their part, carefully balanced their 'dual mandate', though by the 1990s were doing so largely through voluntary environmental measures. By 1994, GCSAA President Joseph Baidy could express a more optimistic view than Nutter once did: "our ongoing contacts with government officials allow us to help shape realistic regulations, responsibly minimizing the burden of compliance where possible" (Baidy, 1994: 7).

Thinking across our analysis in *The greening of golf*, the developments described in Chapters 5, 6, and 7 constitute an 'alter-golf' response to concerns over golf's environmental impacts (see Figure 1 from Chapter 2). The Promethean, or pro-golf – response described in Chapters 3 and 4 hinged on a belief in humankind's implicit right to manipulate the earth and to reign over surrounding non-humans. The alter-golf response described since then places tremendous value on nature. But it also values humankind's ability to protect nature where necessary, and to improve it where possible. A golf course, by Audubon International's telling, can be a sanctuary for wildlife. Said otherwise, this is a vision of *reformism* bound together with the principles of ecological modernization: golf's potential flaws are recognized, but are counter-balanced by industry's ability to adopt a leadership position on environmental issues. Were governments not willing to recognize industry leadership in this case, golf's professed environmental stewardship would be moot. Golf's 'light-greening' has been a two-way street.

To be sure, some things remain in place from golf's earlier Promethean age. This is not an outright rejection of golf – an 'anti-golf' response – as the dominant view remains that golf is good, and that the golf industry should continue to grow unabated. Neither is this a transformative 'alter-golf' response in which synthetic chemicals are fully excised from the superintendent's 'arsenal'. In the two chapters that follow, we turn our attention to these 'darker-green' points of view.

PART IV
The dark-greening of golf

8

Anti-golfers across the world unite! Global and local forms of resistance to golf course development

In the previous three chapters we illustrated how and why members of the golf industry changed their environment-related practices over time. We focused especially on the strategies industry members used to frame and promote their now dominant 'light-green' position. One of our key findings was that industry was especially effective in their attempts to position light-green responses to environmental problems as the 'only' reasonable responses to these problems and, in turn, to position golf industry members as natural leaders in the quest for improved environmental outcomes. In this way, it would appear that representatives of the golf industry – along with a legion of other sport management environmentalists – have effectively incorporated and redefined environmentalism. In other words, a light-green consensus has emerged; the activities and perspectives of more 'traditional' (i.e. darker-green) environmentalists are effectively cast aside.

Yet darker-green forms of environmentalism have not disappeared, even if they now exist in a complex environmental landscape where claims of environmental leadership abound. In this fourth section of *The greening of golf*, we explore how these darker-green environmental groups have responded to golf in general, and to golf's 'green' credentials in particular. We focus in this chapter on movements against golf involving either resistance to particular golf-related development projects or, more radically, to the very idea that golf should exist. Our examination of these 'anti-golf' responses includes a description of key groups mounting such responses, an outline of their undergirding assumptions, and commentary on how anti-golf messaging has been 'framed' – that is, how it has been presented to key audiences such as the public. We also consider the level of success that golf protest groups have achieved and strive to explain why these groups may or may not have attained their desired outcomes or level of influence. This chapter, in other words, is devoted to 'industry unfriendly' environmental stances and their successes and failures.

In carrying out this analysis, we focus on two anti-golf movements in particular: the Global Anti-Golf Movement (GAGM), a very broad and flexible movement against golf; and Tripping up Trump (TUT), which arose in response to one particular course development project. GAGM is noteworthy, as we shall see, for its staunch and outright rejection of golf. TUT presents an interesting case too, first in its high-profile nature. Indeed, at the centre of the TUT controversy was celebrity businessman (and, recently, US Presidential candidate) Donald Trump, who hoped to build a championship-level golf course on the Scottish coast, and in the process encountered an entrenched group of protesters concerned in part about the environmental impacts of Trump's proposed development. GAGM and TUT are furthermore indicative of golf's global 'journey'. For GAGM, this much is suggested in the movement's very name. The TUT case involved an American entrepreneur venturing back to golf's 'homeland' in Scotland to build a course that could attract tourists from across the world. In addition, the Trump course, now completed, can be considered an archetypal 'glocalized' development: by integrating generic standards of golf course beauty with a distinctly Scottish landscape, the course is both familiar and unique at the same time. The confrontation between Trump and TUT was likewise a classic encounter between local and global forces. Altogether, this chapter helps advance our interest in this book in assessing golf's environmental implications and their relationship to globalization.

The Global Anti-Golf Movement: a virtual movement and a 'movement of movements'

With its official launch on what they proclaimed to be 'No Golf Day' in April 1993, GAGM became a recognized critic of the golf industry and positioned itself as the only sustained social and environmental movement focused specifically on golf (to our knowledge). Although we suggest later in this chapter that GAGM is in some respects an unofficial 'movement of movements' – and we say 'unofficial' because not all of the movements that resist golf explicitly associate themselves with GAGM or GAGM's values – GAGM itself has become a reference point for many who have written about golf-related problems of all kinds because of its ability to keep its message 'on the radar'. This follows from the movement's early adoption of the Internet for promoting its message, as well as its clearly defined mission statement and set of objectives. People may not agree with all of GAGM's viewpoints, but for anyone searching online for anti-golf initiatives, GAGM cannot be ignored.

So, just what is GAGM, and what does GAGM (hope to) do? The GAGM website explains that the movement emerged "following a three-day conference on Golf Course and Resort Development in the Asia-Pacific Region in Panang, Malaysia from April 26 to 28, 1993", and that the movement was initially sponsored by three organizations: "the Global Network for Anti-Golf Course Action (GNAGA) based in Japan, the Asian Tourism Network (ANTENNA) based in Thailand and the Asian-Pacific People and Environmental Network (AEN) based in Malaysia" (as summarized in Jarvie, 2006: 247). The GAGM website contains a manifesto that includes an overview of social and environmental concerns related to golf along with a set of proposed changes that follow on from these concerns. As sociologist Grant Jarvie recounts, for GAGM:

> (i) golf courses and golf tourism are part of a global package that is capitalist-oriented with most of the money being exported out of the locality; (ii) the speculative nature of the industry makes it a high-risk investment for small countries and localities with many golf courses, resorts and companies becoming bankrupt; (iii) the environmental impact of golf course development is negative in that it facilitates water depletion and toxic contamination to such an extent that the golf green is fraught with ecological problems; (iv) [golf] promotes an elitist and exclusive leisure class with the globalisation of this lifestyle encouraging wealthy urban elites to absorb a particular way of life regardless of the environment and other members of society; and (v) in the face of growing criticism the golf industry is falsely promoting the notion of pesticide-free, environmentally friendly golf courses in the knowledge that such a golf course does not exist. (Jarvie, 2006: 247)

This last point – that the golf industry falsely promotes environmentally friendly golf courses – is particularly noteworthy in light of what we know from previous chapters about the golf industry's comprehensive campaign to publicize their leadership on environmental issues. GAGM offers more specific criticism on this matter, contending that

> the creation and maintenance of the "perfect [putting] green" comprising exotic grass inevitably requires intensive use of chemicals [and that] the increasingly touted integrated pest management system as an alternative to the use of pesticides on golf courses is not a solution [because] application of pest control through IPM is impossible to achieve and should be viewed as nothing more than a hollow attempt to make golf courses appear less toxic than they are.[1]

For GAGM, IPM is easily discreditable: "the danger is that IPM will be taken seriously by officials involved in the approval of golf courses."[2]

These are pointed critiques. The recommendations contained in GAGM's manifesto are equally drastic. These recommendations include: a call for an immediate moratorium on new golf course development projects; a public environmental and social audit of all existing courses; the conversion of golf courses into public parks or, where they lie in forests, wetlands, or on islands, their conversion back to their natural state; prosecution of members of the golf industry as appropriate (for example, in the case of illegal occupation of public land); and laws banning the promotion of golf courses and golf tourism.[3] These recommendations of course mark a radical departure from the moderate and golf-friendly environmental strategies that are promoted and implemented by many golf industry members themselves. GAGM essentially has no tolerance for industry-led solutions to environmental problems. They are flagrantly distrustful of 'green' initiatives such as IPM and indeed have been for some time – remembering that GAGM emerged on the scene in 1993. GAGM furthermore calls on governments to take on greater responsibility in regulating the golf industry. This is especially noteworthy in a context that has seen the emergence of voluntarism as a regulatory mechanism, as described in Chapter 7.

What kind of social movement is GAGM?

With its manifesto in tow, GAGM is a 'social movement' in a general sense: it is 'a political entity that aims to create social change' (see Staggenborg, 2008; Wilson, 2012b). More specifically, GAGM can be deemed a 'new social movement' – a general form of movement dominant since the 1960s. New social movements are unlike 'older social movements' in the sense that older movements are concerned primarily with economic matters, while 'newer' ones are generally interested in politics and power in a wider sense. Harvey and Houle offer a useful definition of new social movements that includes reference to both the structure and broad mandates of these sorts of groups. They say they differ from older ones in that they:

> (a) are not linked to specific economic interests, (b) work towards change in society's values, and (c) work for the collective good. They are fluid, their membership diverse, they take different organizational forms, and they vary in size, composition, and forms of actions. They are often active at local, national and transnational levels in the form of loose networks of groups and organizations. (Harvey and Houle, 1994: 347)

More recently, Harvey *et al.* (2009) examined the anti- and alter-global social movements emerging from dissatisfaction with neoliberal globalization and its promotion of deregulation and the near-unimpeded 'flow' of labour and capital. Harvey *et al.* depicted these anti- and alter-globalization movements as largely devoid of hierarchical structure and as focused less on state-level issues and more on those that span from 'the local' to 'the global' (i.e. they adhere to what sociologist Alain Touraine (1977) has called the principle of 'totality'). Harvey *et al.* (2009) include 'ecological' movements alongside those associated with, for example, civil rights, peace, human security, workers' rights, and children's rights among those fitting this description.

GAGM fits the new social movement label well. Its concerns transcend economics. It aims to change how golf is valued socially, especially in comparison to spaces that in GAGM's view better serve the collective good (such as public parks). Having been founded by the Global Network for Anti-Golf Course Action, the Asian Tourism Network, and the Asian-Pacific People and Environmental Network, GAGM's structure now appears quite fluid (or, at least, it seems quite easy for people and groups to affiliate with GAGM). Most of all, and as noted above, GAGM moves from local to global concerns in addressing golf, making reference to specific protests against course construction while also delivering broad and bold claims about golf that in their view apply *irrespective of context*. GAGM, therefore, is not just a political entity that aims to create social change – it is one that strives to do so without the easily discernable structure or approach of social movements of old.

What does GAGM 'do', and is it effective?

On 30 April 2008, the day following the fifteenth anniversary of the Global Anti-Golf Movement's launch, sports journalist William K. Wolfrum wrote a short column for the Golf Channel's WORLDGOLF website with the satirical title 'The Global Anti-Golf Movement: golf's ultimate enemy celebrates 15 years of having a manifesto' (Wolfrum, 2008). Wolfrum's column is based on the idea that while GAGM has outlined a forceful plan for taking on the golf establishment, the group has apparently been completely ineffective. As he states: "There has been a war going on right under your noses. For 15 years now, golf has been under a sustained attack. Not a very effective attack, mind you, but an attack, nonetheless." Wolfrum goes on to say (satirically) that, in fifteen years, GAGM's accomplishments comprised inclusion in Wolfrum's blog post: "And that's only in 15 years, mind you. Imagine what the next 15 years will bring" (Wolfrum, 2008). This is of course intended to be humorous, though Wolfrum does raise interesting questions about what GAGM has actually accomplished. Below, we discuss how we might evaluate the success of a movement like GAGM, and consider how Wolfrum's point might be complemented by a more in-depth and nuanced consideration of what GAGM has done, what it could do, and what could reasonably be considered 'success' for a movement of its kind.

Our evaluation of GAGM was aided by literature describing the various ways that social movements define success. Looking at success as a flexible concept is important in this context because success for these sorts of groups often (necessarily) means much more than directly and obviously influencing environmental policy or industry behaviour. Indeed, a more nuanced view of success is crucial for those who are working against the institutionalized interests and activities of dominant groups because challenges to the extant system are unlikely to lead to quick and readily apparent transformations. Moreover, those affiliating with new social movements might have differing goals and motivations among themselves, again making success harder to judge compared to 'older' social movements that, to a greater extent, speak in a unified voice. For example, some affiliating with GAGM may be concerned with golf's environmental impacts near their own homes, while others may be focused more broadly on golf's uptake of ostensibly 'green' practices such as IPM. Put simply, evaluating the success of a movement that is connected to so many issues and has a presence (or desired presence) in so many contexts is not so straightforward.

To be sure, Wolfrum's dismissal of GAGM has merit based on a strict reading of GAGM's manifesto. GAGM clearly has not inspired the complete abolition of golf courses in favour of public parks, for example. Yet below we outline a set of criteria that have been devised to help evaluate the success of social movements in more nuanced fashion (adapted from Wilson, 2012b: 94; see Staggenborg, 2008), applying these criteria along the way to the case of golf. Our intention here is not to celebrate GAGM, but to note that, in a complex environmental landscape, success (and failure) should equally be understood as complex in nature. These criteria are as follows:

- The movement raised awareness about golf-related social and environmental issues;
- The movement effectively promoted a sense of belonging and community for those involved in anti-golf resistance work;
- The movement has become a recognized representative for golf-related social and environmental issues;
- The movement offered inspiration and a sense of empowerment for those who have felt marginalized and/or oppressed by pro-golf developers, industry members and other golf advocates;

- The movement brought attention to an alternative approach to the practice of sport (e.g. to chemical-free golf);
- The movement's activities led to desirable changes in government policies and/or changes in cultural norms and practices pertaining to golf's environmental and social impacts;
- The movement interrupted the activities of powerful groups whose goals and actions are unacceptable to the activist group.

With these criteria in mind, it would be fair to suggest that although GAGM seems to be an often-dormant 'group',[4] GAGM has also made progress on at least some of these fronts. GAGM's positioning as a source of (radical) information on golf and its social and environmental implications is first noteworthy in this regard. The movement has, in one sense, been a subject of discussion among and source of information for scholars writing about golf's social and environmental dimensions for some time (e.g. see Jarvie, 2006; Maguire et al., 2002; Stolle-McCallister, 2004; Wheeler and Nauright, 2006). So too have mainstream media outlets made reference to GAGM's politics and practices since the movement's early days. For instance, a 1995 article in the UK newspaper *The Independent* entitled "How about bunking off for the day? Best lie low in the clubhouse tomorrow: It's World No Golf Day and the backlash is gathering strength" included a description and history of the then-nascent GAGM and an overview of various golf-related social and environmental concerns (Fox, 1995). Even William K. Wolfrum, in dismissing GAGM, still implicitly recognized this movement as a source of anti-establishment information. We feel safe in assuming too that a wider audience has also accessed GAGM's online materials, especially given that these include materials on local protests around the world.

It is worth noting here that if GAGM had emerged pre-Internet, it would seem that their ability to have a sustained impact and presence would have been almost completely diminished. With this in mind, and as one of us has argued elsewhere, sport-related social movements – even smaller and poorly resourced ones – have unprecedented potential through the uptake of new media for disseminating information. This was especially the case in the years before corporate saturation of the web became so prominent (see Wilson, 2007). GAGM seems to have benefited immensely from their early adoption of online communication. That the scholarly and news media articles examining GAGM mentioned throughout this section appear to have drawn almost exclusively on the same resource – GAGM's webpage – is testament to this.

Perhaps more significant than this awareness-raising is the extent to which GAGM has indeed interrupted – or, at least, helped interrupt – the activities of powerful groups whose goals and actions they deem unacceptable. As we have seen, GAGM is certainly directed towards this end. The final statement of the updated GAGM manifesto – a take on the famous line of Karl Marx and Friedrich Engel's *The Communist Manifesto* – speaks to the goal of inspiring, uniting, and resisting: "Anti-golfers throughout Italy, Europe and the world, unite!" (translated from Italian; see www.antigolf.org/storia.htm). As Horne (1998) recounts, by the late 1990s GAGM's original leader, Gen Morita, had claimed responsibility for halting the construction of more than a hundred courses in Japan. Tactics for accomplishing this included electing anti-golf sympathizers to government positions, raising awareness among the public on the local impacts of golf, and adopting a standing tree trust that prohibits the development of the land on which the tree stands (Horne, 1998: 178). Stolle-McAllister gives another example along these same lines – one that speaks more to GAGM's wide-ranging influence. GAGM was one of several groups, along with Greenpeace, the Sierra Club, and others, that supported anti-golf activists in Tepoztlán, Mexico by providing information on golf's environmental impacts and by publicizing the activist campaign in Mexico City. "Tepoztlán became, for a while, a center of regional ecological activism and a national and even transnational symbol of resisting unsustainable development projects" (Stolle-McAllister, 2004: 150). GAGM, it can be added, was acting on its manifesto.

Local anti-golf movements: 'tripping up' golf?

Beyond the Tepoztlán case, even a cursory search for local, golf-related activism reveals that collective action in the face of golf-related developments has been plentiful over the years, and has emerged in various regions of the world. Indeed, the 'relevant links' part of the GAGM website shows movements in Italy, the UK, Crete, Japan, Canada, Greece, China, and the Philippines. Journalists especially have covered and offered commentary on golf-related conflicts and issues in these regions.

Take one confrontation from the Philippines as a case in point. A 2009 article entitled 'Turf wars' in *Australian Golf Digest* recounted the tense encounter that emerged around a major development planned in the coastal village of Hacienda Looc in the 1990s. The plans included a luxury beach resort, a new subdivision, and a yacht marina. Four championship golf courses would also be built, in the process demanding a 'moulding' of the hills around the village. Todd Pitock, the article's author, described the situation:

> Greg Norman and Jack Nicklaus were on board. Hacienda Looc would be the next hot spot. Everyone loved the plans. Everyone, that is, who didn't already live in Hacienda Looc. No one had bothered to ask the 7,000 farmers, fishermen and villagers who faced eviction from ancestral lands in what the project's critics say amounted to a nefarious land grab orchestrated by corrupt officials and unscrupulous developers. (Pitock, 2009: 91)

Pitock went on to describe the conflicts that followed the proposed development:

> Hacienda Looc residents organised themselves, first rebuffing bulldozers by forming human chains. Eventually they formed an organisation called "Break Free" and mounted legal challenges. Then things got ugly. The government sent in military and police, and the developers hired their own para-military personnel whom villagers say harassed and assaulted them. Then, in two separate incidents, three of Break Free's leaders were shot dead. Two shooters, the developer's private guards, were arrested, then released without charges being filed. No one was accused in the third killing. The events engendered outrage and threats of retaliation from a guerrilla movement called the New People's Army. As the stakes and the embarrassment heightened, the plans were scuttled, and for more than a decade residents have continued to fight off developers in Philippine courts. (Pitock, 2009: 91)

Seemingly less dramatic but still significant conflicts have been identified in China, where a golf course development boom has been taking place in recent years.[5] An investigative report in the UK's *Guardian* described how the tropical island of Hainan in the southeast of China, a region known to be a "a rare conservation success story in China" with clouded leopards and black gibbons among the 300 endangered species in this area, has become an area for golf course development – though not without controversy (Watts, 2010). The article describes the dissatisfaction and concern expressed by local villagers, although it appears that locals were collectively unable to alter the direction of developers:

> In Changyong village on the edge of the course, residents said they have been flooded for the past two years by water than runs off of plastic sheeting under the huge course. "It's had a huge impact," said Deng Zhenhe. "We never had flooding in the past. Now it comes three months every year. The water comes up to our waists sometimes. Cars can't get through." At Bopian village, a crowd gathers to express their grievances. "The golf club has cut down many big trees

and the lychee and longan trees we used to farm. Our sheep and cows have nowhere to graze," said a man who gave only the surname Wu. "I was cheated of some of my land." (Watts, 2010)

This example, along with the case in the Philippines, is effectively the tip of the iceberg. The golf industry has faced resistance of this kind many times over.

Our main concern here, though, is not with the number of anti-golf movements of this sort, nor with the precise places in which they arise – but instead with questions about what we can learn about local forms of citizen resistance through focused examination. We are especially interested in the processes through which local movements might be more or less successful in their attempts to resist what they see as imminent social and environmental threats. Looking at these processes can offer in-depth insight into some of the 'big picture' questions we posed about golf and development in the introductory chapter of this book – especially questions about how and when it is that hegemonic groups are able to generate consent for particular ideas and activities and, equally, how and when *counter*-hegemonic groups are able to successfully challenge the status quo. Here we employ a second case study, this time of the aforementioned group Tripping up Trump, as a way into these issues. The following examination of TUT is informed by a range of materials, including media coverage, the TUT website, and especially our own interviews with Michael Forbes – key adversary of Donald Trump – and others affiliated with the TUT group.

Tripping up Trump: backstory

In 2006, planning for the development of a resort known as 'Trump International Golf Links' was initiated. The proposed location for the resort – which was to include two golf courses, a collection of hotel rooms, villas, residential units, and a resort village – was Menie Estate on the North Sea Coast of Aberdeenshire, Scotland. In 2007, the initial proposal was rejected by a local planning body representing Aberdeenshire Council known as the Infrastructure Services Committee. This was not an uncontroversial decision. Councillor Martin Ford, who was Chair of the committee at the time and cast the deciding vote to reject the proposal, was subsequently ousted from his Chair position through an emergency meeting of and vote by the Council. The BBC reported that the ousting was justified by councillors who felt that the economic benefits of Trump's plan outweighed its potential environmental costs, and that Ford was not acting in the best interest of the region by opposing the course proposal (BBC, 2007). Ford argued – and still maintains – that the the Infrastructure Services Committee's position was sound, as the new development would effectively destroy what was a legally protected Site of Special Scientific Interest (SSSI): a unique and dynamic dune system on the site of the proposed development. Ford spoke to his decision in an interview for the documentary *You've Been Trumped*:

> You could apply the tests of sustainable development to the Trump proposal and it failed them, it failed them in spades. It [Trump's proposal] was predicated on people flying across the Atlantic ... playing a few games of golf and flying back over the Atlantic. It was predicated on utilizing an irreplaceable and diminishing resource, effectively natural habitat. (Baxter, 2012)

The Scottish government did not see things this way, which is why government officials decided to designate the Trump proposal an issue of national importance. In doing so, the decision to reject Trump's proposal by the the Infrastructure Services Committee became reviewable in the national parliament, and thus reversible. In 2008, the Scottish government made the decision to overturn the the Committee's verdict, thus allowing Trump International to continue with development plans.

The tensions between Trump's team and TUT continued into 2010, when Trump International came into conflict with local fisherman and farmer, Michael Forbes. Forbes's house is located on a parse of land that Trump desired for the development. Despite buyout offers, Forbes refused to sell. The conflict became hostile as Trump claimed that Forbes lived like a "pig" and that his property was a "slum". Forbes indicated in response that he did not care what Trump thought, and was quoted as saying that Trump could "shove his money up his arse" (Miller, 2010). Trump's team subsequently raised the possibility of requesting that Aberdeenshire Council forcibly purchase Forbes's home and those of his neighbours (which would all be resold to Trump International for development purposes) under what is known as Compulsory Purchase Order (CPO) legislation. According to the Scottish government website, CPO legislation makes it possible for "organisations to acquire land without the owner's permission, if there is a strong enough case for this in the public interest" (The Scottish Government, n.d.). The point of debate around this issue was whether Trump's development would bring enough benefits to the region to justify a CPO intervention. Although the CPO was never formally commenced by Trump's group, making formal government deliberations unnecessary, the threat of CPO was a significant concern for Forbes and the wider anti-Trump movement (Dennys, 2013).[6]

Indeed, the activist group TUT was proactive on this issue. In an attempt to undermine the CPO before an order was initiated, Forbes sold a plot of his land (given the name 'the Bunker') located in a place of particular value to the development project to a range of TUT members and others. This tactic – one that would complicate any attempts to proceed with a CPO – is reminiscent of the standing tree trust tactic noted above in relation to GAGM. An article in *The Scotsman* offers a succinct description of the background and rationale for the response:

> Tripping Up Trump (TUT) said it had implemented the same legal framework used by the Heathrow [airport] anti-expansion protesters to buy a plot of land near the airport to block the construction of a third runway. TUT spokesman Martin Glegg said Mr Forbes had sold the group a plot of land on his estate. Thousands of members of the public will have the chance to sign up and have their names placed on the deeds, creating a major legal headache for any compulsory purchase plans. (The Scotsman, 2010)

In essence, the sale of the land to multiple people would mean that each person would need to be dealt with individually for a CPO to be approved. It would appear that this strategy was effective, or, at least, that its intended outcome was achieved, as the CPO was not pursued.

In recent years, Trump's group has expressed concern about proposals to build wind farms off the cost of Menie near the Trump International Golf Links course. Trump himself indicated that the massive energy-generating windmills were a noise nuisance and visually unappealing and that, as such, they would negatively impact tourism around the course. Trump has (unsuccessfully) attempted to stop the windmills through legal action (Carrell, 2014). In a February 2014 press release from the UK's Green Party, it was reported that Trump's organization had "withdrawn its planning application to build a second golf course at Menie and has abandoned its scheme to construct a large golf resort at the site" (Kennedy, 2014). The release included comments from Green Party member Martin Ford – the same Martin Ford who led the committee that recommended rejecting the development in the first place. In Ford's words:

> Of course, the Scottish Government should never have stepped in to grant Mr Trump planning permission in the first place. We have lost an important and beautiful natural area that was legally protected as a Site of Special Scientific Interest. Our duty, as I saw it, was to hand this natural heritage over to following

generations intact, so they could enjoy it and wonder at and better understand nature. Instead, it has become a golf course. The justification for allowing this damage to the environment was the jobs and economic benefit the proposed golf resort would bring. While the scale of the economic benefit promised by Mr Trump was clearly ridiculously exaggerated, there is no doubt that, had the resort gone ahead, there would have been some job creation and economic activity as a result. As it is, the north-east has got the worst of all possible worlds. We have lost our irreplaceable, natural, mobile dune system – for negligible economic return. (Kennedy, 2014)

The Trump golf development saga is ongoing in the sense that further development in Menie remains a possibility – Trump could still choose to pursue the CPO – and in that Menie residents and those sympathizing with their cause continue to voice their displeasure, especially online. Having said this, however, the 'high point' of the Trump-TUT confrontation seems to have passed. To the extent that Trump International Golf Links now welcomes golfers the world over, Trump seems to have won.

Assessing the successes and failures of Trump and TUT

Again, though, we would emphasize the importance of recognizing nuance in assessing success and failure as they pertain to (new) social movements. Both Trump and TUT gained support at different times in their quarrel. To understand how they each accomplished this, it is useful to evaluate how each group 'framed' their position – especially as these positions pertained to the environmental impacts of Trump's golf course development. Frame analysis helps us see how particular versions of reality are strategically mobilized, leaving other realities in the background or 'outside the picture' entirely. Entman put it this way in his foundational article on framing:

> To frame is to select some aspects of a perceived reality and make them more salient in a communicating text. Frames, then, define problems – determine what a causal agent is doing and costs and benefits, usually measured in terms of cultural values; diagnose causes – identify the forces creating the problem; make moral judgments – evaluate causal agents and their effects; and suggest remedies – offer and justify treatments for the problem and predict their likely effects. (Entman, 1993: 52, 55)

To be sure, framing is not all there is in confrontations such as this. Important too is the ability among different groups to mobilize resources in support of their work and to take advantage of political opportunities (Wilson, 2012b). Yet framing is key in making an issue intelligible in particular ways and thus in arriving at desired outcomes. This is true for both Trump and TUT.

Trump's frames

On the one side, then, were Trump's frames (or, at least, the frames of those affiliated with the Trump project). When it comes to the environment, Trump and his team attempted to offset critiques of the development's environmental impacts by suggesting that his golf course would not only be constructed with environmental principles in mind, but that it would, in fact, be *helpful* for the environment. For example, Trump was quoted in one instance as saying, "from an environmental standpoint, it is in a much better situation than it was before we bought the site." On another occasion he indicated that his group "saved the dunes" (Baxter, 2012). Trump's framing in this case thus included a novel spin on the impact of this development on the dynamic sand dune system, which he proudly claimed to have stabilized. This is an intriguing (and from an environmental perspective, dubious) spin in the sense that the very reason that the dunes were classified as a Site of Special Scientific Interest was *because they were a dynamic system*. Trump framed the dunes as follows: "I've stabilized the dunes. That means the dunes will be with us forever and that's good, because dunes can be gone with the wind" (Baxter, 2012).

Perhaps unsurprisingly, Trump and his team also emphasized the economic benefits of their proposal. In early coverage of the controversial development (before it was approved), Trump and his team mentioned the "one billion pound development" (instead of just 'the development') when referring to the project. Linking the development with a large monetary sum would seem to be a strategy for highlighting the vast economic implications of the project – as well as the major economic downside of not catering to Trump's requests. A BBC report in 2007 offers some early evidence of this interpretation of Trump's economic frame: "Mr Trump's spokesman George Sorial had warned failure by Aberdeenshire Council to endorse £1bn golf resort plans on Wednesday would put the entire project in jeopardy" (BBC, 2007).

In another effort to frame the proposed development as beneficial for the local region – and, perhaps, in an attempt to counter TUT's protests and any support TUT was accruing – Trump also stressed the robust 'popularity' of the proposal. In an interview appearing in the 'Tripping up Trump' documentary, Trump contends that "this [the development] is a very popular project, we've had great support from the Council, [and] great support from the political leaders" (Baxter, 2012). Indeed, this is true! It was only with the Scottish government's decision to overturn the local Infrastructure Services Committee's original verdict disallowing the course that Trump International Golf Links was made possible. Elsewhere in the 'Tripping up Trump' documentary, Trump claims that his group had "tremendous support from the environmental groups". To buttress these assertions of support, Trump framed Michael Forbes, his main public rival in building the course, as 'unpopular' – indicating in one instance that he had come to learn that "Forbes is not a respected man among the people that he lives with" (Baxter, 2012).

Anti-Trump and anti-development frames

Just as Trump and his team framed the development as favourable for the environment, TUT and its allies offered strategic messages intended to highlight the negative environmental impacts of the proposed project. A main strategy was to consistently use the term "Site of Special Scientific Interest" (SSSI) when describing the proposed development area, since the dynamic dune system had in fact received this designation.

What does it mean to receive SSSI designation? Scottish Natural Heritage, the public body that represents the Scottish government on environment- and conservation-related issues and that verifies and offers this designation, describes SSSIs as "those areas of land and water (to the seaward limits of local authority areas) that Scottish Natural Heritage considers to best represent our natural heritage – its diversity of plants, animals and habitats, rocks and landforms, or a combinations of such natural features" (Scottish Natural Heritage, n.d.). The goal of giving particular areas SSSI status is to "[make] sure that decision makers, managers of land and their advisers, as well as the planning authorities and other public bodies, are aware of them when considering changes in land-use or other activities which might affect them" (Popham, 2012). SSSIs can, therefore, be developed for reasons that are considered crucial and in the public interest – which is how Trump's course ultimately received approval. Yet by consistently referring to the dunes as an SSSI, anti-Trump activists were reframing the proposed golf course and the wider development as an environmental threat. The film *You've Been Trumped* includes interviews with environmental experts like Dr Jim Hansom, a geomorphologist at the University of Glasgow, who is quoted as saying that the dunes "are our [i.e. Scotland's] equivalent of the

Amazon Rainforest" (Baxter, 2012). Although Hansom is positioned as a scientist who is simply offering an assessment of what the dunes represent, equating the Amazon and the dunes is precisely the kind of powerful imagery that is helpful in the process of framing. In discussing the Trump course, Hansom also attests in the film to knowing of "no credible environmental organization that favoured such a development" (Baxter, 2012). It is relevant here that *You've Been Trumped*'s director Anthony Baxter is described as a "friend of TUT" on TUT's website. Baxter indeed turned out to be an excellent resource for the TUT campaign.

Another tactic used by TUT and anti-Trump protesters was to mobilize a discourse of authentic Scottish heritage. In this case, those standing up to Trump were framed as 'locals' defending their turf in the face of an American billionaire tycoon. This frame is significant in its capacity for drawing support from people who may not be concerned with environmental issues, but are moved by their concern for the rights of local people. It is the classic David and Goliath story. One of the ways that TUT developed this frame was to feature stories about the local residents impacted by Trump's development on their webpage and in a newspaper/newsletter created by TUT called *Menie Voices*. One excerpt from the newspaper describing the experiences of some of those near the Trump development reads as follows:

> Homeowners described how their water had been turned off for ten days and now security guards drive through and past their property 24/7, almost every day. One resident Susan Munro described how the events had affected her. "I feel helpless; it seems nobody wants to know. You phone the council and nobody wants to speak to you or hear your questions. Even the police seem to be on Trump's side." Michael Forbes of the Mill of Menie also had to watch as Trump's men and heavy machinery forcibly removed his salmon nets from land his family had used for generations. (Anon, 2010)

A powerful portrayal of the history and culture of the residents in and around Menie was also offered in Baxter's *You've Been Trumped*, which includes interviews with and life histories of some of those negatively impacted by Trump's development. It offered a brief history of salmon fishing in the area – a history that included Michael Forbes and his ancestors. The film invokes a sense of nostalgia for a simpler moment when global mega-developments were not so common.

Of course, such histories are always socially constructed in the sense that people are necessarily selective and partial when choosing what to include in and what to exclude from their messaging. With this in mind, scholars such as

Nauright and White (1996) have shown how these stories and how nostalgia itself can be tools for those attempting to retain or defend a cultural artefact or institution – a stadium about to be razed, for example, or sports team that may be moved or disbanded (see Wilson and White, 2002). What the Trump protesters were effectively mounting in this regard was a 'collective action frame': a narrative told and retold in an attempt to create a connection with potential social movement members, and to remind existing movement members of the injustice they are responding to (and who is to blame for the injustice). Through a message of collective past experience, Menie's residents are framed as the rightful inhabitants of the Menie area – even as its stewards – while Trump and his team are made to be uncaring and avaricious outsiders. As noted above, it would appear that this story was designed to provoke an emotional response among those who see Trump and his team as bullies, and the Menie residents as courageous underdogs. Researchers interested in understanding the characteristics of successful acts of resistance recognize the importance of this sort of emotion – what Italian social theorist Antonio Gramsci (1971) called 'emotion-passion' – when attempting to generate consent for a particular (in this case counter-hegemonic) position.

The championing of Michael Forbes as an anti-Trump figure was especially crucial to this framing of the 'local and authentic' residents of Menie as preferable to the 'global and ostentatious' Trump. TUT strategically mobilized images of the heroic Forbes as a principled man standing up to an incorrigible bully. The first image one sees when landing on the TUT webpage is a close-up of the stoic Forbes standing against the backdrop of his Menie property, accompanied by the caption "a voice for the local residents and a community of people who care."[7] In his documentary *You've Been Trumped*, Baxter included an interview with TUT member (and former producer for the British band The Clash) Mickey Foote, who nicely encapsulates TUT's preferred framing of Forbes:

> A lot of local people don't see Michael as a particular problem [i.e. the problem Trump makes him out to be]. They see him as standing up for what is rightfully his, and they don't believe in all the claptrap that Trump's PR machine put out. (Baxter, 2012)

Baxter's *You've Been Trumped* further dramatized the David and Goliath story of Forbes versus Trump by inserting clips from the 1983 film *Local Hero* throughout his documentary. *Local Hero*, directed by Glasgow-born Bill Forsyth, is about an American oil company that sends a powerful executive "to Scotland to buy up an entire village where they want to build a refinery."[8] The film champions the Scottish locals, who resist the advances of the executive and the company he works for.⁹ Through this frame, the Trump confrontation becomes a case of life imitating art.

Evidently, the framing of Forbes as a noble underdog resonated beyond the protest movement, as Forbes won the 'Top Scot' award in 2012 at the renowned Glenfiddich Spirit of Scotland Awards. The award, given annually to recognize a Scottish person who "has made the greatest impact in furthering Scotland's reputation at home and abroad", has also been offered previously to people such as tennis star Andy Murray and author J. K. Rowling (The Huffington Post, Inc., 2012).

Mobilizing resources and pursuing political opportunities

As noted above, beyond framing, resource mobilization and political opportunism are important to the success of social movements as well. The same could certainly be said of those whom social movements are opposing, though in social movement studies it is more common to consider how less powerful groups mobilize resources and political opportunities since these groups are often working 'against the grain' and must be especially entrepreneurial to make political and social inroads. In hindsight, there were indeed key instances where TUT and their supporters made especially astute political manoeuvers to either act on their mission and/or call attention to their cause.

One key instance in this regard was the creation of the 'Bunker', the aforementioned plot of land sold to a host of course opponents to subvert a potential CPO on Forbes's land. The Bunker idea was also publicized at a strategic (i.e. a politically opportune) moment, as TUT spokesperson Martin Glegg noted in our interview with him:

> We released the Bunker the day Trump was coming to town … He was in a press conference, and everybody was saying, you know, "what's all this?" … Then that [the Bunker and Michael Forbes's farm] ended up being the story. (Personal interview, July 2012)

Another example in this regard is TUT's response to the announcement that Donald Trump was to receive an honorary degree from Robert Gordon University in Glasgow. Leading up to the announcement, TUT was contacted by a former Robert Gordon Principal (a high-ranking position in the university) who had decided to hand back the honorary degree he had previously received from the university as an act of protest against Trump's honour. In an interview, TUT spokesperson Martin Glegg described the situation, and how TUT took advantage of the opportunity:

> Trump got offered an honorary degree before he'd actually basically delivered anything in Aberdeenshire ... A lot of people didn't think that was right, even people that thought the golf course should go ahead. Well ... one of the ex-principals [of the university] phoned up Tripping Up Trump ... and I spoke to him on the phone and he said, "listen, I'm gonna hand in my honorary degree, I'm gonna hand it in – how do you want to do this?" So we were like, "ok, brilliant", so it was like, we phoned David Milne and David Milne and him met outside the university one day and we organized it ... [We] got the press down and there was just, there was a lot of energy then, and when Trump got his honorary degree, that was the same day we released our papers [highlighting the problems with the Trump development]. So the camera crews were out already – otherwise, we might not have got it [the coverage of TUT and their concerns]. (Personal interview, July 2012)

The media attention that the anti-Trump campaign received also brought celebrity supporters into contact with TUT, including actress Tilda Swinton, Brian May of the band Queen, and director David Puttnam. Glegg explained how TUT was strategic in their attempts to utilize celebrity support:

> We just got quotes from them specifically. Like [we'd ask them], "could you give us a quote?" and say, you know, that you support the campaign ... and then it'd be like, "oh, Tilda Swinton" [supported us] ... It was kind of fun as well what was going on. But obviously the seriousness of it behind it was kind of there as well. But if we put information that was dry, that was just kind of fact-based, or, well that wouldn't get in the papers. (Personal interview, July 2012)

TUT also benefited in this sense from the work of Scottish artist David McCue, who held an art show in a barn on Michael Forbes's property. The show included various paintings celebrating Forbes and TUT's resistance campaign, as well as paintings that depicted a "very angry, very self-motivated, very self-interested" Trump (from an interview with Mickey Foote in *You've Been Trumped*; Baxter, 2012).[10] Along with these paintings, the exhibit included an interactive 'mini-golf' hole that invited people to putt a golf ball through a large dollar sign (painted in United States red, white and blue) into the mouth of an image of Donald Trump. The exhibit was also featured in *You've Been Trumped*, along with an interview with McCue – who described the Menie locals making up the resistance campaign as "lovely, genuine, honest, authentic people" (Baxter, 2012). The exhibit itself, in bringing together like-minded members of the community, served as a 'resource' in the wider anti-Trump movement.

Conclusion: anti-golf in light-green times

In many ways TUT can be considered a successful social movement. Most obviously, and in much the same way that GAGM's very existence puts anti-golf messaging 'on the radar', TUT became *the* voice of opposition to Trump's development project – a unique and still lasting position. In framing Trump's course in counter-hegemonic ways and in mobilizing resources and political opportunities in furthering their cause, we feel it safe to say that TUT raised awareness not only around issues pertaining to Trump International Golf Links but on golf's potential social and environmental impacts in general. The campaign's work was also crucial in supporting the families impacted by the threat of the CPO. That Michael Forbes and others remained in their homes despite the spectre of the CPO can certainly be construed as a 'win', even if Trump's building of the course was a 'loss' given TUT's overall objectives.

In assessing its successes and failures, our examination of TUT in this chapter is in some ways reminiscent of research by the few others who have studied golf-related resistance movements. For example, based on her research exploring golf-related protests in Greece, Briassoulis contends that social movements gain momentum when sometimes diverse interests are intentionally or accidentally aligned. She adds that context is of high importance when trying to understand when and how these synergies emerge:

> Opposition does not arise in a vacuum; it concerns specific proposals for golf development in often ecologically and culturally valuable locations. Specialist and nonspecialist signees [of the petition against the golf development] alike did not react to abstract images but to an elitist, exclusionary image of golf and golf tourism *in conjunction with* the negative environmental, social and economic impacts of golf development *at the particular location*. (Briassoulis, 2009: 308, emphasis in original)

The Trump case, as we have seen, brought together many narratives – from the course's environmental impacts to the perceived invaluableness of local heritage to Trump's purported inauthenticity in comparison to Michael Forbes, among others. It thus presented TUT sympathizers with many contextually specific reasons to rally around the TUT cause. In this regard, by keeping a wide focus, new social movements have the ability to pull together and harmonize a range of different voices. This becomes crucial when the time arises to (for example) have supporters purchase a share of 'the Bunker' in defending against a looming CPO.

And yet, while we came to better understand the dynamics of a 'somewhat successful' social and environmental movement by looking at TUT, this same case aptly demonstrates the barriers that new social movements can face, and why it is that such movements sometimes fail to achieve key goals. Most of all, TUT protesters failed to protect the dynamic dune system on the Scottish coastline. The most direct explanation here returns us to the concept of 'environmental managerialism', discussed in the preceding chapter as well. The decision made by the Scottish government to overrule the initial decision by the committee working on behalf of Aberdeenshire Council to deny Trump's request for permission (an initial decision based on a sustainability assessment of the proposal) would seem to be a clear example of a government weighing economic against environmental concerns – and coming out in favour of the former. This point is (unintentionally) confirmed by Alex Salmond, Member of Scottish Parliament at the time, in his explanation for his support for the Trump proposal: "we can see social and economic benefits, I think, that outweigh environmental concerns" (from Baxter, 2012).

What many critics are noting in retrospect is that Trump's promise for a billion pound development remains unrealized, partly because of Trump's frustration about the wind farms near the golf course. Perhaps, in cases like these, a precautionary approach should also be taken towards economic as well as environment-related decisions. Even though Trump himself was commonly portrayed as the villain in this context, it is important to keep in mind that the decisions to support the development proposal were ultimately made by government, and that Trump's attempts to secure further profits are understandable and should be expected.

In another sense, the very ways in which the environment is typically perceived can be deemed a barrier to groups such as Tripping up Trump as well. As one member of TUT said to us in an interview, the threat of the CPO was a crucial force in rallying public support around Trump's cause:

> I had people coming up to me after seeing that documentary [describing the CPO] saying, "we didn't realize how bad it was", and I said, "well I've been telling you for long enough," you know? "That's terrible, that's terrible putting people out of their homes for a golf course", and that won people. People who had either never thought about [the Trump course] or had said, "well, it'll be a good thing," actually came and said, "no, he's gone too far." And I think when he realized …

he was losing sympathy, I think that's when he [Trump] backed down about the Compulsory Purchase Orders. I think he always hoped it would go away but in Scotland too, you just have to mention pushing people out of their own homes and, you know, it's kind of a really emotive stuff. (Personal interview, July 2012)

A backlash against the CPO is understandable, as an order of this kind would indeed move local people off their land. But the Trump course was to have quite significant effects on the coastal sand dunes as well, at least in the view of course opponents like TUT. Thus, in achieving success on the CPO but not on the sand dunes, TUT was 'winning' mainly *to the extent that environmental concerns aligned with the concerns of people*. This is not quite the manifestation of a Promethean discourse – the idea that humans have an inherent right to manipulate the earth, as discussed in Chapters 3 and 4. But it is a 'light-green' inclination; the 'darker-green' idea that the environment is *inherently* valuable is outside the frame. The point for these purposes is that this is a barrier in the sense that groups like TUT are working within this wider context, and so some issues with which they are concerned may be less likely to resonate from the outset. To say this another way, if we grant the above account from our interviewee, Trump only went 'too far' in the eyes of much of the public when his development aspirations impacted on people like Michael Forbes. In this case the environment itself has no voice – no agency – in the matter.

Looking across this chapter, our analysis herein speaks ultimately to one of the main foci of this book: the relationship between golf, environmental issues, and globalization. Indeed, the two primary cases outlined above shed valuable light onto this relationship. The very decision by the Scottish government to support Trump's proposal aligns with a neoliberal style of governance that sees the opening of borders to the movement of capital (i.e. Trump's US dollars) as highly beneficial. Meanwhile, as we have seen, TUT framed the process of a US businessman putting his imprint on the Scottish coastline through a different lens – one stressing the direct impacts of this on the local context and its deep-rooted history. GAGM is, at the same time, a global movement by definition. GAGM itself embodies aspects of globalization in the sense that its website is an attempt to link anti-golf advocates from around the world.

What all of the conflicts outlined in this chapter have in common is that they are between those who support golf-related developments and those who resist them. The question remains: what about 'radical', darker-green responses to golf's environmental problems *that include golf*? Does an 'alter-golf' alternative exist that is not reformist (i.e, largely industry/chemical-friendly)? We explore this possibility in the next chapter.

Notes

1 Quotation taken from http://www.antigolf.org/english.html.
2 Same as note 1.
3 Same as note 1.
4 According to a 2010 update of GAGM's website, an Italian journalist named Andrea Atzori – whose background includes a political science degree from the University of Cagliari and a Master's thesis on the politics of the environment – took over from Mr Gen Morita of Japan as figurehead and leader of GAGM. This change meant that the 'base' for the movement moved from Japan to Italy. We say the movement may be dormant because the website's latest update appeared to be in 2012, and an email we sent to the contact address of Atzori received no response. We also used the term 'group' tentatively here since the website seems to be run, ultimately, by Atzori, and it is unclear how involved others are in the day-to-day or even periodic operations of the movement.
5 A 2010 article in *The Guardian* indicates that Jack Nicklaus claimed the country is planning to build 1,400 public courses over the next five years (Watts, 2010).
6 There appears to be some uncertainty over whether Trump and his group actually applied for the CPO. Martin Ford quotes Trump as saying he never applied for a CPO, but Ford also says that this is untrue – that Trump's lawyers wrote to Aberdeenshire Council on 4 March 2009 asking the Council to exert its CPO power on behalf of Trump International Golf Links Scotland (Ford, 2011). At the very least, the *potential* of a compulsory purchase was a very real threat to those residents of Menie who might be affected by it.
7 See http://www.trippinguptrump.co.uk.
8 Quoted from http://www.imdb.com/title/tt0085859.
9 The TUT website also includes interview footage with Michael Forbes's mother, Molly Forbes, who shares the challenged land with Michael and his wife. The interview begins with Molly saying "My name is Molly Forbes, and this is my home, which I call paradise," followed by Molly's emotional reflections on the difficulties she and Michael have met in their dealings with those working on Trump's development. This includes comments on the frequent drive-by visits of security from Trump's property and the cut-off of water on Forbes's property because of the development – both well documented in Baxter's film (see http://www.trippinguptrump.co.uk/molly-forbes-interview).
10 To view the paintings, see http://www.davidmccue.info.

9

Organic golf 'on the fringe': the potential and challenges of a chemical-free golf alternative

Throughout this book we have described responses to golf-related environmental problems that are intended to 'alter' golf – that is, responses intended to revise and improve environment-related practices within the golf industry. For the most part, the 'alter-golf' responses we highlighted were led by mainstream golf industry members and their affiliates. We labelled these particular changes to golf course maintenance and construction 'light green' as a way of highlighting that these changes are ultimately moderate responses to environmental issues, based as they are around the 'latest science', around technology-driven strategies for dealing with environmental problems, and on the view that chemicals are still useful and necessary so long as they are used responsibly. Put another way, these strategies for making golf 'greener' are ultimately industry-friendly, do not require a radical shift in business practices, and require only modest and measured changes to the way that golf's relationship with the environment is perceived. In the last chapter we outlined how some individuals and groups have fully rejected this responsible turn.

To be sure, the light-greening of golf is, on the one hand, innovative and in many respects progressive in its attempts to make golf more environmentally friendly. On the other hand, we have pointed to problems with being overly reliant on the 'latest science' when making decisions about synthetic chemical use, recognizing that such an approach has important limitations when it comes to negotiating necessary and unnecessary health- and environment-related risks. Across our analysis to this point there is a question as to why, if golf is considered a crucial leisure and tourism activity (i.e. economically important and, perhaps ironically, health-promoting), other non-chemical alternatives are not being pursued with the same vigour as the 'light-green' solutions described to this point.

This chapter is about just this sort alternative to the mainstream 'light-green' turn – an alter-golf response *that both values golf and, generally speaking, seeks to excise synthetic chemicals*. This more radical alter-golf approach – as compared to the moderate approaches adopted by industry members – is known as 'organic golf'. Below, we describe what organic golf is and why we think it is, in fact, a more radical alternative to even the most progressive industry-led responses to environmental problems. We also address questions about why this alternative to more chemical-intensive forms of golf is not being pursued as vigorously as it might be. Organic golf, for all its potential, remains on the industry's 'fringe'.

This chapter is specifically organized into the following sections. First, we define organic golf and offer an overview of approaches to and basic techniques for maintaining an organic golf course. Following this, we discuss the problems with, merits of, and feasibility of organic golf. In the process, we engage with key debates about organic golf that in some ways extend to debates about the organic movement in general. The next part of the chapter includes an extended discussion of the various (possible) reasons that the organic golf movement has not made more progress. Unlike the environmental feasibility issues outlined earlier in the chapter, this section focuses especially on sociological explanations for the organic golf 'movement's' overall lack of success to date. Included here is a discussion of the incentive systems that underlie decision-making by governments and the behaviours of golf industry members and chemical industry members – as well as challenges faced by (and contradictions within) the organic golf movement itself. We conclude by arguing that organic golf is one of the more intriguing solutions to golf-related environmental problems that we came across in our research because it embodies perspectives and practices that are both 'light green' and 'dark green' in their inclination. That is to say, proponents of organic golf embrace certain kinds of science and technology-driven responses to environmental problems while at the same time championing a more radical anti-chemical stance and a somewhat alternative view of what counts as an acceptable golf course aesthetic. Our commentary on this will highlight one of the main arguments we offer in the final chapter of this book – an argument for remaining open to a diversity of options when it comes to golf's environmental future.

To help us carry out these steps, we draw on interviews we conducted with key figures at two organic golf courses – one on Salt Spring Island, British Columbia, Canada and one in the town of Royston (near Cambridge) in the United Kingdom. Our discussion herein is also informed by published information about organics and golf, online interviews with organic golf advocates, and presentations made available to the public pertaining to the practice of maintaining an organic course. Our particular focus when looking at courses apart from those we visited is the renowned Vineyard (organic) Golf Club near

Martha's Vineyard in Massachusetts, USA. The Vineyard has received a great deal of publicity, at least partly because US President Barack Obama has been known to play there. Vineyard's course superintendent, Jeff Carlson, is a noteworthy figure too – one who is both highly regarded in the mainstream golf industry (where light-green ideas and practices prevail) but is also working at the industry's dark-green periphery by way of his involvement with organic golf.

What is organic golf?

In exploring the world of organic golf, we came across a range of views on what it means to be an authentically 'organic' golf course in the first place. The most straightforward definition of an organic golf course is a course that does not use "a single synthetic pesticide, fertilizer, herbicide or other artificial chemical treatment" (Pennington, 2010). Those we interviewed who work at organic golf courses went beyond this standard definition, however, suggesting that chemical-free course maintenance is only one aspect of organic care. As the superintendent at Blackburn Golf Course on Salt Spring Island, British Columbia explained:

> For me, organics mean something wholly derivative of a natural process ... of a non-chemical, non-synthesized basis ... [But] for me, it's not just soil and grasses, it's everything. I mean it's from attitude and thinking to products that we have here to [our] building to everything that we do, all the processes and operations ... There's no use going halfway, I think if you're going to go that way, you may as well go that whole, you know, as natural as possible. (Personal interview, September 2011)

This holistic vision of organic maintenance is in turn realized in many ways:

> From recycling to, we try to go as much electric as we can, try to stay away from petroleum products. There's a lot of little things that we do. Say downed trees for instance. We put vegetable oil in the chainsaws to cut up the branches and whatnot. We try to take all the branches that have come down and we chip them and recycle them back into the golf course and pathways and we try and, it's almost like a cycle, trying to keep everything healthy and hand it off to another generation where it's [in a] a great place and healthy. (Personal interview, September 2011)

Similar to our interviewee at Blackburn Meadows, one of the employees we spoke with at New Malton organic golf course in the UK saw the anti-chemical side of organic golf as part of a broader effort to be environmentally and (in this case) socially sustainable:

> Organic courses [involve] purely no chemicals whatsoever ... [But organic, for us, also means] self-sufficiency, it's about creating a good junior section, allowing everyone to play golf whether you're male, female, junior, disabled, whatever, you know. (Personal interview, July 2012)

Another New Malton employee noted the role that golf courses can play as wildlife sanctuaries:

> Ecology-wise, it doesn't matter what you think about the organics, whether you believe in it, or whether you believe it works, the ecology side of it, you can do it on any golf course. I'm not saying you can go on the scale we've gone to, because we have got acres and acres for the wildlife. See those areas there [points to an area on the course] are fantastic for wildlife. Not every golf course can do that – they haven't got the spare land to do it. But every hole [on most courses] has an area where the golfers don't have to go, or won't go. And what I'm saying to the greenkeepers is, keep that back for the wildlife. And at the end of the day, it's about sustainability, because if they're not going to look after that area, they're not gonna cut it down every week ... they're not using diesel, they're not wearing the machinery out and that relieves them to go out and do something else. They can then look after the greens for an extra half hour [rather] than basically cutting down grass, which is just destroying habitat for wildlife. So, the benefits are incredible, but it's getting a message through and this is the best way of doing it. (Personal interview, July 2012)

Taken together, this is indeed a loose assemblage of values and practices. In constructing a sense of what organic means, 'chemical-free' maintenance fits together with recycling, alternative energy, wildlife conservation, and, for New Malton, even inclusivity in terms of membership. This is not unlike how the new social movements we saw in the last chapter were quite diverse in their intentions and goals.

Underlying the organic golf movement – and we use the term 'movement' loosely, noting that the organic golf practitioners we identified in our research were not actively working together as part of an organized collective – is the idea that synthetic chemicals pose unnecessary risks, and that these risks can be avoided by those working within the golf industry. Jeff Carlson of the Vineyard (organic) Golf Club makes this point explicitly during an interview published in *Golf Digest* (Barton, 2008). His opinion here is noteworthy in that Carlson has expressed openness to both the limited uses of synthetic chemicals (for reasons outlined below), and to the idea that pesticides can be used safely.

Carlson has thus effectively moved between lighter and darker-green positions. Still, on this occasion, when asked, "If pesticides are safe, why is there a movement to use less of them?" Carlson outlined the risks accompanying any form of chemical use:

> I guess because of that absolute – because we don't know they're absolutely OK. Because I was told in the 1970s that mercury-based fungicides were safe. So, they were wrong. And maybe there are some pesticides out there that aren't good. (Barton, 2008)

This perspective aligns with our own critical reflections from the end of Chapter 5, in which we noted historical contradictions in the golf industry's defence of chemical applications. Golf industry representatives, we said at the time, have defended chemicals almost as a default position, even though such a stance looks misguided in the light of hindsight for many once-popular chemicals. Here Carlson is likewise outlining the rationale for a more precautionary approach.

Techniques and products for 'doing' organic golf

Although the techniques and products used to manage organic golf courses vary and are of course complex, we will offer a brief overview of some particularly noteworthy practices. The main aim of this section, however, is not to exhaustively describe the range of organic course management techniques that are available to those inclined to use them. Instead, our goal is to demonstrate that alternative/organic techniques are being used and developed on an ongoing basis, and to point out that although organic golf remains a work in progress, it certainly seems to be a potentially viable alternative.

With this background, then, we found that those who manage organic courses often referred to both the *cultural practices* that are used to maintain courses and the particular *organic inputs* used to deal with turfgrass-related problems. Below we identify and describe two key cultural practices:

- *Focusing on drainage and dew accumulation on courses*. This means getting rid of excess sitting water, which can lead to course damage and/or plant/insect infestation (and ice formation on courses in the winter). Choosing sites for golf courses where good drainage is possible is key here. Grass cutting and running rollers over the greens early in the morning are also useful practices for reducing sitting dew. In a presentation on the topic, Jeff Carlson mentioned 'whipping' greens (i.e. manually taking the dew off of greens) along with the use of wetting agents, which we discuss further below. (Carlson, 2010)

- *Managing micro-climates.* This means attending to the unique challenges associated with having different temperature zones on a course – a challenge linked to the mix of shade and sun exposure in different areas. Carlson noted how trees and shade are a source of problems like pythium (a.k.a. 'root rot'). He goes so far to as to suggest that the an ideal course has no trees because tree-related problems are so difficult to manage organically. (Carlson, 2010)

Other things to take into account when developing and/or maintaining an organic course include: choosing grasses that are easiest to maintain organically (according to Carlson, fescue and bentgrass are good, and the commonly used blue grass is problematic); having a compact course layout, which helps minimize overall inputs into the course; fertilizing enough to keep grasses healthy and vigorous (recognizing that too much or too little fertilizer puts grasses at risk); monitoring the pH levels of soils (high and low levels are indicators of risk); hand weeding and hand watering (instead of using inputs to kill weeds); and attending to areas of the golf course where it is not necessary to cut grass as often (e.g. where golf balls are rarely hit). In these ways, organic golf provision ideally begins from course design and follows all the way through to particular maintenance practices. The practices outlined above in many cases veer away from trends that, over time, became commonplace in the golf industry (acknowledging that some also align with the principles of 'responsible golf', as per earlier chapters). Eschewing chemicals is the most obvious example of this. The making of compact courses is another case in point. As we saw in earlier chapters, improvements in equipment over time, among other trends, have helped expand golf's occupation of land.

In addition to these sorts of on-course cultural practices, those managing organic golf courses also emphasized the need for tolerance of some visual on-course imperfections – and that education for golfers who play organic courses is needed to foster this tolerance. Carlson suggested that his goal is to maintain a high level of 'playability' on the course while (hopefully) changing the way that golfers 'see' courses – since visual imperfections are inevitable with organic care (Carlson, 2010). That said, the organic golf managers that we studied (through our interviews and document analyses) also recounted their efforts to maintain courses that were essentially indistinguishable from one treated with synthetic chemicals. Organic courses from this perspective should have no trouble competing in the crowded golf marketplace. As one of our interviewees from New Malton noted:

> The biggest compliment someone, a non-believer, can give you is [to] come in and say, "Actually, I enjoyed the course, that was good" and you say, "actually, we're organic, we use no chemicals," and they say, "really! Oh I didn't know that." And that is a massive compliment because they're comparing us with other golf courses that can use chemicals, who've got a massive advantage. (Personal interview, July 2012)

The cultural practices noted above are carried out in addition to the application of organic turfgrass products that are intended to eliminate diseases and infestations and promote healthy growth. One of the main inputs are organic 'wetting agents', aimed at helping the absorption of water into the turf, thus avoiding the above-noted problems of dew and sitting water. Carlson (2010) referred to the use of hot water and foam to control crabgrass and other weeds – which is applied using machinery developed to deliver "super-heated water from a boom or spray nozzle" (Riley, 1995: 9). As part of his discussion of wetting agents and organic inputs, Carlson also referred to experiments he is running with the support of turfgrass researcher Dr Frank Rossi of Columbia University, which focus on matters such as the alteration of potassium and nitrogen inputs as a way of dealing with turfgrass problems (Carlson, 2010). Elsewhere, the owner of the (now defunct) Grand Forks organic course in Grand Forks, British Columbia, owned and maintained by a husband and wife team who had previously run an organic vineyard in Switzerland, described their use of "organic fertilizer such as bone meal, blood meal, kelp, humate, composted turkey manure and so on", and their application of rock glacial dust to deal with grub worms (Ziemer, 2009). Our interviewees at both New Malton Golf Club and Blackburn Meadows were similarly inclined towards experimentation in fertilizing and in dealing with turfgrass-related challenges.

The inputs described above can also be complemented by the application of organic pesticides available on the market for turfgrass maintenance. The approved organic products Carlson uses and referred to in his presentation at the University of Guelph's Turfgrass Institute include applications with the brand names 'Civitas', 'Spotless', 'Ecoguard', 'Rhapsody', and 'Safe-Tea' (compost tea). Looking closer at the first of these, Civitas was formulated by Petro Canada – itself a Suncor Energy business, with Suncor said to be the first company to develop Canada's oil sands (Suncor Energy Inc., n.d.a). The aim with Civitas is evidently to strengthen turf, thus preventing insects and pathogens from taking hold in a host plant to begin with (i.e. as opposed to killing off fungus directly). This much was said in a press release from 2009 announcing Civitas' unveiling: "Unlike traditional chemical fungicides, CIVITAS is a synthetic isoparaffin-based product that works to prime the turf's genes, stimulate its natural defences and kill or inhibit fungal diseases" (Suncor Energy Inc., 2009; also see Suncor Energy Inc., n.d.b; GCSAA, n.d.g). The upshot for proponents of Civitas is that the product can in turn guard against turf diseases such as anthracnose, dollar spot, and brown patch, among others, while also protecting against insects such as cutworms and annual bluegrass weevils (Suncor Energy Inc., n.d.b). Both Civitas and the more recent product Civitas One are Organic Materials Review Institute Listed®, meaning they have been reviewed against organic standards and deemed acceptable by the Institute (see http://www.omri.org; also see Golfdom Staff, 2013). Moreover, and of significance to the wider themes of *The Greening of Golf*, Civitas was said to be the 'technological breakthrough' that golf superintendents have been waiting for upon its release. A company spokesperson added: "The science behind our product is revolutionary" (Suncor Energy Inc., 2009). Here organic golf veers into the territory of ecological modernization (EM), replete as EM is with faith in science and technology in solving environmental problems (see Chapter 2). Hence our above claim that organic golf, depending on how it is practised, can potentially blend both lighter- and darker-green sensibilities.

Different understandings of the 'organic applications' approach

Although we (unsurprisingly) found that those working on organic golf courses were generally committed to the chemical-free principles that underlie organic golf, there were different views on how strictly organic principles should be followed. On one side, those we spoke with at Blackburn Meadows and New Malton seemed especially committed to a strict application of organic principles (i.e. a 'no synthetic chemicals, no matter what' philosophy). One of our interviewees at Blackburn illuminated this position in suggesting that chemical-intensive golf is simply not feasible going forward: "most mainstream golf courses cannot continue to operate the way they are, just pumping chemicals underneath their soils, leaching it into the groundwater." (Personal interview, September 2011)

By contrast, Jeff Carlson has suggested that environmentally friendly golf course maintenance is ultimately about the activities of superintendents, and not just the ingredients used on courses. Carlson's point, which he emphasized in the presentation at Guelph's Turfgrass Institute mentioned earlier, is that the haphazard use of organic ingredients can also cause environment- and health-related problems. 'Natural' (i.e. non-synthetic) inputs can be poisonous, for example, meaning problems can ensue even when organic ingredients are put in the hands of non-experts (Carlson, 2010). These observations sit alongside Carlson's expressed view that it is 'virtually impossible' for pesticides to affect groundwater (contra the above comments from our Blackburn interviewee). Carlson has also reflected fondly on the effectiveness of chemicals in the mainstream golf industry: "I terribly miss the opportunity to be able to use an insecticide occasionally. Right now I would sell my soul for a one-time application of a pre-emergent weed control" (Barton, 2008). All told, then, and even though Carlson is himself an organic golf practitioner and advocate, his philosophy on course maintenance in general evidently cannot be distilled down to 'no synthetic chemicals, no matter what'.

Furthermore, and recognizing that chemical companies have identified the need to cater to the organic market and attempted to create products that have been approved as 'organic', it appears that those in the organic golf movement are facing questions about what can be counted as organic. As the owner of Blackburn Meadows notes:

> We have customers that as soon as they hear organic, they know [it means] no chemicals … But when you talk to industry people, fertilizer reps or whoever else, they want to know to what step of organic we're talking about, because there are those intermediate organic products and different practices. Yes, [all products] came from the earth one way or another and they're put together, so would you consider that organic? Well no, if they're changed to see better results and that sort of thing, then no, they're not necessarily organic. (Personal interview, September 2011)

While there is at least some agreement on what 'counts' as an organic golf course, it would be a stretch to suggest that anything resembling an organized organic golf 'movement' currently exists – and it is important to acknowledge here that contradictions around organic golf itself are ever present. As Carlson (2010) admits in his Guelph lecture, it is worth considering whether the costs associated with doing organic work – which, at times, require the construction and frequent usage of the new equipment – may ironically lead to an especially large environmental footprint, all in the name of maintaining an organic golf course. These are the same sorts of questions that have been asked for years of those producing organic foods and other products.

We conclude this section by highlighting an intriguing metaphor offered by the superintendent at Blackburn Meadows Golf Club to distinguish the approach taken by his course to organic golf from those managing non-organic golf courses. He used the metaphor of medicine, distinguishing his own holistic (or 'naturopathic') approach from the perceived 'pharmaceutical' approach at the industry's core. As he stated:

> The last fifty years, [we] have been educated that, "ok, this is what we do, this pasture, this weed, we apply this". It's like a doctor now, you know? All you've got is this element, you've got to use this pill, [in an] encyclopaedia, right, of pharmacology and go from there. Versus a naturopath, I mean we're the naturopath of golf courses. I look at it in a holistic manner and that's an analogy. (Personal interview, September 2011)

Of course, given the various approaches to and reasons for managing organic golf courses, it is not clear that this naturopathic metaphor would be adopted by other organic golf practitioners. Conversely, those committed to the sustainability methods associated with IPM might also identify with a holistic approach, noting that IPM also includes a range of cultural as well as chemical course management practices. Still, the naturopathic metaphor is intriguing as a way of highlighting the 'natural' and system-focused emphasis of at least some organic golf advocates. As we have seen, the military metaphor – the 'war' on pests – of the 'pro-golf' era eventually gave way to medical imagery: pesticides have at times been seen as medicine for the earth. In the Blackburn Meadows view, this 'medicine' can be relied on too heavily. Hence the need for a different 'alter-golf' solution.

Reflections on organic practices: considerations, debates, and hope

So far, we have described some of the practices and perceptions of those who manage organic golf courses and those who have a stake in organic golf's success. We highlighted a range of positions and reflected on some of the ambiguities of the 'organic movement' generally. Through our overview, a few important and stable themes emerged, including:

- *That, according to superintendents who use them, organic methods 'work'.* Moreover, as resources have been invested in testing and utilizing organic methods, further successes have been and continue to be attained. According to Carlson (2010), they especially work when it comes to the playability of golf courses.

- *That the level and type of success with organic management is context-dependent.* That is to say, it was uniformly recognized that organic management strategies are 'more or less' effective depending on many factors. These include factors related to the golf course in question itself, such as the extent to which the course has been treated with synthetic chemicals in the past and the types of grasses it features. But broader circumstances are important here too. The Vineyard organic course, for example, is primarily set in a moderate climate more favourable to organic golf than places experiencing weather extremes. Those behind the course also appear to have had greater resources at their disposal than those working at other organic sites. Maybe most significantly of all, there was heavy input from the local community, which required the course to be organic from the very outset.

- *That continuing to develop organic management techniques – and organic courses – requires time, further experimentation, and investment.* The time factor here is key, as the natural defences of grasses need time to redevelop on golf courses where synthetic pesticides have been used previously. In the same way, some applications and methods just will not work immediately. This is not to say that these methods/applications are faulty, but it does mean that the desired results may not be evident right away for reasons that are not always apparent – and that time for experimentation is important. Furthermore, and given the need for more 'on-course' work by superintendents and workers to maintain organic courses, such courses often require long hours of intensive labour.

- *That strict regulation of chemical usage can be helpful for superintendents attempting to implement a successful organic programme.* That is to say, as superintendents face pressures to maintain pristine golf courses, it would seem that in a regulated environment – where the use of organic methods that may not have immediate impacts on disease, weeds, and pests – golfers (and undoubtedly course owners who would not voluntarily 'go organic') may be more patient with and perhaps supportive of superintendents efforts, struggles, and successes. Jeff Carlson (2010) indicated that this was his experience when dealing with golfers at the highly regulated Vineyard golf course – golfers who were remarkably patient with the efforts of his course maintenance team when they understood the team's goals and tactics.

In sum then, it seems that organic golf is, technically speaking, a plausible option for course owners/superintendents. There is clear evidence that organic methods work – and also that the potential of organic golf, in terms of the knowledge and products needed to effectively manage organic courses, is only beginning to be realized. While it is unclear how golfers would respond to the aesthetic and playability adaptations that would be required of them in an organic-only environment, we would venture to suggest golfers might be quite open to such changes – especially in light of the long tradition of links-style golf that is played in more rugged conditions.

Moreover, Jeff Carlson's (2010) view that the regulations on his course were enabling in the sense that golfers became more tolerant of some variable course conditions and educated about the benefits of organic golf is instructive here as well. Namely, Carlson's experience is relevant as we consider what golfers 'could do' if public and environmental health concerns were widely known, and if organic golf was widely available (and mandated). In the same way, mandating 'organic-only' golf courses would undoubtedly inspire the development of a culture of more environmentally knowledgeable, innovative, and motivated course owners and superintendents. In fact, Carlson has specifically suggested that superintendents would likely be quite supportive of a move towards organic course management. As he states in an interview with *Golf Digest*:

> Superintendents would be totally supportive of it. I've noticed a tremendous interest in managing golf courses more organically, especially among younger superintendents. They'd do a great job. The golf courses would be terrific, but they'd have some visual blemishes. (Barton, 2008)

In citing Carlson in this way, we do of course recognize that it is presently not viable for many course owners to 'go organic' because the investment and time needed to make organic golf work might be too financially risky. Part of the problem is that 'going organic' is currently optional, which means that adopting organic methods requires investments that non-organic competitors do not have to deal with, making the endeavour especially risky in a competitive leisure industry.

On reflection then, and remembering the various risks associated with pesticides outlined in Chapter 1, we find it curious that organic golf is not taken more seriously as an option and goal for those responsible for environmental and public health-related issues. Put simply, and addressing one of the overarching questions of this book, if organic golf is generally considered to be less impactful/'risky' than 'responsible' golf, the question arises as to why organic golf is not the dominant response to golf-related environmental concerns. Why has the golf industry settled on strategies that are intended to reform the industry, but not *transform* it through more radical health- and environment-friendly measures? Why are there not more regulations in place promoting the development and adoption of organic practices, thus 'evening the playing field' for those already moving in an organic direction? In the next part of this chapter we address these sorts of questions as we consider the barriers and challenges that would seem to prevent the expansion of organic golf. We also highlight ways that existing sociological theory and research might explain the existence and persistence of these barriers and challenges.

Why hasn't organic golf caught on? Barriers and challenges

It is always difficult to know for sure why a particular set of values or practices catch on, and others do not. Acknowledging this, we think in this case there are identifiable barriers, challenges, and circumstances that make it very difficult for pro-organic golf advocates to make the sort of progress that would be needed for an organic golf movement to thrive or become the status quo.

Time, money and Augusta National syndrome

According to our interviews with superintendents working at Audubon-certified golf courses – that is, those receiving external accreditation for their attentiveness to environmental issues, though still working within the 'responsible golf' paradigm (see Chapters 5, 6 and 7) – the main barrier to going organic is the time and cost associated with maintaining a course using organic methods. The following comment from an assistant superintendent at an Audubon-certified course in British Columbia speaks to this: "I'd like to go organic, but for one, it's very expensive. Organic products don't offer a lot of nutrients usually. They're very low analysis so you have to use a lot more of them, which increases the cost" (Personal interview, October 2011).

This seems straightforward, though assessing the comment in full requires attention to the set of expectations that superintendents are faced with, specifically over the visual aesthetic and perceived playability of their courses. We are of course referring here, again, to the Augusta National ideal – the perhaps unrealistic standard set by the course that hosts the annual Masters tournament. Jeff Carlson makes this point in his interview in *Golf Digest*, recounting a story whereby a tee box he was assessing measured near perfectly in terms of insect damage and disease. The visual appearance of the tee, however, would suggest to an outsider that the course superintendent could be fired for poor performance. Carlson's point is that the standard of success for a golf course is extremely high; he names Augusta National specifically in recounting this story (see Barton, 2008).

To be sure, not all courses are the same, and many courses owners and superintendents will have differing expectations depending on their target market, competition, and resources. Still, it is not a stretch to suggest that for many golf course superintendents, and for seemingly most of those working on higher-end tourist-oriented courses, this expectation is standard.

The organic golf movement is still 'finding its voice'

As we noted in the previous chapter, there are various reasons that some social movements succeed and others fail. It is similarly important to acknowledge that it can take time for movements that eventually become successful to 'find their voice' – to mobilize the right kind and right amount of resources, at the right moment, and in the right circumstances. Social historian Eric Hobsbawn made a similar point many years ago, when describing how particular groups are 'pre-political', referring to the idea that those working in a movement often need time to "find a language to express themselves and their concerns, to prepare themselves for active engagement with politics" (Wilson, 2012b: 85). Of course, even if a movement becomes more organized, this does not ensure that it will achieve its goals, or that it will avoid internal divisions that inhibit its success. Still, to become more organized means that particular steps need be taken.

It was clear from our research that the organic golf movement is still 'finding its voice' in the sense that those engaged in organic care – the superintendents and course owners who are taking leadership through local course management activities – have not banded together and have not articulated or promoted any kind of unified vision. This is not to say that this will not happen or that progress has been totally elusive to date. In fact, those we interviewed expressed an interest in moving ahead with a collective vision of organic golf at some point. They have also taken some steps towards promoting organic golf to public audiences. The following comments are evidence of this:

> I definitely feel like we're leaders in this and that we have to continue to lead and educate as well. There's just been a lot on the plate this year but in the year or two to come we'd like to integrate more with, and connect more with other golf courses and recreation, on a similar path. We have to, it's only going to help everyone and help ourselves and increase our knowledge base. (Owner, Blackburn Meadows Golf Club; Personal interview, September 2011)

> In the last 12 years there's been numerous occasions that we've been featured in media or [been] of interest for magazines and things like that. I think it's important for people to hear once in a while, you know, that there's a golf course doing this sort of thing. So yeah, I think we are part of the organic movement and have established ourselves in the industry that way, with certain groups and certain people in the golf course maintenance industry … they know what we're all about and they know not to push things they shouldn't on us and that's, that's what we want to see. We don't want someone coming and pushing chemicals on us, we want them to know that we are organic and we're standing strong on that and so in that fashion. Yes, we are I'd say a strong part of that movement. (Superintendent, Blackburn Meadows Golf Club; Personal interview, September 2011)

The suggestion here that the organic work taking place at Blackburn Meadows is part of the broader organic movement is certainly relevant in the sense that this broader movement might be a resource to help lend credibility to and facilitate the growth of organic golf. Process-wise, this is akin in many respects to the linkages that local anti-golf resistance movements attempted to forge with global environmental and human rights-related movements – and, at times, with the far-reaching Global Anti-Golf Movement as well. It is relevant too that the owners of (the now defunct) Grand Forks organic golf course came to organic golf after a career working with organic wine vineyards in Switzerland.

Similarly, interviewees at New Malton discussed how organic golf has attained more credibility over the years from its indirect linkages with other sport-related organic ventures:

> I think seventy percent of football pitches [in the UK], I think it's seventy percent, are actually organic … It's funny, in football, because players are worth so much, talking about millions of pounds obviously, they're now worried about injuries. So if they pick up an injury with an open wound, and there's chemicals on the floor, and it's infected or something happens, a reaction, it could put a player out of work … It will cost them a lot of money. And again, these football pitches are going organic, not because they're interested in organics and want to do it, want to save money. It's because they're being forced into doing it because they're worried about being sued by the players and by other teams. … It's getting

the ball moving. You know, that could turn out to be one of the best things ever. If football turns organic, then, how many football fans in this country? Millions of them. Most popular sport in the world, in England I think. That movement's there. It'll help. But what I'm saying is, it'd be nice for a sport or a company to want to do it like we do, rather than feel that they have to. That's what'll happen. It'll take someone that has to do it in golf, forced to do it to get them to do it. (Golf professional and course worker, New Malton Golf Club; Personal interview, June 2012)

Ultimately, and acknowledging this guarded optimism, it was evident that those we interviewed were using most of their time and resources to keep their organic golf courses afloat. To do much more than this without additional resources would seem unlikely in the near future. Moreover, the fact that the two organic courses we were aware of in British Columbia, Canada folded since we began our study – including Blackburn Meadows – would seem to confirm that promoting the broader organic golf movement would be a secondary concern for those running these courses. So, while the success of the organic golf movement generally and the success of individual organic courses are likely to be, in the long run, interrelated, recognizing this does not provide much assistance to those dealing with immediate economic issues.

Another potential barrier along these lines could be the existence of differing viewpoints on the need to completely ban synthetic chemicals from golf courses – remembering how Jeff Carlson's stance on synthetic chemicals slightly differed from the position taken by those at Blackburn Meadows and New Malton. Of course, these sorts of nuanced differences are common to social movements of all kinds and can ultimately lead to fractioning and internal dissent (Wilson, 2012b). The organic golf movement, however, has apparently not developed to the point that these sorts of questions have been discussed among movement members.

Golf's 'integrated circus'

What has not been mentioned so far are the broader set of structures and reasons that striving for Augusta National-like conditions remains desirable – and why 'doing what it takes' (perhaps using synthetic pesticides) to maintain such an aesthetic is generally favoured despite the risks it brings into play. A related question is why the organic movement would face such difficulty when organic golf seems to makes so much sense for environmental and public health-inspired reasons.

One potential explanation is that organic golf poses a threat to those who are an integral part of the economic interrelationships between the golf industry, the chemical industry, the global tourism industry and many governments. The idea that a set of highly integrated and economically motivated relationships would be difficult to break – and that 'alternative' and seemingly less profitable possibilities would be trivialized by those with a vested interest in the status quo – would not be surprising for sociologists like Whitson and Gruneau (1997). Whitson and Gruneau have observed how power and influence are generated and secured when different sport-related industries sharing economic goals work together to achieve these goals as part of what they refer to as sport's 'integrated circus' (following Marchak, 1993). Whitson and Gruneau are specifically attuned to relationships between media conglomerates, sport franchises, and corporate sponsors, exploring how such linkages lead to the hyper-promotion of products (e.g. beer – think Coors baseball field in Colorado) and various media technologies and services (think Rogers Centre in Toronto, which hosts gridiron football, baseball, and other events).

Yet a similar logic can be applied in the case of golf. Consider, for example, that pristine and predictable golf experiences that are enabled by chemical applications on courses are thought to support a global golf tourist industry – and that such tourism is beneficial for local economies and their governments (or, at least, is imagined as beneficial in this way). Likewise, the close ties between the golf and chemical industries is a key factor in this regard. Beyond the use of chemicals on golf courses, chemical companies are among the key donors to the GCSAA's Environmental Institute for Golf (EIFG), as noted in Chapter 5.

The point here is that even if members of the golf industry were interested in decoupling from the chemical or tourism industries, this would seem to be a financially risky proposition. Not only would it be difficult to replace existing sponsors, but the risk of losing paying golfers to courses that continue along the chemical-friendly route would likely, for many in the industry, be considered too high. For governments that have the decision-making power to make across-the-board decisions to ban cosmetic pesticides, this might also be considered too politically risky for their liking – recognizing that if golfers did indeed 'stay home' because golf courses were not (literally) green enough, there would undoubtedly by negative backlash from the leisure and tourism industries. There would also, of course, be direct economic implications for governments too – recognizing the increased strain on the public purse associated with replacing voluntary regulatory mechanisms with more direct and stringent ones.

Of course, there are also risks associated with *not* taking a more precautionary regulatory approach, though these risks fall under the banner of environmental and public health and not economics. In the end, it would seem unlikely that governments working with an 'environmental managerialist' sensibility, as per Chapter 7, would stand firmly behind the organic golf movement unless an especially compelling pro-organic golf lobby were to emerge.

Undermining the treadmill, embracing science? Final reflections on the organic golf movement

Although the organic response to golf-related environmental problems has its own issues and challenges, there were many aspects of the movement that we found quite promising. Perhaps more than anything, we were impressed with the eclectic and creative approach to dealing with concerns about chemicals. What we mean by this is that the organic golf pioneers we studied were, on the one hand, open to solutions to turfgrass issues that derived from their own experimentation with non-synthetic fertilizers and applications. This 'science and technology' approach to dealing with on-course problems – problems that have commonly been dealt with using synthetic pesticides – would certainly seem to align with the principles that underlie an ecological modernist response to environmental problems. In this sense, organic golf leaders are not out of step with their mainstream counterparts in pursuing solutions through experimentation and innovation.

At the same time, conversely, these organic golf leaders were adopting anti-chemical practices that are transformative in the sense that they destabilize the integrated circus at the core of the 'chemical industry–golf industry' relationship. One interviewee from New Malton in 2012 made this point in stark terms: "If you think about the implication of what we're doing here, if I'm right [about the viability of organic golf], then we don't need a chemical industry." Organic golf in this sense is mounting a challenge to mainstream responsible golf, what with its lasting fondness for pesticides. At the very least, organic golf disrupts golf's chemical supply chain (though without discarding the innovative aspects of an EM-driven approach). At most, as per our New Malton interviewee, this supply chain will eventually become altogether obsolete.

To return a final time to our PAAR continuum (see Figure 1 from Chapter 2), the practices and perspectives described in this chapter implicitly, and at times explicitly, call into question the post-political consensus of responsible golf. Post-politics rest on the notion that a particular solution – in this case, an ecological modernist one – is the only viable solution in a given context. Recognizing the many barriers and challenges faced by the purveyors of organic golf – Blackburn Meadows has shut its doors since our research began – advocates of 'alter-golf' are at the very least putting an alternative, transformative model of golf provision 'on the table' for consideration. This is the best (and in some respects the only) example we encountered of a transformative, but still golf-friendly, response to golf's environmental impacts. GAGM and the local golf protests described in Chapter 8 belong on our spectrum as well, but these are anti-golf responses (as GAGM's name makes clear) in that they call for the blockage of golf course developments and/or the elimination of golf altogether.

What is ultimately perhaps most interesting about organic golf is its place within golf's historical trajectory. We noted above that hand weeding and hand watering can be considered part of the organic superintendent's ('naturopathic') toolkit – acknowledging that organic golf can also employ heavy machinery depending on the superintendent's preferences and budget. In this regard, we are brought back to the image of the basket- and fork-wielding superintendent, as described in 1916 in the trade publication *The Golf Course* (see Chapter 3).

In theoretical terms, in earlier chapters we assessed golf's post-war Promethean inclination through the lens of the 'treadmill of production'. The treadmill is an economic change theory highlighting how, in industrial pursuits, human labour power gives way to mechanical labour power, yielding higher profit margins and further investment in mechanical tools. Of course, all of this often comes with heightened environmental impact as well – for example, when the golf industry shifted from course maintenance by hand to course maintenance by DDT and broad-based spraying equipment. To some extent, organic golf puts the treadmill in reverse. Golf returns to its pre-modern roots.

In the next and final chapter of this book, we reflect on the place of organic golf in the sport's potential 'utopian' future.

PART V
Conclusion

10

Reflections, recommendations, and minor utopian visions for a game we love

In 2008, the magazine *Golf Digest* published a special feature on 'golf and environmental issues' that included an interview with Brent Blackwelder, a Duke University golf team alumnus who went on to become president of the American branch of the environmental non-governmental organization Friends of the Earth. To conclude the interview, Blackwelder was asked, "What would golf be like in a perfect world?" He responded as follows:

> You'd be playing on an organic course. The maintenance equipment would be charged by solar power. Recycled water would be used for irrigation, and used efficiently and sparingly. There'd be a great variety of wildlife habitats. This idea that you've got to make everything look like a miniature golf course with a green carpet is crazy. It's the same problem that we see with these lawn fetishes – all the water and chemicals and energy that are used for a lawn that just sits there. So let's get back to the rugged qualities of the game. People ought to read the history of golf. (Quoted in Barton, 2008)

We have referred to this *Golf Digest* special issue at other points in this book, given that it includes candid interviews with key figures in and around the golf industry such as course superintendent Jeff Carlson, course architect Mike Hurdzan, and pesticide activist Jay Feldman. At this point in our analysis, we see Blackwelder's idea of what golf 'could be' as particularly provocative and valuable. Most of all, Blackwelder's vision of golf's (organic) future can be seen as a step towards unsettling established wisdom on golf's relationship with the environment in a '*radical but non-partisan*' and '*utopian but realistic*' way. It is radical because it suggests a transformational response to golf-related environmental problems: to carry out Blackwelder's vision would mean to undermine existing relationships between the chemical industry and golf industry, thus upending a major profit-oriented and corporate-driven relationship. This is not insignificant if we remember the relationships currently in place between the chemical industry, the golf industry, and governments, as outlined in Chapters 5, 6, and 7. At the same time, while Blackwelder is critical of the culture and incentive systems that underlie the ongoing drive for pristine golf courses, we also see Blackwelder's vision as non-partisan in the sense that he is also embracing the pro-environment innovations that emerge from the development of new technologies (e.g. solar powered maintenance equipment). In one short passage, then, Blackwelder offers an assessment of golf that is in line with a critical 'treadmill of production' perspective *and* reflects the faith in technological innovation favoured by advocates of 'responsible golf' and ecological modernization. This is a vision of environmentally friendly golf that appears to be relatively unclouded by a commitment to any particular ideological stance. It brings together perspectives on our environmental future generally considered to be incompatible.[1]

We also think Blackwelder's response is thoughtful in the sense that it is sensitive to the contexts within which the golf industry currently exists and the contexts from which it evolved. In fact, Blackwelder's vision reminds us in some ways of C. Wright Mills classic book *The Sociological Imagination* – a book that included Mills' argument that rigorous sociological analysis requires 'historical and comparative sensitivity'. What Mills (1959) was suggesting was that being sensitive to different social and historical contexts *makes it easier for sociologists to see and show why the institutional arrangements that we take for granted – arrangements that seem unchangeable, even 'natural' – are much easier to modify, even transform, than might seem apparent on the surface*. In this case, Blackwelder 'imagined' a time in history when chemical-aided golf was not the status quo. This would seem to imply that there is nothing 'natural' about golf's present-day status quo and that, as such, what we have called responsible golf need not remain hegemonic going forward. Furthermore, and by implicitly comparing chemical-intensive golf to organic golf, Blackwelder is drawing attention to the fact that another kind of golf – a more environmentally friendly version of golf – is not only possible, but it exists (albeit not in the exact form Blackwelder describes).

Ultimately, we would argue that Blackwelder's vision is reminiscent of what historian Jay Winter (2006) calls a 'minor Utopia'. For Winter, to seek a minor Utopia does not mean to attempt to create a 'perfect' situation – since attempts to seek perfection (what he calls a 'major Utopia') are unrealistic and can be quite dangerous (remembering here, for example, the utopian projects of Nazi Germany). Instead, Winter describes minor Utopias as "partial transformations" and "steps on the way to less violent and less unjust societies" (Winter, 2006: 208).

In a similar way, sociologist Erik Olin Wright (2007, 2010) has argued that it is important to visualize what the world 'could be like' and to identify instances where versions of what he calls 'Real Utopias" already exist. The idea here is that 'social dreaming' of this sort is a crucial step towards the attainment of the radical social and environmental changes needed at the contemporary moment (see Claeys and Tower Sargent, 1999). Wright further suggests that effectively visualizing, and ultimately realizing, some version of a Real Utopia requires an initial assessment and critique of existing institutional arrangements. Only then, with a better understanding of existing problems, does it make sense to try social and environmental experiments that are intended to create a more equitable and sustainable world. As he states:

> To be a radical critic of existing institutions and social structures is to identify harms that are generated by existing arrangements, to formulate alternatives which mitigate those harms, and to propose transformative strategies for realizing those alternatives. (Wright, 2007: 26)

Wright uses the metaphor of a pond to help us think about how a dominant 'ecosystem' (e.g. responsible golf) might begin to change when the pond is exposed to 'alien species' (e.g. chemical-free golf). He argues that thinking of society as an ecosystem where "everything is interdependent, but interactions do not constitute a tightly functionalized totality" can also help us imagine alternatives and inspire hope for change (Wright, 2013: 9). His point is that an ecosystem can be transformed by introducing "an alien species that initially finds a niche and then gradually displaces certain other species" (Wright, 2013: 9). While Wright recognizes that there are never guarantees about the positive results of such experiments – new/alien species often die or are eliminated – the idea is that attempts to offer alternatives and inspire thinking about what is possible are crucial if we have any hope of triggering radical social and cultural changes.

Inspired by Blackwelder's vision for golf going forward and by academic conceptions of 'utopian' possibilities, we spend this final chapter reviewing golf's environmental past and present – and thinking with some imagination about its future. Initially, we offer an overview of what we see as the main findings that emerged from our research, as presented over the course of this book. Following this, we present a set of recommendations that are intended to inspire concrete thinking about how to promote healthier and more ethical relationships between the golf industry and its numerous stakeholders – paying particular attention, of course, to environmental issues. As you would expect from reading to this point, the list of stakeholders we are concerned with in making these recommendations is quite lengthy. It includes the multitude of people who golf or who live near or work on golf courses, people generally concerned with the health- and environment-related impacts of practices such as pesticide spraying; and – not to be forgotten – the voiceless flora and fauna impacted by golf's occupation of land. In this chapter, we intend therefore to offer suggestions for translating the problems and opportunities we identified through our research into concrete actions, and thus into social and cultural changes – and then, even further, into 'minor' or 'real' golf Utopias. With Wright's vision of the pond in mind, our goal is to consider how the dominant ecosystems in and around golf might be altered through interventions that are both smaller and larger in scope. Finally, we conclude this chapter by acknowledging the many relevant topics and issues we were unable or chose not to pursue in this book. At this time we also outline an agenda for future research on golf, the environment, and globalization.

The greening of golf: a summary of key findings

Below we outline the main findings that emerged during our research. These findings shed light on the 'greening of golf' across the twentieth and early twenty-first century and, by our assessment, lingering concerns and nascent possibilities pertaining to the golf industry's relationship with the environment.

Finding 1: Members of the golf industry have embraced environmentalism, especially since the late 1970s

It is perhaps easy to overlook this finding, given that the past two chapters centred on radical responses to golf-related environmental questions (organic golf and anti-golf protests) and given that we ourselves highlighted lingering issues with responsible golf. Yet our analysis in Chapters 5, 6 and 7 indeed identified important changes in the golf industry, as well as an overall shift from a pro-golf (i.e. Promethean) position marked by denialism on environmental matters to a 'responsible', ecological modernist position that situates the environment as a crucial matter of concern. IPM, for example, while still a source of consternation for some, marks a point of departure from an earlier time when golf courses were allegedly 'plastered' with synthetic chemicals – the spectre of Augusta National syndrome a driving force. The education and certification programmes adopted by organizations such as the GCSAA are, in principle, steps towards improved environmental outcomes.

Finding 2: There are limits to the 'green' sensibilities of those representing the mainstream golf industry

A common refrain for activists and environmental groups is that minimizing pesticide exposure (as per IPM) is still not precautionary enough. Our introductory chapter highlighted research suggesting that synthetic chemicals still pose risks, even if these risks are not quite as clear or as pressing as they were in the case of products such as DDT.

What a historical analysis – the likes of which we have undertaken – reveals is how the golf industry has come to defend synthetic chemicals almost as a default position over time (recognizing the occasional presence of counter-hegemonic views as well). As we said in Chapter 5, the golf industry has seemingly known the answer – pesticides are needed – before the question is even asked. The close relationship between the chemical and golf industries is not irrelevant in this regard, with the former helping the latter by, for example, lending financial support to the Environmental Institute for Golf.

The 'limits' on the greening of golf also pertain to the economic growth agenda that, understandably, is cherished by industry representatives. The desire to build new golf courses at a rapid pace is one that dates back at least a century. What it means in a time of responsible golf, however, is that the efficiencies won through precision irrigation, among other tactics, are potentially offset by golf's expansionary imperative (which includes a desire for global expansion). Does it truly matter that golf courses can be watered with greater efficiency when new courses can, at the same time, be built on Sites of Special Scientific Interest, as in Menie, Scotland?

Finding 3: In a time of responsible golf, appearing 'green' is just as important as being 'green'

Chapter 6 showed that professionalization in the golf industry in North America has meant enhancing educational programmes and devising formal mechanisms for liaising with the public and with governments. Of course, it is perfectly acceptable for an industry to develop in this way. The concern that arises, however, is when internal and external messaging are at odds. We cited the rather candid reflections of former GCSAA President Timothy O'Neill in making this point: "Existing environmental data is limited and not complete, uniform or centralized. *Information provided to the media, government and industry often is inaccurate or misleading.* This is not a healthy state of affairs" (O'Neill, 2006: 13, emphasis added).

Finding 4: Governments have responded in kind to the golf industry's leadership on environmental matters

This is the realization of post-politics: whereas industry has become more responsible in managing the environment and developing mechanisms for communicating their ethos of responsibility, governments (in Canada especially) have been keen to accept industry leadership in a wider context where volunteerism has emerged as a key environmental policy instrument. The 'consensus' that this is the best way forward rests on the alleged balancing of economic and environmental priorities – though from a critical perspective (one evinced, for example, by a government committee formed to review pesticide legislation in Canada in the year 2000), regulatory systems of this kind tilt the balance between economic and environmental sustainability to the side of the former. In other words, and as Hannigan (2006) says in describing the notion of 'environmental managerialism', governments are apt to create policies and oversight systems that gesture towards environmental protection while in fact privileging industry's economic well-being. The outcome in the case of Ontario's ostensibly stringent Cosmetic Pesticides Ban Act is a situation whereby those contesting cosmetic pesticide legislation in the courtroom in the past are now themselves involved in systems of environmental oversight.

Finding 5: Local and global 'anti-golf' movements have emerged over time, with varying goals and varying levels of success

Said otherwise, the 'light-green' post-political consensus described in Chapters 5–7 of this book has not been readily accepted by all. The most radical response to golf's post-war development – including its global expansion – is GAGM, which questions the merits of tactics such as IPM and calls for golf courses to be abolished. More local 'anti-golf' responses question golf course development projects within *particular* contexts. In Chapter 8, we featured the Tripping up Trump movement as a case in point – one that was successful in some modest ways, though ultimately failed in the task of blocking Donald Trump's course construction project on an environmental SSSI.

Finding 6: 'Organic golf' has gained some traction and publicity as an alternative to responsible golf, though there are barriers that currently prevent organic golf from becoming a more mainstream option

These barriers include: the overall cost of maintaining an organic golf course that can compete (on an aesthetic level especially, and to a certain extent playability level) with non-organic courses; a lack of organization among organic golf advocates; a lack of support from the broader golf industry; and a reluctance on the part of many governments to mandate chemical-free golf. Difficulties faced by organic golf advocates are also no doubt a reflection of the difficulties faced by the golf industry more generally – an industry that has struggled in the recent recession years to remain profitable in particular areas (although the industry continues to expand in other areas). It is also well known that maintaining an organic golf course comes with unique challenges dependent on the geographic context in which the course is situated, with moderate climates being preferable.

Nonetheless, if we revisit our PAAR continuum (see Figure 1 from Chapter 2), organic golf presents us with an 'alter-golf' response that is different from that preferred by the mainstream golf industry. Organic golf is *transformative* in that it effectively seeks to disentangle the golf and chemical industries. In Chapter 9, we suggested that organic golf to some extent returns the sport of golf to its roots – for example, in privileging 'pre-modern' tactics such as hand weeding. Organic golf might also undermine Augusta National syndrome – the 'illness' whereby consumers come to expect playing conditions on par with those at Augusta National Golf Club, home of the Master's tournament – in the sense that on-course 'blemishes' are not deemed grounds for synthetic chemical applications. That said, it is noteworthy in this regard that one representative from an organic golf course told us that he hoped consumers would fail to distinguish between his course and a non-organic alternative.

Seeking 'minor Utopias': recommendations for a greener and more ethical golf culture

These six findings form the central narrative of *The greening of golf*. With these findings in mind, we now offer a set of recommendations for changing current environment-related practices as they pertain to golf – recommendations that are driven by our ultimate concern with environmental and public health. These recommendations are responses to the problems and opportunities for change that emerged from our research.

Recommendation 1: Move towards a 'phased in' ban on the use of cosmetic non-organic chemicals on all golf courses

Although there are various ways of inspiring behavioural and cultural change, we think that elected officials who have been mandated to work in the best interest of those they represent – which means attending to environmental and public health concerns – should be compelled to ban non-essential pesticide use across the board, as this is the most straightforward strategy for creating change. Such bans of chemical usage, guided by and justified through a precautionary approach to environmental and public health, are becoming commonplace, as we noted in Chapter 7. In the same chapter we also argued that the reasons for exempting golf courses from such bans are, in our view, uncompelling and problematic; hence our recommendation.

This recommendation is obviously aimed at governments (e.g. provincial governments in Canada) that centre their chemical-use policies on reducing cosmetic chemical applications on golf courses, but not eliminating them. Our suggestion is inspired by lawmakers in Denmark who recently developed binding regulations aimed at phasing out chemical usage on golf courses over time (Beyond Pesticides, 2011; also see R&A, 2013). This approach ostensibly recognizes the difficult challenge the golf industry faces in changing now well-established course maintenance practices, while also offering a clear statement that radical change in the name of environmental and public health is the most precautionary way forward.

In making this suggestion, we are advocating for what we call 'rear-view mirror' policy making as a way of guiding public policy away from mistakes of the past. As noted throughout this book, when governments take an 'environmental managerialist' approach, they create policies and structures that are favourable to industry, and, in theory, to economic growth. To use a car metaphor, they see mainly through the windshield to what lies ahead economically, and rely heavily on industry-produced knowledge (e.g. on the risks associated with chemicals) as the engine to propel them forward. Indeed, debates over pesticides tend to centre on scientific claims regarding their safety (or, at least, their 'riskiness'), with chemical advocates and critics advancing evidence in support of their respective causes.

We do not suggest that chemical research is irrelevant by any means, but we do contend that historical insights should be more heavily weighted in deciding future policy directions. When it comes to golf and the environment, there are three germane points that this 'rear-view mirror' approach unveils. First, and as one of our respondents from an organic course pointed out, the use of turfgrass chemicals is a relatively new phenomenon – for centuries golf courses fared quite well without their use. A turn to chemical-free golf, then, is in fact then a *return* to an older style of course management. Second, the time period from the late 1960s to the present is marked by growing public scrutiny over the necessity of chemicals, and, indeed, by the reduced usage of chemicals on many noteworthy golf courses. The logical conclusion of these trends is to ultimately excise chemicals completely, even if this takes some time to achieve. The long arc of golf's pesticide usage – from a time of helicopter-aided DDT spraying in the 1960s to IPM's *de jure* guidelines for restrained pesticide usage in the present moment – points in the direction of outright elimination of synthetic chemicals from golf courses anyway. Third, and most important, a historical view reveals that the science surrounding turfgrass products is always in flux, for the chemicals deemed 'unrisky' at one point (e.g. DDT in the 1960s and 1970s) are sometimes later revealed to be more toxic than once thought. This means that even the precautionary principle favoured by environmentalists might not be stringent enough, since proving the absolute safety of chemicals (required under this principle) is perhaps impossible. Based on our interviews with golf course superintendents, we recognize the stresses that would come from an immediate excising of turfgrass chemicals from golf course management; we thus suggest that the Danish model and its gradual phasing out of chemicals stands as a useful template for other governments. Indeed, even if the 'sunsetting' of pesticides has an 'end by' date far in the distance, it would expedite the process of finding innovative management solutions. In other words, an impending ban of this kind would direct the incredible resourcefulness, innovation, and empirical wherewithal of individuals such as golf superintendents towards fully precautionary measures, as opposed to achieving the seemingly impossible standard of Augusta National syndrome.

Of course, we remain attentive to the very real impediments to achieving policy changes. For example, and as the Standing Committee formed in the Canadian House of Commons in 2000 pointed out, those with decision-making power often have a vested interest in maintaining the status quo. Our decision to lead with this recommendation is a way of inspiring a revisiting of the arguments offered by the Standing Committee, since the suggestion made by this committee to dissolve conflicts of interest in environmental regulation is as relevant today as it was at the time it was made.

To be sure, we cannot know with complete certainty the impacts of this sort of policy change. What we do know, however, is that those who are compelled to use chemicals on golf courses for fear of losing customers (and perhaps for fear of losing their jobs) are unlikely to engage in voluntary non-chemical experiments any time soon, even if the potential benefits of a successful transition to an organic course are recognized. The economic stakes, it would seem, are too high unless the playing field is levelled (at least when it comes to chemical versus non-chemical courses) through an across-the-board ban.

With Wright's metaphor of 'the pond' in mind, we suggest that introducing a non-chemical mandate to golf's ecosystem would be most likely to result in an adaptation that would, over time, be scarcely noticeable. Ironically, and given the results of other scenarios that might play out *without* such a mandate, there is little risk for government here – noting that the chemical industry will undoubtedly adapt to this new scenario, as they are already doing through the production of organic inputs.

Recommendation 2: To support recommendation 1, begin an education campaign and website called 'Seeing Golfscapes Differently' that features outstanding chemical-free golf courses around the world that do not conform to the 'pristine and predictable' image associated with Augusta National

We think the Seeing Golfscapes Differently project would be an excellent venue for the promotion of organic golf courses especially – and could perhaps be considered a strategy for inspiring more superintendents and owners who are 'close to organic' to make a full transition to this end point.[2] The idea here would be to demonstrate what is possible when it comes to offering alternative forms of aesthetically pleasing chemical-free golf and to inspire local golfers to seek out these alternatives. The goal is not to promote global tourism, which comes with its own travel-related environmental issues – although we recognize that this could be an unintended consequence of this initiative. We appreciate the paradoxes embedded in this last point, since while we would hope that these courses would be economically viable by catering to local golfers (thereby reducing their environmental footprint), we recognize that global golf tourism aids with the issue of economic viability.

Recommendation 3: Until a chemical ban is fully instituted, require every golf course to prominently post on its website and scorecard a list of 'ingredients' that are used on the course

This would feature a list of chemical inputs, with direct links from this list to the website of a non-partisan health organization that describes each chemical and its potential risks (e.g. the World Health Organization, or government-based websites reviewed by impartial experts on chemical risk assessments). The ingredients would also list the amount of water used on the course and the source from which water is derived. This information would also be linked to a non-partisan website that offers information about best practices in terms of water usage, and a list of risks and concerns. Indeed, the Cosmetic Pesticides Ban Act in Ontario already requires golf courses to list their chemical usage online, though we doubt that many golfers in fact access this information.

Recommendation 4: Place higher priority on community voices in the decision to build golf courses in the first place

Even if golf were to become fully organic, there would still be environmental issues for industry members to contemplate. In theory, Donald Trump might have pledged that his course in Menie, Scotland would be chemical free ahead of its development. Even so, it is unlikely that this would have satisfied community residents concerned for the sand dunes along Scotland's shoreline, deemed a SSSI.

There are surely many cases where golf courses are built only after community dialogue. Indeed, this recommendation stems from the making of the Vineyard organic golf course whose chemical-free ethos was built on the back of community demands (see Chapter 9). In making this recommendation, we also have in mind Harvey Neo's (2010) research on golf in Singapore, and specifically his finding that the integration of multiple stakeholders in dialogue on golf course development is not always as effective as it seems on the surface. The taken-for-granted starting point (or post-political consensus) that a golf course will in fact be built can undermine more radical perspectives. Still, there is a need to address environmental issues beyond chemical usage on golf courses, such as the occupation of green space that comes with an expansionary industry agenda. Giving agency to communities is a potential solution in this regard, and speaks to our vision of 'contextual golf' outlined below.

Championing the local and the political: seeking contextual golf in a globalizing world

All told, we view these recommendations as modest in nature: environmental issues are incredibly complex – made more so in contexts where economic growth is the highest of priorities – and so we see small steps and 'minor Utopias' as the only way forward. The spirit underlying these suggestions is that the range of actors involved in addressing golf-related environmental issues can and should be made as diverse as possible, and that the range of *possible outcomes* can and should be diversified as well. Both caveats are important. The rejoinder to this 'spirit' might be that multiple actors are already involved in environmental decision-making as it pertains to golf. For example, both environmental groups and the EPA participated in the making of the 'Environmental Principles for Golf Courses in the United States' in the mid-1990s (see Chapter 7). Still, as articulated above and throughout this book, we see limits on the extent to which 'green' initiatives can be adopted: this is a time where 'light-green' responses reign in the end. The golf industry's innovativeness in constructing and managing golf courses is most welcome, but we do not see the golf industry itself as best positioned to 'lead' the transformational changes that are needed in achieving a precautionary, chemical-free version of golf. Indeed, and following Robbins (2007), even though individuals such as golf superintendents are on the surface 'acting freely' – for example, in *choosing* to apply chemicals – there are also pressures to 'submit fully' to the ethereal but ever-present and powerful demands of a network of industries (or 'integrated circus', as per Chapter 9). The problem here is that the 'freedom to choose' to *not* use chemicals is often not really a viable choice. This is part of the reason that we have expressed empathy across this book for golf superintendents who must grapple with Augusta National syndrome while also accounting for their own green sensibilities.

But many of those elected to government positions are not subjects in this system in the same way as golf superintendents or others working in the golf industry. And although we recognize that governments have their own dual incentive system, whereby environmental and economic concerns must be dealt with simultaneously, we see 'environmental managerialism' as comparatively easier to overcome. At the very least, and in theory, governments are accountable to the public in ways that private businesses are not – thus targeting those who are ultimately mandated to deal with environmental concerns would seem to be the best use of resources.

Underlying these recommendations too is an acknowledgement that in some geographical locations and environmental conditions, discontinuing a golf course or choosing not to develop a new one should be considered the best option available. Playing golf is not a human right. It is a luxury and is only one way to be physically active, enjoy a leisure experience, and/or make a living. With this in mind, why would we take any chemical-related risks to maintain a golf course? Why should excessive water use on any course be acceptable?

What we are calling for, therefore, is contextual golf – the existence of golf courses only in circumstances where the sort of organic golf outlined by Blackwelder is environmentally and economically feasible – and a 'championing of the local'. We say this because we think the pressures associated with the modernization and globalization of golf – pressures to offer predictable leisure experiences for global tourists – are challenged when an ethics of environmental precaution is prioritized. This is also a 'championing of the political' (as opposed to the post-political) in the sense that questioning the viability of golf in particular contexts would lead to important and *contentious* debates. Our view is that reintroducing contentious debates about golf and environmental issues is important and necessary, and is reflective of a highly democratic and open (i.e. not foreclosed) political context. This is much different from a context where the most important decisions about how to deal with key sustainability-related issues are already made before consultation that effectively involves 'ironing out the details'. In fact, we think that openness to the notion that building or maintaining a golf course can be a bad idea also creates space for alternative recreational options that might be more inclusive and more socially and environmentally sustainable than golf is at present. Consider frisbee golf – an activity that is less reliant on space and does not require pristine settings. We find this alternative especially intriguing considering that frisbee golf courses have emerged on some former golf courses, including courses that have been left to grow over, and thus left for use by those not requiring a manicured space.

Golf, globalization, and the future

In the first chapter of this book, we indicated that our analysis herein was designed to make a contribution to the nascent research area known as critical golf studies – a body of literature that is just beginning to account for the range of golf-related issues noted above, among others. Our hope is that future research in this area will continue to explore topics examined in the preceding chapters while also assessing the linkages between these topics and other social issues. The latter include, for example: race-, ethnicity-, and gender-related inequalities that have been perpetuated through policies dictating who is allowed to play on particular golf courses; economic inequalities that have been reinforced through the private ownership of vast quantities of land for a sport that many cannot afford to play; and global inequalities that manifest through the exploitation of scarce water and land resources in countries of the Global South for sport and leisure tourism purposes.

These problems are centrally relevant to our study of environmental issues in the sense that the implicit rationale for preserving golf in the first place is that it is somehow a public good. We recognize here that there are ways in which golf is indeed a public good, noting the physical activity-related benefits for those who have access to and an interest in golf (e.g. see Parkkari *et al.*, 2000) and the economic benefits that can be earned by those in the golf industry itself (e.g. course owners) and those featured in golf's wider 'integrated circus' (e.g. the apparel and equipment industry, the chemical industry, and the tourism industry). Still, if we weigh these benefits against the concerns that have been raised in this book about the potential health- and environment-related risks associated with golf, the 'golf is good for us' argument seems far less compelling. Moreover, if these benefits are only accessible to a small number of stakeholders, questions must be raised about the incredible space requirements for a game that remains exclusive in some ways.

Globalization, golf, and the Olympics

During our research we became especially cognizant of how our study of one of the major global issues of our time – environmental sustainability – has differing implications for those in different parts of the world. The movement of 'Americanized' versions of golf into less wealthy areas is reminiscent of concerns expressed by many scholars about the implications of sport-related global expansions more generally (Andrews *et al.*, 2014). These issues were raised most explicitly in our discussion of social movements and sport, and especially the Global Anti-Golf Movement, in Chapter 8.

There is no better example of a global sport-related initiative that has for many years been the focal point of debates regarding social and environmental issues than the Olympic Games. In fact, the upcoming Rio 2016 Games has particular relevance here in the sense that it is being hosted in a city and country that is ostensibly a good 'fit' with the stated development-related goals of the International Olympic Committee (IOC). Rio is the city of the Global South that will, according to Olympic advocates, benefit from the apparent economic, social, and environmental gains that hosting a sport mega-event supposedly provides. In fact, and as Pentifallo and VanWynsberghe (2012) have argued, the choice of Rio for the Games reflects what many see as a trend towards the hosting of events in cities considered to be especially underdeveloped and 'in need' of help from Global North organizations such as the IOC. Of particular pertinence here is that the sport of golf has been (also controversially) reintroduced to the Olympic Games after being an official Olympic sport in 1900 and 1904. This reintroduction meant that a new golf course would be constructed for use during the Games.

The links between the critiques of the IOC and the range of global issues underlying golf, tourism, and environmental problems has not been lost on commentators focused on Rio 2016. Elena Hodges, writer for the activist news website Rio Olympics Neighborhood Watch (found at RioOnWatch.com) offered a compelling examination of this issue. The Olympic golf course, Hodges writes, is a microcosm for the problems with Rio 2016's infrastructure development:

> The site chosen for the golf course sits on 1 million square meters of protected Atlantic Forest on the edge of the Marapendi lagoon in Barra da Tijuca. A mix of fragile mangroves, marshes, and sandbanks, the area contains about 300 identified species. A whole host of different animals will be threatened by new development in Marapendi, from herons to capybaras to endangered species such as the yellow-necked alligator, the beach lizard, and the crested guan. (Hodges, 2014)

Hodges goes on to problematize Complementary Law 125, which by her recounting was passed by Rio's city council to enable access to this land:

> [T]he law passed in December 2012 is extreme in its provisions. First, it authorizes the construction of the golf course within the borders of the Marapendi Reserve, using the justification that building a golf course qualifies as sustainable use of the land. Additionally, it redraws the borders of the Marapendi Municipal Reserve in order to completely cut out the section that fell within the intended golf course site. The law effectively nullifies the area's "permanent protection" status, handing this piece of public land over to a private developer, RJZ Cyrela. (Hodges, 2014)

Hodges also adds that the law in question gives the developer the right to build twenty-three new luxury on-site condominiums.

Implicit to this commentary on the whole is that those in Rio who are charged with organizing and hosting the Games must do major infrastructure upgrades *to satisfy the requirements of the IOC* – a global 'super NGO' that has no particular inherent interest in the range of local stakeholders that are impacted by the Games. In fact, it is well established that the intended and unintended consequences of preparing for and holding the Olympics can be understood as an impact of globalizing forces on local (host) cities (Hayes and Horne, 2011). Of course, the IOC has immense influence on local planning and governance decisions in cities around the world; the Games themselves also mobilize global capital and tourism (VanWynsberghe *et al.*, 2013). That golf is implicated in the vortex of concerns associated with the Games is but another example of how golf is inseparable from broader concerns about global tourism and economic globalization – all issues examined in Chapter 8 especially.

Why we are hopeful: globalization, activism, and political opportunity

Although it would be easy to dismiss our vision for 'contextual golf' and related suggestions for change as unrealistic and unattainable, we think that there are good sociologically based reasons for optimism. For instance, and remembering from Chapters 2, 8 and 9 that social movements are most likely to be successful when the socio-political context is one that offers opportunities for change, we think that it is relevant that (in Canada especially) governments have demonstrated a willingness to make some hard decisions to regulate the cosmetic usage of chemicals. Although the golf industry is commonly exempt from these regulations, from a precautionary perspective this is still a move in the right direction. Demonstrating why the current industry-friendly system of regulation for golf is flawed (as we sought to do in Chapter 7) could ultimately compel decision makers to phase in regulations for golf courses just as they did for "lawns, vegetable and ornamental gardens, patios, driveways, cemeteries, and in parks and school yards" in Ontario (Ontario Ministry of the Environment, 2009).

It was also evident from our findings that regulatory changes around golf (e.g. mandating chemical-free courses) would potentially be embraced by many people working on golf courses. The pressure evidently faced by many superintendents to maintain pristine conditions on courses would undoubtedly be alleviated if regulations made it essentially impossible to achieve the pristine aesthetic. This would, we think, be one way to initiate cultural change around golf. We are also aware from our interviews that many superintendents are genuinely concerned about environmental issues. In fact, and if we remember research findings from scholars like Robbins (2007), who described how and why people used lawn chemicals despite their knowledge of the health risks associated with their usage, we might also see why regulating chemical inputs could effectively alter a system that 'produced' particular kinds of behaviours. Regulation, thought about this way, would 'produce' more ethical and less risky forms of behaviour in this case. It seems that the only group that would lose out with the sorts of regulations we are suggesting is the chemical industry – a point that would seem to be confirmed if we consider the lobbying efforts of chemical advocates when decisions about chemical bans are 'on the table' for discussion.

We are also aware that successful social movements have strong, active, and tactical leaders – what sociologists call 'social movement entrepreneurs' (Wilson et al., 2013). In Chapter 9, we featured the work and commentary of influential and respected golf course superintendent Jeff Carlson, a leading advocate of organic golf. Although Carlson is not anti-chemical per se – contending as he has that measured inputs of inorganic chemicals at key moments may reduce the need for other environmentally damaging activities – he could certainly be viewed as a social movement entrepreneur in the sense that he is demonstrating what is possible when it comes to the upkeep of a highly playable golf course that maintains a particular aesthetic, and is advocating for a more innovative and environmentally friendly form of golf. Although our vision of 'contextual golf' is more radical than this, and would require more extensive cultural changes when it comes to pursuing the pristine aesthetic that is still the dominant 'look' in the golf world, there is no doubt that Carlson is an influential figure.

So too is Brent Blackwelder, as a respected environmentalist who weighed in on golf and environmental issues in *Golf Digest*, an important figure in linking golf with the broader environmental movement. A profile of the recently retired Blackwelder speaks of the public education and advocacy work that is needed by leaders of a movement towards real Utopias of golf (and sport). The profile specifically outlines Blackwelder's work in testifying in front of Congress more than a hundred times on pressing environmental issues, in founding American Rivers, an organization that helped drastically expand the National Wild and Scenic Rivers System, and in initiating reform at the World Bank that directed the Bank to pay greater attention to environmental issues. In general, in his work as president of Friends of the Earth, Blackwelder was "renowned for speaking truth to power" (Centre for the Advancement of the Steady State Economy, n.d.).

Inspired by environmental social movement entrepreneurs such as Blackwelder, we remain hopeful that with a better understanding of the problems plaguing status quo responses to golf-related environmental problems, and with a developing plan for 'real Utopias' of golf (e.g. contextual golf), that even greener golf is possible. We also draw hope from our knowledge of successful globally connected movements for change that have emerged in recent years, as these movements have effectively connected global issues to local experiences as a way of inspiring social- and environmental justice-inspired changes (see Castells, 2012). While one book alone cannot make the difference, our hope is that the information and arguments contained herein might indeed be one piece in a larger movement towards a more socially and environmentally just game of golf.

Notes

1 Moreover, Blackwelder's vision, if carried out, would also have implications for many who currently maintain organic golf courses – not just those who manage non-organic courses. For example, organic golf superintendents would in many cases need to find solutions to problems with carbon-emitting maintenance equipment, water overuse, and in some cases the excessive input of potentially damaging organic materials – all the while attending to the needs of the flora and fauna that are sharing the land through the protection of wildlife habitat spaces. Noting the current problems with economic viability and workload for those on most organic courses, Blackwelder's vision is, therefore, not exactly friendly to the organic course superintendent/owner either, although those working organic courses would likely be in philosophical agreement with Blackwelder.
2 The idea here is also to promote courses (or even golf holes) that were designed in ways that work with and feature the indigenous features of the settings the courses were created within – and are chemical free. While the principles underlying 'indigenous designs' have been championed by golf architects like Bill Coor and his partner golfer/designer Ben Crenshaw (who do what has been termed 'minimalist golf'), we suggest that to be featured on the site courses would need to be chemical free.

References

Adams, R. and Rooney, J. R., Jr. (1985). Evolution of American golf facilities. *Geographic Review*, 75(4), 419–438.
AGSA. (n.d.). About us. Retrieved 18 November 2014 from http://www.agsa.ca/atrf/about-us/.
Alavanja, M. and Bonner, M. (2012). Occupational pesticide exposures and cancer risk: a review. *Journal of Toxicology and Environmental Health, Part B*, 15(4), 238–263.
Alexander, M. (1970). Now is the time. *The Golf Course Superintendent*, September/October, 20–21.
Althusser, L. (1971). *Lenin and Philosophy*. New York: Monthly Review.
American Society of Golf Course Architects (n.d.). Environmental case studies. Retrieved 15 December 2014 from http://www.asgca.org/environmental-case-studies.
Andrews, D. L., Batts, C., and Silk, M. (2014). Sport, glocalization and the new Indian middle class. *International Journal of Cultural Studies*, 17(3), 259–276.
Andrews, R. N. L. (1998). Environmental regulation and business 'self-regulation'. *Policy Sciences*, 31(3), 177–197.
Andrews, R. N. L. (2006). *Managing the Environment, Managing Ourselves: A History of American Environmental Policy*, second edn. New Haven, CT: Yale University Press.
Anon. (1916a). No title. *The Golf Course*, January, 2.
Anon. (1916b). No title. *The Golf Course*, November, 114.
Anon. (1916c). Greenkeeping notes. *The Golf Course*, August, 81.
Anon. (1916d). No title. *The Golf Course*, November, 114.
Anon. (1916e). No title. *The Golf Course*, July, 67–68.
Anon. (1918). The use of dynamite in golf course construction. *The Golf Course*, January–February, 53–63.
Anon. (1921). Cornell University establishes a course to train men to superintend parks and golf courses. *Bulletin of the Green Section of the US Golf Association*, July, 141.
Anon. (1930). Investigations in greenkeeping problems. *Nature*, 125(3140), 30.
Anon. (1936a). A 15-year miracle. *Turf Culture*, June, 1.
Anon. (1936b). Reviewing the library of grass. *Turf Culture*, June, 2–12.
Anon. (1946). DDT. *Timely Turf Topics*, January, 3.
Anon. (1950). Turf and greenkeeping. St Ives Research Station. *Nature*, 166(4209), 22–24.
Anon. (1966). Poisons. *The Golf Superintendent*, June, 30–40.
Anon. (1967). Golf course chemical warfare takes to the air. *Golf Superintendent*, July, 8–9.
Anon. (1968). GCSAA public relations program begins. *The Golf Superintendent*, July, 23–24.
Anon. (1977). Insect update: turf insect control programs changing from shotgun to rifle shot. *Golf Superintendent*, February, 17–22.
Anon. (1980). Conservation … our key to the future. *Golf Course Management*, January/February, 59.
Anon. (1982a). Game-plan for golf. The first zillion years. *Golf Course Management*, September, 70–76.

Anon. (1982b). A logo with a message. Golf is one of the good guys! *Golf Course Management*, July, 21–23.
Anon. (1985). With vital commitment to the future. *Golf Course Management*, February, 18–28.
Anon. (1986). New GCSAA TV spots to be released. *Golf Course Management*, December, 67–68.
Anon. (1987a). EPA announces action on cadmium. *Golf Course Management*, September, 96.
Anon. (1987b). GCSAA's newest member service: government relations. *Golf Course Management*, June, 6–12.
Anon. (1988a). Presenting a case for golf courses. *Golf Course Management*, May, 76–78.
Anon. (1988b). Environmental auditing: the EPA perspective. *Golf Course Management*, November, 54.
Anon. (1988c). Partnership for the future. *Golf Course Management*, November, 49–52.
Anon. (1988d). Diazinon cancellation reversed by judge. *Golf Course Management*, March, 132.
Anon. (1990a). Government relations in practice. *Golf Course Management*, May, 54–56.
Anon. (1990b). Executive summary. Turfgrass: an environmental hero. *Golf Course Management*, February, 153.
Anon. (1991a). Brief stresses benefits of managed greenspace. *GreenMaster*, January/February, 21–29.
Anon. (1991b). GCSAA responds to report from New York. *Golf Course Management*, September, 98.
Anon. (1991c). GCSAA's environmental award. *Golf Course Management*, January, 84.
Anon. (1992). Corporate awards program promotes environmental stewardship. *Golf Course Management*, September, 94.
Anon. (1993a). Sanctuary program available. *GreenMaster*, January/February, 31–32.
Anon. (1993b). Special recognition for environmental leadership. *Golf Course Management*, January, 64.
Anon. (1994). Facts about golf course pesticides. *GreenMaster*, August, 16–17.
Anon. (1995a). Collier's reserve: state-of-the-art from the start. *Golf Course Management*, January, 36–42.
Anon. (1995b). GCSAA on ESPN. *Golf Course Management*, February, 142–144.
Anon. (2000). McMaster wins environmental award. *GreenMaster*, February/March, 12.
Anon. (2003). GCSAA picks up honor from EPA. *Golf Course Management*, March, 17.
Anon. (2010). Intimidation at Menie. *Menie Voices*. Retrieved 29 December 2014 from http://www.trippinguptrump.co.uk/wp-content/uploads/2014/04/Menie-Voices-final-Issue-1-Oct-Nov-2010-1500KB.pdf.
Appadurai, A. (1996). *Modernity at Large: Cultural Dimensions of Globalization*. Minneapolis, MN: University of Minnesota Press.
Arcury-Quandt, A.E., Gentry, A.L., and Marín, A.J. (2011). Hazardous materials on golf courses: experience and knowledge of golf course superintendents and grounds maintenance workers from seven states. *American Journal of Industrial Medicine*, 54(6), 474–485.
Arnold, R. (1982). The politics of environmentalism. *Golf Course Management*, August, 45–60.
Arya, N. (2005). Pesticides and human health: why public health officials should support a ban on non-essential residential use. *Canadian Journal of Public Health*, 96(2), 89–92.
Audubon International (n.d.). Audubon Cooperative Sanctuary Program for Golf Courses. Retrieved 17 December 2014 from http://www.auduboninternational.org/acspgolf.

Augustin, B. J. (1982). Does your irrigation system know there's a water crisis? *Golf Course Management*, February, 22–25.
Bachand, N. and Gue, L. (2011). Pesticide free? Oui! 2011 progress report: a comparison of provincial cosmetic pesticide bans. Retrieved 28 July 2013 from http://www.david-suzuki.org/publications/downloads/2011/pesticide-free-oui-2011.pdf.
Baidy, J. G. (1994). Message from your president. Unseen benefits. *Golf Course Management*, November, 7.
Bale, J. (1993). *Sport, Space and the City*. London: Routledge.
Bale, J. (1994). *Landscapes of Modern Sport*. London: Leicester University Press.
Barclay, J. A. (1992). *Golf in Canada. A History*. McClelland & Stewart.
Barton, J. (2008). How green is golf? *Golf Digest*. Retrieved 8 July 2014 from http://www.golfdigest.com/magazine/2008-05/environment_intro.
Baskin, C. (1984). Chemical usages and controversies. *Golf Course Management*, March, 29–37.
Baxter, A. (Director) (2012). *You've been Trumped*. Montrose, UK: Montrose Pictures.
BBC. (2007, December 12). Trump rejection councillor sacked. Retrieved 29 December 2014 from http://news.bbc.co.uk/2/hi/uk_news/scotland/north_east/7139605.stm.
Beck, U. (1992) *Risk Society*, Beverly Hills, CA: SAGE.
Beditz, J. F. (2000). The development and growth of the of the US golf market. In A. J. Cochran and M. Farrally (eds), *Science and Golf II: Proceedings of the World Scientific Congress of Golf*. London: M.R.E. & F.F. Spon.
Benbrook, C. (2008). Prevention, not profit, should drive pest management. *Pesticide News*, 83, December.
Berger G., Flynn A., Hines, F., and Johns, R. (2001). Ecological modernization as a basis for environmental policy: current environmental discourse and policy and the implications on environmental supply chain management. *Innovation: The European Journal of Social Science Research*, 14(1), 55–72.
Berndt, W. L. (1996). For the record … *Golf Course Management*, February, 68.
Bethune, G. (1980). The thinking superintendent. Agronomy … plus a whole lot more. *Golf Course Management*, January/February, 46–49.
Beyond Pesticides (n.d.). IPM: an historical perspective. Retrieved 15 December 2014 from http://www.beyondpesticides.org/stateipm/resources/ipm_history.pdf.
Beyond Pesticides (2011). Daily news blog. Danish government agrees to reduce pesticides. Retrieved 14 December 2014 from http://www.beyondpesticides.org/dailynewsblog/?p=4971.
Bicknell, F. (1960). *Chemicals in Food and in Farm Produce: Their Harmful Effects*. London: Faber & Faber.
Blake, R. C. (1971). Reason over emotion. *The Golf Superintendent*, March, 7.
Bliss, L. (2015, April 8). Will California's golf courses survive the drought? Long a symbol of water profligacy, some courses have been conserving for years. Others have not. *CITYLAB*. Retrieved 7 May 2015 from http://www.citylab.com/weather/2015/04/how-will-californias-golf-courses-survive-the-drought/389994/.
Boudway, I. (2013, April 12). The Masters: a sponsorship tradition unlike any other. *Bloomberg Businessweek*. Retrieved 15 December 2014 from http://www.businessweek.com/articles/2013-04-12/the-masters-a-sponsorship-tradition-unlike-any-other.
Bowen, W. R., Gibeault, V. A., Ohr, H. D. and Thomason, I. J. (1979). IPM. An alternate approach to solving pest problems. Golf Course Management, February, 16–23.
Boyd, D. R. (2003). *Unnatural Law: Rethinking Canadian Environmental Law and Policy*. Vancouver: UBC Press.
Brandt, J. W. (1968). President's message. *The Golf Superintendent*, July, 7.

Briassoulis, H. (2010). 'Sorry golfers, this is not your spot!' Exploring public opposition to golf development. *Journal of Sport and Social Issues*, 34(3), 288–311.

Brickell, B. (1969). Guest editorial. *The Golf Superintendent*, January, 103.

British Golf Museum (n.d.). FAQs. Retrieved 17 December 2014 from http://www.britishgolfmuseum.co.uk/faqs/.

Britton, B. (1988). President's message. *GreenMaster*, September/October, 6.

Bryant, J. and Holt, A. M. (2006). A historical overview of sports and media in the United States. In A. A. Raney and J. Bryant (eds), *Handbook of Sports and Media* (pp. 22–45). Mahwah, NJ: Lawrence Erlbaum Associates.

Buttel, F. H. (2000). Ecological modernization as social theory. *Geoforum*, 31(1), 57–65.

Campbell, M. (2009, March 30). Ontario bans lawn and garden pesticides. *The Globe and Mail*. Retrieved 17 December 2014 from http://www.theglobeandmail.com/news/national/ontario-bans-lawn-and-garden-pesticides/article18449302/.

Campbell, M. (2002). *The Scottish golf book*. Champaign: Sports Publishing LLC.

Campbell, S. (1996). Green cities, growing cities, just cities? Urban planning and the contradictions of sustainable development. *Journal of the American Planning Association*, 62(3), 296–312.

Canadian Cancer Society (2013). Our position on pesticides. Retrieved 28 July 2013 from http://www.cancer.ca/en/prevention-and-screening/be-aware/harmful-substances-and-environmental-risks/pesticides/our-position/?region=onandacc=true#ixzz2ZCzOMPHp.

Canadian Cancer Society (n.d.). Pesticides. Retrieved 23 December 2014 from: http://www.cancer.ca/en/cancer-information/cancer-101/what-is-a-risk-factor/environmental-risks/pesticides/?region=on.

Canadian Environmental Law Association (2012a). The precautionary principle. Retrieved 28 July 2013 from http://www.cela.ca/collections/pollution/precautionary-principle.

Canadian Environmental Law Association (2012b). Health and environmental organizations support Ontario-wide ban on cosmetic pesticides. Retrieved 28 July 2013 from http://www.cela.ca/newsevents/joint-statement/health-and-environmental-organizations-support-ontario-wide-ban-cosmetic-.

Carlson, J. (2010, March 24). *The Vineyard Golf Club: Seven years of organic management*. 2010 Superintendent-in-Residence Lecture, Guelph Turfgrass Institute. Guelph, Ontario, Canada. Retrieved 29 December 2014 from https://uoguelph.adobeconnect.com/_a838360559/p99443919/?launcher=falseandfcsContent=trueandpbMode=normal.

Carrell, S. (2014). Donald Trump loses legal challenge to windfarm near his Scottish golf resort. *The Guardian*. Retrieved 29 December 2014 from http://www.theguardian.com/world/2014/feb/11/donald-trump-loses-windfarm-scottish-golf-resort.

Carrow, R. N., Duncan, R. R., and Wienecke, D. (2005). BMPs: critical for the golf industry. *Golf Course Management*, June, 81–84.

Carson, R. (2002 [originally 1962]). *Silent Spring*. New York: Houghton Mifflin Company.

Castells, M. (1997). *The Information Age: Economy, Society and Culture, vol. 2. The Power of Identity*. Maldon, MA: Blackwell.

Castells, M. (2012). *Networks of Outrage and Hope: Social Movements in the Internet Age*. Malden, MA: Polity.

CBC News (2012). Don't ban cosmetic pesticides, B. C. MLAs recommend. Retrieved 14 December 2014 from http://www.cbc.ca/news/canada/british-columbia/don-t-ban-cosmetic-pesticides-b-c-mlas-recommend-1.1262469.

Centre for the Advancement of the Steady State Economy (n.d.). Brent Blackwelder. Retrieved 14 December 2014 from http://steadystate.org/brent-blackwelder/.

Ceron-Anaya, H. (2010). An approach to the history of golf: business, symbolic capital, and technologies of the self. *Journal of Sport and Social Issues*, 34(3), 339–358.
CGSA (n.d.a). Education. The golf superintendent. Retrieved 17 December 2014 from http://golfsupers.com/en/education.
CGSA (n.d.b). Professional designations. History of the CGSA's professional designation program. Retrieved 17 December 2014 from http://golfsupers.com/en/education/professional-designations.
CGSA (n.d.c). History. Retrieved 14 December 2014 from http://golfsupers.com/en/about-cgsa/history.
CGSA (2007a). CGSA policy paper concerning the use of IPM to manage golf courses. Retrieved 14 December 2014 from http://www.cscm.org/downloads/Approved%20CGSA%20IPM%20Policy%20Paper%202007.pdf.
CGSA (2007b). CGSA statement on the use of pesticides as a component of golf course management. Retrieved 14 December 2014 from http://www.cscm.org/downloads/Approved%20CGSA%20Pesticide%20Policy%20Statement%2007.pdf.
Charters, T. (1989). The golf course pesticides and golfers. *GreenMaster*, May, 12–36.
Chernushenko, D. (1994). *Greening Our Games: Running Sports Events and Facilities that Won't Cost the Earth*. Ottawa: Centurion.
Chernushenko, D., Van der Kamp, A., and Stubbs, D. (2001). *Sustainable Sport Management: Running an Environmentally, Socially, and Economically Responsible Organization*. United Nations Environment Programme.
Christoff, P. (1996). Ecological modernisation, ecological modernities. *Environmental Politics*, 5(3), 476–500.
Clark, M. (1997). IPM and BMP: has anything really changed? *Golf Course Management*, February, 104–108.
Claeys, G. and Tower Sargent, L. (eds) (1999). *The Utopia Reader*. New York: New York University Press.
Cleaver, G. W. (1978a). President's message. Individuality fosters professionalism. *The Golf Superintendent*, July, 9.
Cleaver, G. W. (1978b). President's message. Changing times demand stronger image. *The Golf Superintendent*, March, 9.
Cleverdon, R. (2000). Figure it out. *Tourism in Focus*, 36, 14–15.
CNW Group Ltd (2009). Canadian Cancer Society congratulates Ontario government for passing strong regulations supporting the Cosmetic Pesticide Ban Act. Retrieved 16 December 2014 from http://www.newswire.ca/en/story/451991/canadian-cancer-society-congratulates-ontario-government-for-passing-strong-regulations-supporting-the-cosmetic-pesticide-ban-act.
Colding, J., Lundberg, J., Lundberg, S., and Andersson, E. (2009). Golf courses and wetland fauna. *Ecological Applications*, 19, 1481–1491.
Cousineau, K. (2008). Ontario moves forward on pesticide legislation. *GreenMaster*, April, 45.
CropLife Canada (2009). CropLife Canada submission to Ontario premier on the Cosmetic Pesticides Ban Act. Retrieved 29 July 2013 from http://www.croplife.ca/2009?post_type=policysubmissions.
CropLife Canada (2013a). About us. Retrieved 29 July 2013 from http://www.croplife.ca/about-us.
CropLife Canada (2013b). News releases. CropLife Canada seeks Supreme Court challenge of Toronto pesticide by-law. Retrieved 29 July 2013 from http://www.croplife.ca/newsreleases/croplife-canada-seeks-supreme-court-challenge-of-toronto-pesticide-by-law#sthash.YTKP4XUm.dpuf.

CropLife Canada (2013c). How is industry protecting people and the planet? Retrieved 3 August 2013 from http://www.croplife.ca/protecting-people-and-the-environment/how-is-the-industry-protecting-people-and-the-planet.

Crosset, T. (1995). *Outsiders in the Clubhouse: The World of Women's Professional Golf*. Albany, NY: SUNY.

David Suzuki Foundation (n.d.). Highlights of Ontario's cosmetic pesticide ban. Retrieved 28 July 2013 from http://www.davidsuzuki.org/issues/health/science/pesticides/highlights-of-ontarios-cosmetic-pesticide-ban/.

Davidson, S. (2012). The insuperable imperative: a critique of the ecologically modernizing state. *Capitalism Nature Socialism*, 23(2), 31–50.

Davidson, D. J. and MacKendrick, N. A. (2004). All dressed up with nowhere to go: the discourse of ecological modernization in Alberta, Canada. *Canadian Review of Sociology/Revue Canadienne de Sociologie*, 41(1), 47–65.

Davis, D. (2002). IPM regional portraits (southeast). In G. L. Schumann, J. Vittum, M. L. Elliott, and P. P. Cobb (eds), *IPM Handbook for Golf Courses* (pp. 221–237). New Jersey: John Wiley & Sons.

Dean, M. (1999). *Governmentality – Power and Rule in Modern Society*. London: SAGE.

Dennys, H. (2013, May 1). City Diary: Donald Trump protestors petition the Scottish Parliament over golf resort. *The Telegraph*. Retrieved 29 December 2014 from http://www.telegraph.co.uk/finance/comment/citydiary/10028889/City-Diary-Donald-Trump-protestors-petition-the-Scottish-Parliament-over-golf-resort.html.

Dodson, R. (2001). Fighting for the future. *Golf Course Management*, February, 208.

Dryzek, J. (2005). *The Politics of the Earth: Environmental Discourses*, second edn. Oxford: Oxford University Press.

Dryzek, J. and Schlosberg, D. (eds) (2005). *Debating the Earth: The Environmental Politics Reader*. Oxford: Oxford University Press.

Dufresne, M. (1993). President's message. *GreenMaster*, January/February, 6.

Ede, B. (1990). The Stockley park project. *Landscape Design*, 187, 42–47.

Entman, R. M. (1993). Framing: toward clarification of a fractured paradigm. *Journal of Communication*, 43(4), 51–58.

EPA (1999). 33/50 program: the final record. Environmental Protection Agency. Retrieved 14 December 2014 http://www.epa.gov/oppt/3350/.

EPA (2012). Pestwise. An EPA partnership program. PESP Gold Member highlights. Environmental Protection Agency. Retrieved 16 December 2014 from http://www.epa.gov/pestwise/pesp/members/gold/goldbios.html#GCSAA.

EPA (2013a). Pestwise. An EPA partnership program. About us. Environmental Protection Agency. Retrieved 16 December 2014 from http://www.epa.gov/pestwise/about/index.html.

EPA (2013b). Pestwise. An EPA partnership program. Silver members. Environmental Protection Agency. Retrieved 16 December 2014 from http://www.epa.gov/pestwise/pesp/members/silver/index.html.

EPA (2014a). About Pesticides. Environmental Protection Agency. Retrieved 8 April 2015 from http://www.epa.gov/pesticides/about/.

EPA (2014b). Pesticides: regulating pesticides. Environmental Protection Agency. Retrieved 17 December 2014 from http://www.epa.gov/pesticides/regulating/.

Ewald, J. A., Aebischer, N. J., and Potts, G. R. (1998). Increasing pesticide use: impacts on wildlife based on 30 years of monitoring. In *Proceedings of the Wildlife, Pesticides, and People Conference* (pp. 1–16). Fairfax, VA: Rachel Carson Council Inc.

Finn, G. (1971). Professional all the way. *GreenMaster*, November, 10.

Ford, M. (2011). Trump rules out use of CPOs. *Aberdeen Voice*. Retrieved 14 May 2015 from http://aberdeenvoice.com/2011/01/trump-rules-out-use-of-cpos/.
Foster, J. B. (2009). The vulnerable planet. In L. King and D. McCarthy (eds), *Environmental Sociology: From Analysis to Action* (pp. 25–37). Lanham, MD: Rowman & Littlefield.
Foster, J. B. (2012). The planetary rift and the new human exemptionalism: a political-economic critique of ecological modernization theory. *Organization and Environment*, 25(3), 211–237.
Fox, G. (1995). How about bunking off for the day? Best lie low in the clubhouse tomorrow: It's World No Golf Day and the backlash is gathering strength. *The Independent*. Retrieved 5 May 2014 from: http://www.independent.co.uk/life-style/how-about-bunking-off-for-the-day-1617391.html.
Foy, J. H. (1988). Integrated pest management – A different approach for the same old problems. *USGA Green Section Record*, September/October, 9–11.
Franke, K. J. (1992). Using computer simulations to predict the fate and environmental impact of applied pesticides. *USGA Green Section Record*, March/April, 17–21.
Fushtey, S. (1991). Golf course development in the public eye. *GreenMaster*, November/December, 46–47.
GCM Staff (2001). 20/20 foresight. *Golf Course Management*, February, 130–132.
GCSAA (n.d.a.). Environmental Institute for Golf. How scholarships shape the game. Retrieved 16 December 2014 from http://www.eifg.org/education/scholarships/.
GCSAA (n.d.b.). Sustainability and the bottom line. Retrieved 15 December 2014 from http://www.gcsaa.org/course/environment/sustainability-and-the-bottom-line.
GCSAA (n.d.c.). GCSAA Golf Course Environmental Profile first phase. Retrieved 15 December 2014 from http://www.gcsaa.org/environment/environmental-profile.
GCSAA (n.d.d.). Environmental Institute for Golf. 2013 annual report. Retrieved 16 December 2014 from http://www.eifg.org/wp-content/uploads/2014/06/2013-EIFG-Annual-Report.pdf.
GCSAA (n.d.e). Environmental Institute for Golf. Core competencies. Retrieved 17 December 2014 from http://www.eifg.org/education/core-competencies/.
GCSAA (n.d.f). Environmental Institute for Golf. Outreach efforts. Retrieved 17 December 2014 from http://www.eifg.org/advocacy/gcsaa-outreach-efforts/.
GCSAA (n.d.g). Civitas booth visit. Retrieved 13 May 2015 from http://www.gcsaa.tv/view.php?id=2162.
GCSAA (2007). Golf Course Environmental Profile. Property profile and environmental stewardship of golf courses, vol. I. Retrieved 16 December 2014 from http://www.gcsaa.org/uploadedfiles/environment/environmental-profile/property-profile/golf-course-environmental-profile–property-report.pdf.
GCSAA (2009). GCSAA Golf Course Environmental Profile, Water use and conservation practices on US golf courses, vol. 2. Retrieved 6 May 2015, 2015 from http://www.gcsaa.org/environment/environmental-profile.
GCSAA Staff (1991). Golf's 'hidden' benefits shiningly displayed. *Golf Course Management*, January, 91.
Gibbons, R. (1999). Questions about a gift horse. In R. Gibbons (ed.), *Voluntary Initiatives and the New Politics of Corporate Greening* (pp. 3–12). Peterborough, ON: Broadview Press.
Gillis, R. V. (1993). RVG report. *GreenMaster*, January/February, 8.
Goldsmith, L. (1981). The politics of water. *Golf Course Management*, June, 14–17.
Goldsmith, L. (1982). Our concern for the '80s. Water. Will it become as precious as oil? *Golf Course Management*, January, 29–33.

Golf Canada (n.d.). History of golf. Retrieved October 2012 from http://www.rcga.org/innerpage.aspx?x=6u0mMawITYS62eG2ZX3wHzXU3NNZfipQlHsBWlOwcg%2FM%2BukTXecJEt11zqppmVXC.

Golfdom Staff (2013, 17 September). CIVITAS ONE approved for organic golf course maintenance. *Golfdom*. Retrieved from 29 December 2014 from http://www.golfdom.com/civitas-one-approved-for-organic-golf-course-maintenance/.

Golf Environment Organization (n.d.a). Recognition of sustainability. Retrieved 14 December 2014 from http://www.golfenvironment.org/get_involved/real_results/263_recognition_of_sustainability.

Golf Environment Organization (n.d.b). Action. Retrieved 17 December 2014 from http://www.golfenvironment.org/vision/action.

Golf Environment Organization (n.d.c.). Water. Retrieved 8 May 2015 from https://www.golfenvironment.org/sustainable_golf/water/.

Goodman, S. (1999). The computer age. *Golf Course Management*, January, 302–305.

Gould, K. A., Pellow, D. N., and Schnaiberg, A. (2004). Interrogating the Treadmill of Production: everything you wanted to know about the treadmill but were afraid to ask. *Organization and Environment*, 17(3), 296–316.

Government of Canada (n.d.). Government of Canada publications. Canada's climate change: voluntary challenge and registry (VCR). Retrieved 17 December 2014 from http://publications.gc.ca/site/eng/53756/publication.html.

Gramsci, A. (1971). *Selections from the Prison Notebooks*. New York: International.

Grant, Z. (1987a). Integrated pest management update: the Sherman Hollow story. *Golf Course Management*, November, 6–82.

Grant, Z. (1987b). What is integrated pest management. *Golf Course Management*, November, 10–12.

Green Cross Products (1970). Killex Turf Herbicide (advertisement). *GreenMaster*, January, 7.

Greenberg, J., Knight, G., and Westersund, E. (2011). Spinning climate change: corporate and NGO public relations strategies in Canada and the United States. *International Communication Gazette*, 73(1–2), 65–82.

Griffiths, D. (1997). Letters. Must we always demand perfection? *GreenMaster*, February/March, 38.

Gurney, M. (1987). New President launches accreditation program. *GreenMaster*, May, 9–11.

Hajer, M. A. (1995). *The Politics of Environmental Discourse: Ecological Modernization and the Policy Process*. Oxford: Clarendon Press.

Haass, R. N. (2009, September 2). Haass: what golf teaches us about geopolitics. *Newsweek*. Retrieved 2 October 2014 from http://www.newsweek.com/haass-what-golf-teaches-us-about-geopolitics-79489.

Hannigan, J. (2006). *Environmental Sociology*, second edn. New York: Routledge.

Hansen, A. A. (1921). The use of chemical weed killers on golf courses. *Bulletin of the Green Section of the US Golf Association*, July, 128–131.

Harrison, J. (2011). *Pesticide Drift and the Pursuit of Environmental Justice*. Cambridge: MIT Press.

Harvey, D. (2005). *A Brief History of Neoliberalism*, New York: Oxford University Press.

Harvey, J., Horne J., and Safai, P. (2009). Alterglobalization, global social movements, and the possibility of political transformation through sport. *Sociology of Sport Journal* 26(3), 383–403.

Harvey, J., Horne, J., Safai, P., Darnell, S., and Courchesne-O'Neill, S. (2013). *Sport and Social Movements: From the Local to the Global*. London: Bloomsbury.

Harvey, J. and Houle, F. (1994). Sport, world economy, global culture, and new social movements. *Sociology of Sport Journal*, 11(4), 337–355.

Hawkins, J. (2014, March 31). Hawk's Nest: 10 reasons why we love the Masters. *Golf Channel*. Retrieved 10 December 2014 from http://www.golfchannel.com/news/john-hawkins/hawks-nest-10-reasons-why-we-love-masters/.

Hayes, G. and Horne, J. (2011). Sustainable development, shock and awe? London 2012 and civil society. *Sociology*, 45(5), 749–764.

Health Canada (2006). Information note: the new Pest Control Products Act. Retrieved 16 December 2014 from http://www.hc-sc.gc.ca/cps-spc/pubs/pest/_fact-fiche/pcpa-lpa/index-eng.php.

Health Canada (2012). Economic Management Advisory Committee – members and participants. Retrieved 29 July 2013 from http://www.hc-sc.gc.ca/cps-spc/pest/part/advise-consult/_emac-cmge/members-membres-eng.php.

Health Canada (2013). For the public. Retrieved 17 December 2014 from http://www.hc-sc.gc.ca/cps-spc/pest/part/index-eng.php.

Hearn, D. E. (1987a). Message from your president. Pesticide usage today: The need to listen and learn. *Golf Course Management*, April, 5.

Hearn, D. E. (1987b). GCSAA, government relations and the world about us. *Golf Course Management*, June, 5.

Hercules Turf and Horticultural Products (1966). Me ready to trade medicine man for 2,4-D (advertisement). *The Golf Superintendent*, July, 9.

Hitchcock, J. R. (1989). *Sports and Media*. Terre Haute, IN: ML Express.

Hodges, E. (2014). The social and environmental costs of Rio's Olympic golf course. *RioOnWatch: Community Reporting on Rio*. Retrieved from http://www.rioonwatch.org/?p=17283.

Hodgetts, R. (2014, April 9). Masters 2014: 18 reasons to love Augusta – golf's unique event. *BBC*. Retrieved 15 December 2014 from http://www.bbc.com/sport/0/golf/26887265.

Hoffman, A. J. (2001). *From Heresy to Dogma: An Institutional History of Corporate Environmentalism*. Stanford, CA: Stanford University Press.

Hoffman, W. M. (1973). Pesticides in your future. *The Golf Superintendent*, February, 26–28.

Homer-Dixon, T. (2001). *The Ingenuity Gap: Can We Solve the Problems of the Future?* Toronto: Vintage Canada.

Horne, J. (1998). The politics of sport and leisure in Japan: Global power and local resistance. *International Review for the Sociology of Sport*, 33(2), 171–182.

Hoskins, W. M., Borden, A. D., and Michelbacher, A. E. (1939). Recommendations for a more discriminating use of insecticides. *Proc. 6th Pac. Sci. Congr.*, 5, 119–23

Howard, L. O. (2008 [originally 1922]). The war against insects. In T. R. Dunlap (ed.), *DDT, Silent Spring, and the Rise of Environmentalism: Classic Texts* (pp. 20–23). Seattle: University of Washington Press.

Huber, J. (1982). *Die verlorene Unschuld der Ökologie. Neue Technologien und superindustrielle Entwicklung (The Lost Innocence of Ecology. New Technologies and Superindustrial Development)*. Frankfurt am Main, Germany: Fischer.

Huber, J. (1985). *Die Regenbogengesellschaft: Ökologie und Sozialpolitik (The Rainbow Society. Ecology and Social Policy)*. Frankfurt am Main, Germany: Fischer.

Hueber, D. and Worzala, E. (2010). 'Code blue' for US golf course real estate development: 'Code green' for sustainable golf course development. *The Journal of Sustainable Real Estate*, 1–37. Retrieved 15 December 2014 from http://www.josre.org/industry-perspectives/.

Hughes, E. L. (2000). A pesticide primer and the need for federal action. Retrieved 28 July 2013 from http://www.elc.ab.ca/pages/publications/previousissue.aspx?id=450.

Hurdzan, M. J. (1994). Minimizing environmental impact by golf course development: a method and some case studies. In A. R. Leslie (eds), *Handbook of Integrated Pest Management for Turf And Ornamentals* (pp. 185–202). Boca Raton, FL: CRC Press LLC.

Hutchins, B. and Rowe, D. (2012). *Sport Beyond Television: The Internet, Digital Media and the Rise of Networked Media Sport*. New York: Routledge.

Hutheesing, N. (2013, July 31). According to golf, the economy is out of the rough. *Bloomberg Business*. Retrieved 8 April 2015 from http://www.bloomberg.com/news/articles/2013-07-31/according-to-golf-the-economy-is-out-of-the-rough.

IBISWorld (2008). *Golf Courses and Country Clubs in the US*. Los Angeles: IBISWorld.

IPM Council of Canada (2013a). What is IPM?, IPM Council of Canada. Retrieved 29 July 2013 from http://www.ipmcouncilcanada.org/epar/en-CA/Default.aspx.

IPM Council of Canada (2013b). IPM accreditation, IPM certification and accreditation. Retrieved 29 July 2013 from http://www.ipmcouncilcanada.org/epar/en-CA/Default/ipm-accreditation.aspx.

Jackson, J. (2000). Augusta: No. 1 with a snicker. *Golfdom*, July, 22.

Jarvie, G. (2006). *Sport, Culture and Society: An Introduction*. New York: Routledge.

Jhally, S. (1984). The spectacle of accumulation: material and cultural factors in the evolution of the sports/media complex. *The Insurgent Sociologist*, 12(3), 41–57.

Jiggens, M. (n.d.). GTI celebrates 25 years. *Turf and Recreation*. Retrieved 14 December 2014 from http://www.turfandrec.com/index.php?option=com_contentandtask=viewandid=2968andItemid=139.

Johnson, W. O. (1971). *Super Spectator and the Electric Lilliputians*. Boston, MA: Little, Brown & Co.

Jones, P. (1989). A professional first: a compliance auditing package for the course environment. *Golf Course Management*, January, 30–38.

Jones, S. (2012). CGC-yeS! GCSAA changes requirements of certification, renewing interest in the program. *Golfdom*, May, 38–39.

Kaminsky, B. and Seely, K. (2011). Presentation to the Special Committee on Cosmetic Pesticides. Retrieved 6 February 2014 from http://www.leg.bc.ca/pesticidescommittee/presentations/Canadian_Cancer_Society_Presentation.pdf.

Karamichas, J. (2013). *The Olympic Games and the Environment*. New York: Palgrave Macmillan.

Kauffman, S. (1999). 1999: GCSAA certification is route for achievers. *Golfweek*. Retrieved 17 December 2014 from http://golfweek.com/news/1999/nov/30/1999-gcsaa-certification-route-achievers/.

Keil, R. (2007). Sustaining modernity, modernizing nature: the environmental crisis and the survival of capitalism. In R. Krueger and D. Gibbs (eds), *The Sustainable Development Paradox: Urban Political Ecology in the United States and Europe* (pp. 41–65). London: Guilford Press.

Kennedy, P. (2014). Councillor Ford comments on Trump pull-out at Menie Estate. *Aberdeen and Aberdeenshire Greens*. Retrieved December 2014 from http://aberdeengreens.org.uk/news/councillor-ford-comments-on-trump-pull-out-at-menie-estate.

Kerr, C. (1970). A threat to the turf industry. *The Golf Superintendent*, November/December, 28–29.

Kinkela, D. (2005). The question of success and environmental ethics: revisiting the DDT controversy from a transnational perspective, 1967–72. *Ethics, Place and Environment: A Journal of Philosophy and Geography*, 8(2), 159–179.

Kinkela, D. (2011). *DDT and the American Century: Global Health, Environmental Politics, and the Pesticide that Changed the World*. Chapel Hill: University of North Carolina Press.

Klein, B. S. (2012). Green with envy? Don't be. *Golfweek*. Retrieved October 2012 from http://golfweek.com/news/2012/apr/01/green-envy-dont-be-augusta-national-unique/?printandpopup=true.

Knopper, L. D. and Lean, D. R. (2004). Carcinogenic and genotoxic potential of turf pesticides commonly used on golf courses. *Journal of Toxicology and Environmental Health, Part B*, 7(4), 267–279.

Kogan, M. (1998). Integrated pest management: historical perspectives and contemporary developments. *Annual Review of Entomology*, 43, 243–270.

Kramer, N. W. (1970a). Certification – stepping stone or stumbling block? *Golf Superintendent*, June, 9.

Kramer, N. W. (1970b). President's message. *The Golf Superintendent*, April, 9.

Krueger, R. and Gibbs, D. (2007). Introduction: Problematizing the politics of sustainability. In R. Krueger and D. Gibbs (eds), *The Sustainable Development Paradox: Urban Political Economy in the United States and Europe* (pp. 1–11). New York: Guilford Press.

Kross, B., Burmeister, L., Oglivie, L., Fuortes, L., and Fu, C. (1996). Proportional mortality study of golf course superintendents. *American Journal of Industrial Medicine*, 29(5), 501–506.

Krupka, I. (2000). The pest management regulatory agency: the resilience of science in pesticide management. In G. B. Doern and E. J. Reed (eds), *Risky Business: Canada's Changing Science-Based Policy and Regulatory Regime* (pp. 234–260). Toronto: University of Toronto Press.

Kunimatsu, T., Sudo, M. and Kawachi, T. (1999). Loading rates of nutrients discharging from a golf course and a neighboring forested basin. *Water Science and Technology*, 39(12), 99–107.

Labelle, C. (1971a). President's message. To the Canadian Open another champion. *GreenMaster*, August, 2–3.

Labelle, C. (1971b). President's message. *GreenMaster*, November, 2.

Langley, F. (1998). Rhetoric, science and public policy. *Golf Course Management*, January, 320.

Lansner, J. (2013). Golf courses hit rough economics. *Orange County Register*. Retrieved 24 February 2014 from: http://www.ocregister.com/articles/golf-349198-says-courses.html.

Larkin, C. G. (1992). The environmental management program. *Golf Course Management*, March, 58.

Latour, B. (1993). *We Have Never Been Modern* (translated by C. Porter). New York: Harvester Wheatsheaf.

Leach, B. R. (1921). The Japanese Beetle in relation to golf grounds. *Bulletin of the Green Section of the US Golf Association*, October, 210–211.

Leach, B. R. (1925). Improvements in the method of treating golf greens for the control of the Japanese Beetle. *Bulletin of the Green Section of the US Golf Association*, May, 100–102.

Leahy, S. (2011, November 9). Canada cuts environment spending. *The Guardian*. Retrieved 29 July 2013 from http://www.guardian.co.uk/environment/2011/nov/09/canada-cuts-environment-spending.

Legislative Assembly of British Columbia (2012). Report of the Special Committee on Cosmetic Pesticides. Retrieved 17 December 2014 from https://www.leg.bc.ca/cmt/39thparl/session-4/cp/5-39-4-38-5.htm.

Legislative Assembly of Ontario (2008). Committee transcripts: Standing Committee on Social Policy – 9 June 2008 – Bill 64, Cosmetic Pesticides Ban Act, 2008. Retrieved 22 July 2013 from http://www.ontla.on.ca/web/committee-proceedings/committee_transcripts_details.do?locale=enandDate=2008-06-09andParlCommID=8875andBillID=1967andBusiness=andDocumentID=23085#P219_48753

Leiss, W. (2003). How Canada's stumbles with environmental risk management reflect an integrity gap. In E. Lee and A. Perl (eds), *The Integrity Gap: Canada's Environmental Policy and Institutions* (pp. 25–41). Vancouver: UBC Press.

Lemke, T. (1999). 'The birth of bio-politics' – Michel Foucault's lectures at the Collège de France on neo-liberal governmentality. *Economy and Society*, 30(2), 190–207.

Lenskyj, H. (1998). Sport and corporate environmentalism: the case of the Sydney 2000 Olympics. *International Review for the Sociology of Sport*, 33(4), 341–354.

Lenskyj, H. (2002) *The Best Olympics Ever: Social Impacts of Sydney 2000*. Albany, NY: SUNY Press.

Lockyer, A. (2012). From corporate playground to family resort: golf as commodity in post-war Japan. In P. Francks and J. Hunter (eds), *The Historical Consumer: Consumption and Everyday Life in Japan, 1850–2000* (pp. 284–305). New York: Palgrave Macmillan.

Longgood, W. (1960). *The Poisons in Your Food*. New York: Simon & Schuster.

Lowerson, J. (1993). *Sport and the English Middle Class, 1870–1914*. Manchester: Manchester University Press.

Lucas, M. B., Jr. (1980). A history of greenkeeping and GCSAA. *Golf Course Management*, October, 57–62.

Lyle, C. (2008 [originally 1947]). Achievements and possibilities in pest eradication. In T. R. Dunlap (ed.), *DDT, Silent Spring, and the Rise of Environmentalism: Classic Texts* (pp. 44–50). Seattle: University of Washington Press.

MacDonald, D. (2007). *Business and Environmental Politics in Canada*. Toronto: University of Toronto Press.

MacNeill, M. (1996). Networks: producing Olympic ice hockey for a national television audience. *Sociology of Sport Journal*, 13(2), 103–124.

Macomber, L. (1916). Qualifications of an advanced greenkeeper. *The Golf Course*, March, 27.

Magdoff, F. and Foster, J. B. (2011). *What Every Environmentalist Needs to Know About Capitalism: A Citizen's Guide to Capitalism and the Environment*. New York: NYU Press.

Maguire, J., Jarvie, G., Mansfield, L., and Bradley, J. (2002). *Sport Worlds: A Sociological Perspective*. Champaign, IL: Human Kinetics.

Mallin, M. and Wheeler, T. (2000). Nutrient and fecal coliform discharge from coastal North Carolina golf courses. *Journal of Environmental Quality*, 29(3), 979–986.

Maples, P. Jr. (1976). President's page: taking stock of accomplishments. *The Golf Superintendent*, January, 7.

Marchak, P. (1993). *The New Right and the Restructuring of Global Markets*. Montreal and Kingston: McGill-Queen's University Press.

Marks, J. (1970, March 12). Golf courses against chemical ban. *The Globe and Mail*, p. 45.

Marquis, C. E. (1980). Lucas to lead GCSAA in 1980. Meeting today's challenges. *Golf Course Management*, March, 18–23.

May, E. (2012, April 2). Why the 2012 budget is the worst in Canada's history. *TheHuffingtonPost.com, Inc*. Retrieved 14 December 2014 from http://www.huffingtonpost.ca/elizabeth-may/canada-budget-2012-environment_b_1391573.html.

McAllister, M. L. (2004). *Governing Ourselves? The Politics of Canadian Communities*. Vancouver: UBC Press.

McCauley, L. (2005). Immigrant workers in the United States: recent trends, vulnerable populations, and challenges for occupational health. *AAOHN Journal: Official Journal of the American Association of Occupational Health Nurses*, 53(7), 313–319.

McGinnis, L., McQuillan, J., and Chapple, C. L. (2005). I just want to play: women, sexism, and persistence in golf. *Journal of Sport and Social Issues*, 29(3), 313–337.

McKeel, C. (2003). Members rewarded for government relations efforts. *Golf Course Management*, February, 32.

McKenzie, J. I. (2002). *Environmental Politics in Canada: Managing the Commons into the 21st Century*. Toronto: Oxford University Press.

McWhirter, R. (1993). Computerized irrigation saves resources, cuts expenses. *GreenMaster*, May, 29–31.

Meadows, D. H., Meadows, D. L., Randers, J. and Behrens, W. W. III. (1972). *The Limits to Growth*. New York: Universe Books.

Meadows, D., Randers, J., and Meadows, D. (2004). *Limits to Growth: The 30-year Update*. White River Junction, VT: Chelsea Green.

Mellersh, D. (1991). Education key priority for new president. *GreenMaster*, January/February, 18–20.

Metsker, S. E. (1969). How professional are we…? *The Golf Superintendent*, February, 32–36.

Metsker, S. (1990). Backing into professionalization. *USGA Green Section Record*, March/April, 9.

Millington, B. and Wilson, B. (2014). The masters of nature: golf, nonhumans, and consumer culture. In J. Gillett and M. Gilbert (eds), *Sport, Animals, and Society* (pp. 52–66). New York: Routledge.

Miller, C. (Director) (2010). *Donald Trump: All-American Billionaire* [Television documentary]. BBC Television.

Mills, C. W. (1959). *The Sociological Imagination*. London: Oxford.

Misgav, A., Perl, N., and Avnimelech, Y. (2001). Selecting a compatible open space use for a closed landfill site. *Landscape and Urban Planning*, 55(2), 95–111.

Mol, A. P. J. (2003). *Globalization and Environmental Reform: The Ecological Modernization of the Global Economy*. Cambridge, MA: MIT Press.

Mol, A. P. J. (2010). Sustainability as global attractor: the greening of the 2008 Beijing Olympics. *Global Networks*, 10(4), 510–528.

Moss, R. J. (2001). *Golf and the American Country Club*. Urbana: University of Illinois Press.

NAGA (2009). National Allied Golf Association – Environmental position statement. Retrieved 13 December 2014 from http://www.cscm.org/downloads/NAGA%20 Environmental%20Position%20Statement%20April%202009.pdf.

NAGA (2011). National Allied Golf Association – British Columbia pesticide legislation briefing document cover letter. Retrieved 17 December 2014 from http://aga-bc.org/wp-content/uploads/2013/03/NAGA-BC-Pesticide-Briefing-Document.pdf.

Nash, D. (1989). Tourism as a form of imperialism. In V. Smith (ed.), *Host and Guests. The Anthropology of Tourism*, second edn (pp. 37–52). Philadelphia: University of Pennsylvania Press.

NGF [National Golf Foundation]. (2009). *The Future of Public Golf in America*. Jupiter, FL.

Nauright, J. (2012a). Golf, British Isles. In J. Nauright and C. Parrish (eds), *Sports Around the World: History, Culture, and Practice* (pp. 98–105). Oxford: ABC-CLIO.

Nauright, J. (2012b). Golf, United States and Canada. In J. Nauright and C. Parrish (eds), *Sports Around the World: History, Culture, and Practice* (pp. 240–246). Oxford: ABC-CLIO.

Nauright, J. and White, P. (1996). Nostalgia, community, and nation: professional hockey and football in Canada. *Avante*, 2(3), 24–41.

Nelson, J. (2014). From cabinet to CropLife: Menzies avoids ethical scrutiny over new job as top pesticide and GMO lobbyist. *Canadian Centre for Policy Alternatives*. Retrieved 17 December 2014 from https://www.policyalternatives.ca/publications/monitor/cabinet-croplife-menzies-avoids-ethical-scrutiny-over-new-job-top-pesticide-and.

Neo, H. (2010). Unravelling the post-politics of golf course provision in Singapore. *Sport and Social Issues*, 34(3), 272–287.

Neuberger, A. (1967). Control versus confusion and controversy. *USGA Green Section Record*, May, 8–9.

Nimmo, D. and McEwen, L. (1994). Pesticides. In P. Calow (ed.), *Handbook of Ecotoxicology* (pp. 155–203). Oxford: Blackwell Scientific.

Noer, O. J. (1946). How to improve postwar turf maintenance. *Golfdom*, February, 27–61.

Nutter, G. C. (1964). The consequence of 'Silent Spring'. *The Golf Course Reporter*, April, 43–56.

Nylund, D. (2003). Taking a slice at sexism: the controversy over the exclusionary membership practices of the Augusta National Golf Club. *Journal of Sport and Social Issues*, 27(2), 195–202.

O'Connell, R. (1971). Members comment: certification program draws heavy response [Letter submission]. *The Golf Superintendent*, February, 23.

O'Neill, T. T. (2006). President's message. It's a numbers game. *Golf Course Management*, January, 13.

Olivar, C. (1976). Certification program marks 36% increase. *The Golf Superintendent*, February, 41–43.

Ontario Ministry of the Environment (2009). Ontario's Cosmetic Pesticides Ban. Retrieved 29 July 2013 from http://news.ontario.ca/ene/en/2009/03/ontarios-cosmetic-pesticides-ban.html.

Ontario Ministry of the Environment (2013). Pesticides. Retrieved 29 July 2013 from http://www.ene.gov.on.ca/environment/en/category/pesticides/index.htm.

Oosthoek, S. (2012, August 23). How golf courses are getting greener. *The Globe and Mail*. Retrieved October 2012 from http://www.theglobeandmail.com/report-on-business/careers/top-employers/how-golf-courses-are-getting-greener/article577697/.

Ostmeyer, T. (2001). Keepers of the green: 75 for 75. *Golf Course Management*, September, 21–72.

Ostmeyer, T. (2008). It's time to step up! Retrieved 13 September 2015 from http://www.gcsaa.org/gcm/2008/feb/insidegcm.asp.

Owen, D. (2003). *The Making of the Masters: Clifford Roberts, Augusta National, and Golf's Most Prestigious Tournament*. New York: Simon & Schuster.

Owen, D. (2009, September 16). Drying out. America's courses are curbing their addiction to water. *Golf Digest*. Retrieved 6 May 2015 from http://www.golfdigest.com/magazine/2009–11/environment_davidowen_waterconservation.

Palmer, C. (2004). More than just a game: the consequences of golf tourism. In B. W. Ritchie and D. Adair (eds), *Sport Tourism: Interrelationships, Impacts and Issues* (pp. 117–134). Clevedon: Channel View.

Parascenzo, M. (1981). The times they are a-changing. *Golf Course Management*, August, 21–27.

Parkkari, J., Natri, A., Kannus, P., Manttari, A., Laukkanen, R., Haapasalo, H., Nenonen, A., Pasanen, M., Oja, P., and Vuori, I. (2000). A controlled trial of the health benefits of regular walking on a golf course. *American Journal of Medicine*, 109(2), 102–8.

Parliament of Canada (2000). Pesticides. Making the right choice for the protection of health and the environment. Report of the Standing Committee on Environment and Sustainable Development. Retrieved 28 July 2013 from http://www.parl.gc.ca/HousePublications/Publication.aspx?DocId=1031697andLanguage=EandMode=1and Parl=36andSes=2.

Paull, J. (2013). The Rachel Carson letters and the making of *Silent Spring*. *SAGE Open*, 3(July–September), 1–12.

Pate, J. (1993). Television golf and the golf course superintendent. *USGA Green Section Record*, May/June, 19–21.

Peacock, C. H. and Smart, M. M. (1995). IPM, monitoring, and management plans: a mandate for the future. *USGA Green Section Record*, May/June, 10–14.

Pennington, B. (2010). Exclusive golf course is organic, so weeds get in. *The New York Times*. Retrieved December 2014 from http://www.nytimes.com/2010/08/17/sports/golf/17vineyard.html?pagewanted=alland_r=0.

Pentifallo, C. and VanWynsberghe, R. (2012). Blame it on Rio: isomorphism, environmental protection and sustainability in the Olympic Movement. *International Journal of Sport Policy and Politics*, 4(3), 427–446.

Perkins, C. (2010). The performance of golf: landscape, place, and practice in north west England. *Journal of Sport and Social Issues*, 34(3), 312–338.

Perkins, C., Mincyte, D., and Cole, C. L. (2010). Special issue: making the critical links and the links critical in golf studies. *Journal of Sport and Social Issues*, 34(3), 267–375.

Peshin, R., Bandral, R. S., Zhang, W., Wilson, L., and Dhawan, A. K. (2009). Integrated pest management: a global overview of history, programs and adoption. In R. Peshin and A. K. Dhawan (eds), *Integrated Pest Management: Innovation-Development Process* (pp. 1–49). Springer Netherlands.

PGA.com (2011). Timeline of African-American achievements in golf. *PGA*. Retrieved 3 December 2014 from http://www.pga.com/timeline-african-american-achievements-in-golf.

PGA.com (2013). America's first golf club marks a major anniversary. Retrieved 17 December 2014 from http://www.pga.com/golf-courses/golf-buzz/americas-first-golf-club-marks-major-anniversary.

Pick, M. C. (1978). Professional turf varieties for professional turf managers. *GreenMaster*, May, 4–8.

Pitock, T. (2009). Turf wars. *Australia Golf Digest*, 90–94.

PMEP [Pest Management Education Program]. (n.d.). Cadmium compounds EPA Pesticide Fact Sheet 4/91. Retrieved 20 December 2014 from http://pmep.cce.cornell.edu/profiles/fung-nemat/aceticacid-etridiazole/cadmium_chloride/fung-term-cad-chlor.html.

Poellot, J. M. (1991). Striving to attain environmental enchantment: the need for expertise as golf grows globally. *Golf Course Management*, February, 6–159.

Popham, P. (2012). Tee'd off: The residents of Foveran Links speak out about Donald Trump's golf project. *The Independent*. Retrieved December 2014 from http://www.independent.co.uk/news/uk/this-britain/teed-off-the-residents-of-foveran-links-speak-out-about-donald-trumps-golf-project-7939044.html.

Porter, C. (2013, May 31). How a morning stroll led to a pesticide ban. Retrieved 28 July 2013 from http://www.thestar.com/news/insight/2013/05/31/how_a_morning_stroll_led_to_a_pesticide_ban_porter.html.

Post, D., van Veen, T. S., Meyersburg, M., and Bessmer, J. B. (2010). Golf at a crossroads: hazardous or healthy strategies. *Outlooks on Pest Management*, 21(3), 113–121.

Powell, A. J. Jr. (1970a). Beware of 'Satchmo'. *The Golf Superintendent*, May, 54.
Powell, A. J. Jr. (1970b). Beware of 'Satchmo'. *GreenMaster*, June, 21–22.
Prakash, A. and Potoski, M. (2006). *The Voluntary Environmentalists: Green Clubs, ISO 14001, and Voluntary Environmental Regulations*. Cambridge: Cambridge University Press.
Price, S. J., Guzy, J., Witczak, L., and Dorcas, M. E. (2013). Do ponds on golf courses provide suitable habitat for wetland-dependent animals in suburban areas? An assessment of turtle abundances. *Journal of Herpetology*, 47(2), 243–250.
Priestley, G. K. and Ashworth, G. J. (1995). *Sports Tourism: The Case of Golf. Tourism and Spatial Transformations*. Wallingford: CAB.
R&A (n.d.a.). Environmental impact. Retrieved 12 December 2014 from http://golfcoursemanagement.randa.org/en/Environmental-Impact.aspx.
R&A (n.d.b.). Using water efficiently. Retrieved 12 December 2014 from http://golfcoursemanagement.randa.org/en/Environmental-Impact/Using-water-efficiently.aspx.
R&A (n.d.c.). Using chemicals responsibly. Retrieved 12 December 2014 from http://golfcoursemanagement.randa.org/en/Environmental-Impact/Using-chemicals-responsibly.aspx.
R&A (2013). Danes count pesticide applications. Retrieved 17 December 2014 from https://golfcoursemanagement.randa.org/en/Case-studies/2013/03/Danish-pesticides.aspx.
Readman, M. (2003). Golf tourism. In S. Hudson (ed.), *Sport and Adventure Tourism* (pp. 165–201). Binghamton, NY: Haworth.
Record, L. (1967). Fungicides – Forever more? *USGA Green Section Record*, July, 1–5.
Redclift, M. (1986). Redefining the environmental 'crisis' in the South. In J. Weston (ed.), *Red and Green: The New Politics of the Environment* (pp. 80–101). London: Pluto.
Rees, E. (2008). Taking a swing. *The Ecologist*, 38(6), 42–45.
Riley, B. (1995). Hot water: a 'cool' new weed control method. *Journal of Pesticide Reform*, 15(1), 9.
Riordan, C. (2003). Partnership with EPA creates win-win. *Golf Course Management*, October, 32.
Robbins, P. (2007). *Lawn People: How Grasses, Weeds, and Chemicals Make us Who we Are*. Philadelphia: Temple University Press.
Roberts, T. (1966). President's message: an open letter to the agricultural chemical industry. *The Golf Superintendent*, November/December, 6.
Rosillon, J. (1981). Where has all the water gone? *Golf Course Management*, October, 32–35.
Rowe, D. (2013). The sport/media complex: formation, flowering, and future. In D. L. Andrews and B. Carrington (eds), *A Companion to Sport* (pp. 61–77). Malden, MA: Blackwell.
Sampson, C. (1999). *The Masters: Golf, Money, and Power in Augusta, Georgia*. New York: Random House, Inc.
Sandberg, L. A. and Foster, J. (2005). Challenging lawn and order: environmental discourse and lawn care reform in Canada. *Environmental Politics*, 14(4), 478–494.
Sander, B. (1966). The thinking superintendent. No salesmen allowed. *The Golf Superintendent*, April, 40.
Sandomir, R. (2013, August 7). Adding golf to its lineup, Fox Sports acquires rights to United States Open. *The New York Times*. Retrieved 15 December 2014 from http://www.nytimes.com/2013/08/08/sports/golf/adding-golf-to-its-lineup-fox-sports-acquires-rights-to-united-states-open.html?_r=1and.

Schnaiberg, A. (1980). *The Environment: From Surplus to Scarcity*. New York: Oxford University Press.

Schnaiberg, A. and Gould, K. (2000). *Environment and Society: The Enduring Conflict*. West Caldwell, NJ: Blackburn.

Schroeder, K. (2011). *Environmental Law*. New York: Delmar.

Schumann, G. L., Vittum, J., Elliott, M. L., and Cobb, P. (eds) (2002). *IPM Handbook for Golf Courses*. New Jersey: John Wiley & Sons.

Scottish Natural Heritage (n.d.). Sites of special scientific interest. Retrieved December 2014 from http://www.snh.gov.uk/protecting-scotlands-nature/protected-areas/national-designations/sssis/.

Shackelford, G. (2012). The Augusta syndrome revisited. *Golf Digest*. Retrieved October 2012 from http://www.golfdigestcanada.ca/courses-and-travel/the-augusta-syndrome-revisited/.

Sharp, S. (2000). Great expectations. Battling the dreaded 'Augusta National syndrome'. *Golfdom*, May, 20–24.

Shell Vapona Insecticide (1966). A Vapona® fog can reduce a mosquito problem to almost nothing in a matter of minutes (advertisement). *Golf Superintendent*, May, 29.

Sherman, R. C., Bishop, D. M., and Bruneau, A. H. (1983). The turfgrass IPM concept. *Golf Course Management*, April, 45–46.

Shmavonian, K. (2011, April 4). The Masters: schlock unlike any other. *Forbes*. Retrieved 18 September 2014 from http://www.forbes.com/sites/karlshmavonian/2011/04/04/the-masters-schlock-unlike-any-other/.

Simmons, J. S. (2008 [originally 1945]). How magic is DDT? In T. R. Dunlap (ed.), *DDT, Silent Spring, and the Rise of Environmentalism: Classic Texts* (pp. 31–38). Seattle: University of Washington Press.

Smith, M. B. (2001). 'Silence, Miss Carson!' Science, gender, and the reception of 'Silent Spring'. *Feminist Studies*, 27(3), 733–752.

Snow, J. T. (1991). The USGA's environmental program. *USGA Green Section Record*, March/April, 11–13.

St Andrews Links (n.d.). Retrieved 17 December 2014 from http://www.standrews.com.

Staggenborg, S. (2008). *Social Movements*. Don Mills, ON: Oxford University Press.

Steklasa, R. (1977). What do you do when insects start liking the pesticides? *GreenMaster*, July/August, 2.

Strawn, J., Barger, J., and Rogers, J. D. (2011). Earth as medium: the art and engineering of golf course construction. In S. D. Brunn (ed.), *Engineering Earth: The Impacts of Megaengineering Projects, vol. 1* (pp. 1159–1190). London: Springer.

Stoddart, B. (1990). Wide world of golf: a research note on the interdependence of sport, culture, and economy. *Sociology of Sport Journal*, 7(4), 378–388.

Stoddart, M. C. J. (2012). *Making Meaning out of Mountains: The Political Ecology of Skiing*. Vancouver: UBC Press.

Stolle-McAllister, J. (2004). Contingent hybridity: the cultural politics of Tepoztlán's anti-golf movement. *Identities: Global Studies in Culture and Power*, 11, 195–213.

STRI (n.d.). History of STRI. Retrieved 17 December 2014 from http://www.stri.co.uk/about-stri/history-of-stri/.

Suncor Energy Inc. (n.d.a). Oil sands. Retrieved 13 May 2015 from http://www.suncor.com/en/about/242.aspx.

Suncor Energy Inc. (n.d.b). What is Civitas? Retrieved 13 May 2015 from https://www.civitasturf.com/CIVITAS.

Suncor Energy Inc. (2009). CIVITAS™ fungicide unveiled at golf industry show. Retrieved 13 May 2015 from http://lubricants.petro-canada.ca/en/news/2404.aspx?id=2474.

Swyngedouw, E. (2010). Apocalypse forever? Post-political populism and the spectre of climate change. *Theory, Culture and Society*, 27(2–3), 213–232.

The Futures Company (2012). Golf's 2020 vision: the HSBC report. *HSBC*. Retrieved 15 December 2014 from http://thefuturescompany.com/wp-content/uploads/2012/09/The_Future_of_Golf.pdf.

The Huffington Post, Inc. (2012, December 5). Michael Forbes' 'Top Scot' award basically proves Scotland hates Donald Trump. Retrieved December 2014 from http://www.huffingtonpost.com/2012/12/03/michael-forbes-top-scot-a_n_2233927.html.

The Royal Calcutta Golf Club (n.d.). History. Retrieved 17 December 2014 from http://www.rcgc.in/golf_course/history.php.

The Royal Montreal Golf Club (2011). Club history. Retrieved October 2012 from http://www.rmgc.org/history_club/.

The Scotsman (2010). Protesters grab land in bid to foil Trump's estate plan. Retrieved 20 December 2014 from http://www.scotsman.com/news/protesters-grab-land-in-bid-to-foil-trump-s-estate-plan-1-805756.

The Scottish Government (n.d.). Compulsory purchase order. Retrieved 29 December 2014 from http://scotland.gov.uk/Topics/archive/National-Planning-Policy/themes/ComPur).

Tillinghast, A. W. (1916a). Modern golf chats. *The Golf Course*, January, 1–7.

Tillinghast, A. W. (1916b). Modern golf chats. *The Golf Course*, February, 9–19.

Touraine, A. (1977). *The Self-Production of Society*. Chicago: University of Chicago Press.

Turfgrass Information File (n.d.a). About The Golf Course. Retrieved 17 December 2014 from http://archive.lib.msu.edu/tic/gcmb/.

Turgrass Information File (n.d.b). USGA® Green Section Record. About this journal. Retrieved 20 December 2014 from http://gsr.lib.msu.edu/gsr_about.htm.

UNESCO (2006). UNESCO Water e-Newsletter No. 155: water and tourism. Retrieved 7 May 2015 from http://www.unesco.org/water/news/newsletter/155.shtml.

USGA (n.d.). Environmental principles for golf courses in the United States. Retrieved 15 December 2014 http://www.usga.org/course_care/articles/environment/general/environmental-principles-for-golf-courses-in-the-united-states/.

USGA (2009). The USGA's environmental commitment. Retrieved 14 December 2014 from http://www.usga.org/Course-Care/Golf-and-the-Environment/The-USGA-s-Environmental-Commitment/.

Valentine, J. (1947). Efficiency is keynote of better course management. *Golfdom*, Fall, 68–70.

Vamplew, W. (2010). Sharing space: inclusion, exclusion, and accommodation at the British golf club before 1914. *Journal of Sport and Social Issues*, 34(3), 359–375.

Van Buskirk, R. G. (1971). A positive perspective on pesticides. *GreenMaster*, September, 8–16.

Van Riper, T. (2012, March 2). Sports media rights keep rolling – for now. *Forbes*. Retrieved 15 December 2014 from http://www.forbes.com/sites/tomvanriper/2012/03/02/sports-media-rights-keep-rolling-for-now/.

VanWynsberghe, R., Surborg, B., and Wyly, E. (2013). When the games come to town: neoliberalism, mega-events and social inclusion in the Vancouver 2010 winter Olympic games. *International Journal of Urban and Regional Research*. 37(6), 2074–2093.

Wagoner, C. A. (1971). Certification for GCSAA members. *USGA Green Section Record*, September, 6–7.
Wagoner, C. A. (1974). The superintendent in the 70s. *USGA Green Section Record*, March, 5–7.
Watts, J. (2010). All the tees in China: golf boom threatens rainforest. With its 1,000-year-old trees, Hainan was a rare conservation success. But now fairways stretch as far as the eye can see. *The Guardian*. Retrieved 27 December 2014 from: http://www.theguardian.com/environment/2010/apr/23/endangered-habitats-china.
WCED (World Commission on Environment and Development) (1987). *Our Common Future*. Oxford: Oxford University Press.
We Are Golf (n.d.a). A game for all. Retrieved 16 December 2014 from http://wearegolf.org/accessibility/a-game-for-all/.
We Are Golf (n.d.b). Advocacy issues. Retrieved 16 December 2014 from http://wearegolf.org/capitol-hill/advocacy-issues/.
Webb, K. and Clarke, D. (2004). Voluntary codes in the United States, the European Union and developing countries: a preliminary survey. In K. Webb (ed.), *Voluntary Codes: Private Governance, the Public Interest and Innovation* (pp. 335–376). Ottawa: Carleton Research Unit for Innovation, Science and Environment.
West Coast Environmental Law (2011). Memo to Special Committee on Cosmetic Pesticides. Retrieved 15 December 2014 from http://www.leg.bc.ca/pesticidescommittee/presentations/West_Coast_Environmental_Presentation.pdf.
Whannel, G. (1992). *Fields in Vision: Television Sport and Cultural Transformation*. London: Routledge.
Wheeler, K. and Nauright, J. (2006). A global perspective on the environmental impact of golf. *Sport in Society*, 9(3), 427–443.
White-Stevens, R. (1972). A perspective of pesticides. *USGA Green Section Record*, July, 17–21.
Whitson, D. and Gruneau, R. (1997). The (real) integrated circus: political economy, popular culture, and 'major league' sport. In W. Clement (ed.), *Understanding Canada: Building on the New Canadian Political Economy* (pp. 359–385). Montreal and Kingston: McGill-Queen's Press.
Whitten, R. (2010, October 12). The most significant of each decade. *Golf Digest*. Retrieved 20 December 2014 from http://www.golfdigest.com/golf-courses/2010-11/most-important-courses-methodology.
Wickenden, L. (1955). *Our Daily Poison: The Effects of DDT, Fluorides, Hormones and Other Chemicals on Modern Man*. New York: Devin-Adair.
Williams, B. R. (1997). Message from your President. We've come a long way. *Golf Course Management*, February, 7.
Williams, R. (1977). *Marxism and Literature*. Oxford: Oxford University Press.
Williams, S. S. (1983). Thinking superintendent: spray with restraint. *Golf Course Management*, June, 78.
Wilson, B. (2007). New media, social movements, and global sport studies: a revolutionary moment and the sociology of sport. *Sociology of Sport Journal*, 24(4), 457–477.
Wilson, B. (2012a). Growth and nature: reflections on sport, carbon neutrality, and ecological modernization. In D. Andrews and M. Silk (eds), *Sport and Neo-liberalism: Politics, Consumption, and Culture* (pp. 90–108). Philadelphia, PA: Temple University Press.

Wilson, B. (2012b). *Sport and Peace: A Sociological Perspective*. Don Mills, ON: Oxford University Press.

Wilson, B. and Millington, B. (2015). Sport and environmentalism in a post-political era. In R. Giulianotti (ed.), *Sociology of Sport Handbook* (pp. 366-376). New York: Routledge.

Wilson, B. and Millington, B. (2013). Sport, ecological modernization, and the environment. In D. Andrews and B. Carrington (eds), *A Companion to Sport* (pp. 129–142). Malden, MA: Blackwell.

Wilson, B., Van Luijk, N., and Boit, M. (2013). When celebrity athletes are 'social movement entrepreneurs': a study of the role of elite runners in run-for-peace events in post-conflict Kenya in 2008. *International Review for the Sociology of Sport*. Published 'Online First', DOI: 10.1177/1012690213506005.

Wilson, B. and White, P. (2002). Revive the pride: social process, political economy, and a fan-based grassroots movement. *Sociology of Sport Journal*, 19(2), 119–148.

Wilson, H. I. (1925). A proportioning machine for use in applying chemicals. *Bulletin of the Green Section of the US Golf Association*, February, 33–34.

Wind, H. W. (1955). The Masters. *Sports Illustrated*. Retrieved 15 December 2014 from http://www.si.com/vault/1955/04/04/605310/the-masters.

Winter, J. (2006). *Dreams of Peace and Freedom: Utopian Moments in the Twentieth Century*. New Haven, CT: Yale Press.

Winter, J. G., Somers, K. M., Dillon, P. J., Paterson, C. and Reid, R. A. (2002). Impacts of golf courses on macroinvertebrate community structure in precambrian shield streams. *Journal of Environmental Quality*, 31, 2015–2025.

Witteveen, G. (1986). Preparing for play: the look of construction at one northern site. *Golf Course Management*, November, 32–38.

Wolfrum, W. K. (2008). The global anti-golf movement: golf's ultimate enemy celebrates 15 years of having a manifesto. Retrieved 20 December 2014 from http://www.worldgolf.com/blogs/william.wolfrum/2008/04/.

Woods, W. (1985). Construction of a 'new' St. Andrews shows that Golf is thriving in Japan. *GreenMaster*, November/December, 19–20.

World Watch Institute (2004). Matters of scale – planet golf. *World Watch Magazine*, 17(2). Retrieved 7 May 2015 from: http://www.worldwatch.org/node/797.

Wright, E. O. (2007). Guidelines for envisioning real utopias. *Soundings*, 36, 26–39.

Wright, E. O. (2010). *Envisioning Real Utopias*. London: Verso.

Wright, E. O. (2013). Transforming capitalism through real utopias. *American Sociological Review*, 78(1), 1–25.

Wyllie, J. A. (1982). Message from your president: the Masters, a visible standard. *Golf Course Management*, May, 5.

Ziemer, B. (2009). Going green in Grand Forks. *The Vancouver Sun*. Retrieved 29 December 2014 from http://www.vancouversun.com/technology/Going+green+Grand+Forks/1470438/story.html?__federated=1.

Žižek, S. (1999). *The Ticklish Subject*. London: Verso.

Zucker, L. (1988). *Institutional Patterns and Organizations*. New York: Ballinger.

Index

Althusser, Louis, 41–3
Audubon International, 6, 124–5, 127, 129, 144, 146, 149, 189
Augusta National syndrome, xvi, 20, 22, 73–9, 82, 85–7, 95, 106, 117, 147, 189–90, 192, 202, 205, 207–8, 210

Beck, Ulrich, 32, 34
Best Management Practices, 99, 111, 114, 122
Blackburn Meadows (organic) Golf Course, 179, 183–6, 191–2, 195
BMPs *see* Best Management Practices
Boyd, David, 93–4, 134–6, 140
Brundtland Commission, 31, 100

Canadian Association of Physicians for the Environment, 104, 137
Canadian Cancer Society, 11, 104, 132, 137, 141
Carlson, Jeffrey, 105, 179–88, 190, 192, 199, 215
Carson, Rachel, 3, 64–9, 95, 98, 116, 149
Chernushenko, David, 31, 39, 40
China, 84–5
Civitas, 183–4
collective action frame, 169
Cosmetic Pesticides Ban Act in Ontario, 11, 131–3, 135–9, 141, 143, 148–9, 204, 209
Critical Golf Studies, 19–21

DDT, 8, 22, 34, 37, 59–68, 70–1, 77–8, 88, 91–2, 94–5, 104, 116, 133, 144, 195, 203, 207
Dryzek, John S., 32, 35, 36, 69

Earth Day, 131, 144
ecological modernization, 21, 29–35, 38–42, 44, 91–2, 98, 101, 139–40, 184, 194

EIFG *see* Environmental Institute for Golf
EM *see* Ecological Modernization
EPA *see* Environmental Protection Agency (USA)
environmental managerialism, 17, 42, 139–41, 143, 173, 204, 210
    definition, 139
Environmental Institute for Golf, 100, 106, 123–4, 193
Environmental Protection Agency (USA), 68, 71, 91, 96, 116, 117, 122, 128, 144–7, 154, 210

Feldman, Jay, 103, 106, 199
frame analysis, 165
Forbes, Michael, 162–4, 167–72, 174–5
Ford, Martin, 162–4, 175
Foster, John Bellamy, 35, 36, 60, 61, 69
From Heresy to Dogma: An Institutional History of Corporate Environmentalism, xiv, 18, 69

GAGM *see* Global Anti-Golf Movement
GEO *see* Golf Environmental Organization
Golf Environment Organization, 14, 125
Glegg, Martin, 164, 170–1
Global Anti-Golf Movement, 154–60, 172, 174, 195, 204
globalization
    and social movements, 18–19, 44–5
    and golf's international development, 51, 72
Gramsci, Antonio, 41–2, 169
Green Section (USGA publication), 7, 53, 56, 58–9, 62, 66, 68, 71, 77, 91, 95, 97–8, 113

Hagen, Walter, 80
Hannigan, John, 42, 43, 139–41, 148, 204
Harvey, David, 17, 30

Harvey, Jean, xvii, 18, 19, 21, 44–5, 156, 157
Hoffman, Andrew, xiv, 18, 69–70
Homer-Dixon, Thomas, 33–4
Horne, John, vii–viii, 18, 44, 160, 214

ideological state apparatuses, 41
Integrated Pest Management, 22, 32, 92–9, 101–4, 111, 112–14, 118, 122–3, 126, 131, 138–9, 141–2, 144–6, 155–6, 158, 186, 202–4, 207
impression management
    strategies used by the golf industry, 116–23
integrated circus
    and golf promotion, 193
IPM *see* Integrated Pest Management

Japan, 82–4, 86, 160
Jarvie, Grant, 155, 159
Jevons' Paradox, 34
Jhally, Sut, 72, 75

Latour, Bruno, 43, 52
Lenskyj, Helen, 28, 39, 40
limits to growth perspective, 36–8, 42, 64, 69
Local Hero, 169
Loch Marsh Golf Club, 86–7

Macdonald, Douglas, 133, 138, 140–1, 147–8
MacNeill, Margaret, 75
McGuinty, Dalton, 131, 138, 141
Mol, Arthur, 29, 32, 34, 35, 40

NAGA *see* National Allied Golf Association
National Allied Golf Association, 101, 124, 129, 144
Nauright, John, 5, 20, 22, 41, 81–3, 85, 105, 159, 169
New Malton (organic) Golf Club, 179–80, 183–4, 191–2, 194
Neo, Harvey, 19, 44, 128, 209
Nicklaus, Jack, 73, 161
No Golf Day, 154

Obama, Barack, 6, 179

Old Tom Morris, 53–4, 85
organic golf
    cultural practices for course maintenance, 181–2
    definition, 179–81
    why it has not caught on, 189–94

Palmer, Arnold, 73
Palmer, Catherine, 83–5
PESP *see* Pesticide Environmental Stewardship Program
Pest Management Regulatory Agency, 134–6, 142–3, 148
Pesticide Environmental Stewardship Program, 145–7
PMRA *see* Pest Management Regulatory Agency
political opportunity theory, 170–2
post-politics, 44, 111–12, 127–8, 132, 148, 194, 204
precautionary approach, xv, 4, 6, 11, 65, 102–3, 106, 136, 173, 181, 194, 203, 206–7, 210, 214
professionalization
    messages to demonstrate professionalization, 116–23
Promethean environmental discourse, 18, 69–70, 87–8, 91, 102, 102, 120, 149, 174, 195, 202

resource mobilization theory, 170–2
Rio 2016 Olympics, 212–14
Robbins, Paul, 43, 78–9, 210, 215
Reagan, Ronald
    and environmental regulation, 145
Rossi, Frank, 183
Royal Calcutta Golf Club, 51
Royal Montreal Golf Club, 51
Ryder Cup, 84, 125

Safai, Parissa, 18, 44
Sarazen, Gene, 80
Schnaiberg, Allan, 17, 30, 35, 37
social movements
    criteria for success, 158–9
spectacle of accumulation, 75
spectacle of legitimation, 75
sport management environmentalist, 39
sports/media complex, 72, 74–5, 87

St Andrews Links, 51, 83
Staggenborg, Suzanne, 156, 158
Standing Committee on Environment and Sustainable Development, 142–3, 148, 207
Stoddart, Brian, 20
Stoddart, Mark, 43
Stolle-McAllister, John, 159, 160
sustainability, 5, 18, 28–33, 35, 38–41, 100, 102, 121, 186
Swyngedouw, Erik, 128, 148, 149

technology
    and the modern golf superintendent, 96–9
The Ingenuity Gap, 33, 34
tourism
    four golf 'products' aimed at attracting tourists, 84–5
treadmill of production, 17, 21, 29, 35, 37–8, 42, 64, 68, 195, 200

Tripping Up Trump activist group, 154, 162–74
Trump, Donald, 6, 24, 154, 162–75, 204, 209
TUT *see* Tripping Up Trump activist group

United Nations Environmental Program, 40
University of Guelph Turfgrass Institute, 183, 185
Utopian vision for golf, 200–2

Vietnam, 84–5
Vineyard (organic) Golf Club, 6, 178–80, 187, 209

Wheeler, Kit, 5, 20, 22, 41, 82, 83, 105, 159
Williams, Raymond, 44

You've Been Trumped, 163, 167, 168–9, 171

Žižek, Slavoj, 44, 127–8

EU authorised representative for GPSR:
Easy Access System Europe, Mustamäe tee 50,
10621 Tallinn, Estonia
gpsr.requests@easproject.com

www.ingramcontent.com/pod-product-compliance
Ingram Content Group UK Ltd.
Pitfield, Milton Keynes, MK11 3LW, UK
UKHW021848140426
5217IPUK00022B/1650